The Crisis of Public Communication

D0083936

Over the past twenty-five years the role of the mass media in the world of politics has become increasingly influential, controversial and disturbing. Many people feel that the situation has reached crisis point; few would deny that in both America and Britain the modern practice of political communication falls far short of democratic ideals.

In a comprehensive analysis of systems of political communication, Blumler and Gurevitch trace the origins and development of this 'crisis of communication for citizenship'. They provide detailed critiques of the relationship between British and American broadcasters and politicians, and of political communication in election campaigns since the late 1960s.

Blumler and Gurevitch blame neither politicians nor journalists for this crisis. They trace the roots of the problem to our contemporary social and political environment, characterized by an increasingly disaffected public whose ability to make sense of civic problems is increasingly confounded and frustrated. Looking to the future, they consider how political communication might be improved within the context of a restructured public sphere.

Jay G. Blumler is Emeritus Professor of the Social and Political Aspects of Broadcasting at the University of Leeds and Professor of Journalism at the University of Maryland. He is International Editor of the *Journal of Communication* and Founding Co-Editor of the *International Journal of Communication*.

Michael Gurevitch is Professor at the College of Journalism, University of Maryland, and is Associate Editor of the *Journal of Communication*. He is co-author of *The Secularization of Leisure, The Challenge of Election Broadcasting* and *The Formation of Campaign Agendas* and co-editor of *Mass Communications and Society*.

Communication and Society
General Editor: James Curran

The Crisis of Public Communication

Jay G. Blumler and Michael Gurevitch

London and New York

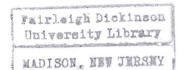
First published 1995
by Routledge
11 New Fetter Lane, London EC4P 4EE

Simultaneously published in the USA and Canada
by Routledge
29 West 35th Street, New York, NY 10001

© 1995 Jay G. Blumler and Michael Gurevitch

Phototypeset in Times by Intype, London
Printed and bound in Great Britain by
Mackays of Chatham PLC, Chatham, Kent

British Library Cataloguing in Publication Data
Blumler, Jay G.
The Crisis of Public Communication
(Communication and Society Series)
I. Title   II. Gurevitch, Michael
III. Series
306.2

Library of Congress Cataloging in Publication Data
A catalogue record for this book has been requested

ISBN 0–415–10851–9 (hbk)
ISBN 0–415–10852–7 (pbk)

Contents

Conclusion

Introduction

Chapter 1

The crisis of civic communication

This book appears at a time of increasing concern about the ways politics is communicated to the public. Such concerns have been expressed by media researchers and other academics engaged in the study of politics, as well as by some media professionals and politicians both in the US and in Britain (the two countries whose political communication systems we have followed most closely) and elsewhere, in many other liberal-democratic societies. It would be no exaggeration to describe this state of affairs as a *crisis of civic communication*.[1]

Its emergence is deeply ironic. With the defeat of the Axis powers in World War II, with the collapse of Communism from the late 1980s, and with the discrediting and toppling of dictatorial and military regimes throughout the Third World, democracy has become the dominant ideology of modern political life (Dunn, 1992). Yet the gaps between ideology and practice are now so glaring that serious observers feel increasingly bound to ask, 'Are we able to believe even in the *possibility* of a role for mass communication in the furtherance of democratic ideals?' (Ettema and Glasser, 1994).

Thus, confidence in the norms of citizenship is waning. Tactics of political campaigning appear ever less savoury. The watchdog role of journalism is often shunted into channels of personalization, dramatization, witch-huntery, soap-operatics and sundry trivialities. It is difficult for unconventional opinions to break into the established 'marketplace of ideas', and political arguments are often reduced to slogans and taunts. Suspicion of manipulation is rife, and cynicism is growing. The public interest in constructive civic communication has been short-changed.

Such problems primarily stem, however, not from the shortcomings and failures of particular individuals or groups but from profound institutional sources. Before they can be properly understood, researched and addressed by reforms, those structural foundations must be clarified.

This book aims to make two main contributions to that task. First, it offers, through an edited collection of some of our past writings, what we regard as an essential way of thinking about communication-in-democracy

– namely, that in large, complex, industrialized societies political messages emanate from firmly formed *political communication systems*. This differs from other prominent orientations to political communication analysis. Ideological approaches, for example, tend to ascribe a subordinate position to the mass media in politics, performing a handmaiden's service to dominant political institutions and ideas. In contrast, we regard political communication as an institution in its own right, interweaving political and media forces and projecting its own characteristic influences, constraints and problems. Second, in one of several freshly written essays, we apply that perspective to the present crisis of civic communication, identifying its systemic origins and gauging the prospects for its easement (Chapter 15).

UNDERLYING SOURCES

At least two processes, one a broad, societal process, the other more specifically media-related, may be identified as having contributed to the crisis of civic communication. The first is a set of transformations in demographic and social relationships and the consequent emergence of what (for want of a better term) may be considered 'mass democracies'. The second has to do with the evolution of the political communication systems in these societies. This may, of course, be regarded not as a separate process but rather as one of the consequences, at the communication level, of the emergence of mass democracies. We nevertheless single it out here because it lies at the heart of the analysis presented in this book.

Most prominent among the surrounding societal trends has been a relative but apparently irreversible dissolution of traditional ties. Institutions that previously organized meaning, identity and authoritative information for many people, structured their political preferences and simplified the process of democratic power-seeking – notably political parties, the nuclear family, mainstream religion, neighbourhood and social-class groupings – all have waned in salience and influence. In their place a more complex and fragmented society has developed, replete with multiplying interest groups and contending value orientations (Luhmann, 1975; Swanson and Mancini, 1995). Such trends have been accompanied by accelerating mobility, not only geographical, occupational and social but also psychic – across cultural attitudes and values, life-style options and social identities; a decline in moral consensus; and an increasing use of communication to participate in imagined communities, stretching beyond one's local doorstep (Mutz, 1992). In these conditions, government is more difficult, popular support is more contingent and effective communication is more vital.

At the same time, the role played by the mass media in politics has also evolved. Over the past quarter of a century, the media have gradually moved from the role of reporting *on and about* politics, 'from the outside' as it were, to that of being an *active participant in*, shaping influence upon, indeed an integral part of, the political process. This kind of intervention is especially visible during election campaigns, since the political functions of the media – and especially of television – assume greater visibility and significance during periods of intensified political communication. But it is by no means confined to election communication. Taken together, these developments have resulted in *the increased dependency of both politicians and voters on the media and the messages they provide*. The kind of democracy we now inhabit as a result is well epitomized by the labels that different scholars have applied to it: 'an age of press-politics' (Kalb, 1992); one of 'media politics' (Arterton, 1985); one of 'mediated politics' (Bennett, 1995); one dominated by a 'political-media complex' (Swanson, 1992). As McLeod, Kosicki and McLeod (1994) have concluded, 'The center of the new political system appears to be the media.'

Various structural consequences flow from this situation. First, organizations have been imported into key positions in the political arena – notably television and the press – whose editorial and reporting policies are not necessarily determined by civic considerations (Patterson, 1980, 1993). Second, this obliges politicians, who wish to attract the attention and support of voters, to do so by first attracting the attention and interest of journalists and editors who are not necessarily politically minded. Third, the difficult and specialized strategic requirements of pursuing such a twofold task have brought forth the increased professionalization of the production and dissemination of political messages, so that election campaigns, for example, are increasingly conducted and controlled by media consultants and campaign managers. Fourth, a highly complex web of relationships has grown up between politicians, their professional advisers and media professionals, which is so mutually preoccupying that ordinary citizens' needs can fall far from sight. Hence (as Weaver (1994, p. 351) notes):

> Regardless of which side seems to be more in control of the campaign agenda, if this agenda is perceived as mostly controlled by politicians and the press without much real input from the public, then increasing alienation and cynicism of citizens is likely to occur.

The reality of the crisis that afflicts our democracies is no secret. The evidence for it is clearly visible. As a *Washington Post* columnist has described it (Harwood, 1994):

> If citizenship is defined as active and informed participation in public affairs and the political process, they – the young in particular – have become non-citizens along with millions of their elders. While our

politicians and editorial writers preach to the world about the joys and successes of democracy, half the American electorate ignores our presidential elections. Voter turnouts in off-year congressional elections of all kinds are an international joke.

The obvious questions are: Whose failure is it? Are the citizens at fault, for being uninterested, lazy, stupid or negligent in the pursuit of their citizenship duty to be politically informed? Does the fault lie with the politicians, who fail in their obligation to inform the citizenry properly? Or are the media, the institutions entrusted with the task of informing the public, guilty of dereliction of duty?

Such a search for the blameworthy is, of course, futile. In a sense the best answer to such a question is probably 'all of the above'. To quote Harwood (1994) again, 'There are close relationships among the decline of citizenship, the decline of interest in traditional definitions of "news" and the decline of journalism's larger role in the life of the society.' But to pose the issues in these terms may point towards a different answer. The roots of the crisis are *systemic* – that is, they inhere in the very structures and functioning of present-day political communication systems. This is why we believe that examining political communication processes in systemic terms is essential for understanding that crisis, and why much of our work in this area over the past two decades has revolved around the concept of political communication systems.

We first developed this notion in an essay published in 1977, entitled 'Linkages between the Mass Media and Politics: A Model for the Analysis of Political Communication Systems' (see Chapter 2 below). In it we explained:

> The position taken in this paper is that the study of political communi-cation could be enriched by adoption of a systems outlook. As con-ceived here, this is regarded not as competitive with other research approaches but as capable of incorporating them. Three benefits could ensue from attempts to place political communication phenomena in a systems framework. First, it links diverse bodies of evidence in broader analytical perspectives. Second, there would be an antidote against the tendency to under- or over-emphasize any single element of the politi-cal communication system (e.g. the audience). Third, by drawing atten-tion to system factors which might have macro-level consequences that could be measured and compared, cross-national investigation would be facilitated.
>
> An underlying assumption of such an approach is that the main features of the political communication process maybe regarded as if they formed a system, such that variation in one of its components would be associated with variation in the behaviour of its other compo-

nents. In very broad terms, the main components of a political communication system may be located in:

1 Political institutions in their communication aspects.
2 Media institutions in their political aspects.
3 Audience orientations to political communication.
4 Communication-relevant aspects of political culture.

Turning back to that statement almost two decades later we might have expected that, given the passage of time, the changes that have transpired over the years in the conduct of political communication almost everywhere, and developments in the academic investigation of political communication processes, would have rendered the above formulation in need of major repairs. Yet looking at it again today, it appears to us to be impressively resilient. In spite of the many changes that have since taken place, the conceptual mapping of the components of the system is, in our judgement, still valid and usefully applicable for conceptualizing the study of political communication systems. Such systems can still be analysed in terms of the triangular relationship between politicians, media organizations and audience members. And the basic structures of the interactions between these components of the system are still those that inspired our thinking in the 1970s.

THE APPROACH AND PLAN OF THE BOOK

In the following pages we flesh out this idea in two broad ways.

The essays in Part I deal largely with the *structures* of political communication systems, both analytically and empirically. Chapter 2 outlines an overall model for their examination. Chapter 3 offers an in-depth examination of relationships between politicians and journalists, treating these as derived from their respective organizational and civic roles. In Chapter 4 that framework guides an empirical analysis of British broadcasters' attitudes to coverage of the UK Parliament, the results of which are then generalized to suggest how journalists might react differentially to a broad range of social and political institutions along 'sacerdotal' and 'pragmatic' dimensions. However, since political communication systems come in different shapes and sizes, varying with different societies' political cultures, political systems and media systems, comparative analysis and research are essential. Chapters 5–7 present a number of dimensions to guide comparative research, along which the political communication processes of different societies may vary, as well as several examples of such research in which the authors have engaged. Finally, the implications of systemically organized political communication arrangements for the realization of democratic values are discussed in Chapter 8.

Although built-in system features of political communication give characteristic shape to a society's public sphere, these are not fixed in cement but develop over time. Part II of the book is consequently devoted to change in the British political communication system between the mid-1960s and the early 1990s, taking advantage of our unique series of observation studies of the operations of BBC Television News and Current Affairs in five election campaigns (1966, 1979, 1983, 1987 and 1992). The individual case-study reports, which form Chapters 9–13, are followed in Chapter 14 by specification of two far-reaching processes of change revealed by a longitudinal analysis of them: the increasing inter-dependence and mutual adaptation to each other of British parties and newscasters; and the gradual routinization and suppression of a ground-breaking 'charisma' that once inspired television journalism at the BBC.

Collecting our own past writings, written over a period of twenty-five years, conveys an assumption on our part that the whole is indeed greater than the sum of the parts. It makes an implicit claim that these past writings are worth revisiting, even if they are a bit frayed and greyer at the edges. It is based on a sense that a measure of continuity and coherence can be found in this cumulative work.

But it is not merely because of pride of parenthood that we saw fit to assemble the essays in this book. They are intended to illustrate a number of points. First, the collection documents our search for, and our confident belief in, the value of a unifying conceptual framework. When we began our joint work in the 1970s political communication research tended to be segmented and fragmented, dealing separately with various topics, and by and large lacking a comprehensive, holistic framework. This was not an accident. It was a reflection of the state of much mass communication research at that time, traceable, perhaps, to Lasswell's (1948) influential definition of the field in terms of 'who says what to whom, with what effect' – a formulation that invited a fragmented analysis of the communication process. The notion of a political communication *system* can thus be seen as an attempt to respond to the fragmented state of the field without jettisoning any more specifically defined lines of enquiry.

Second, throughout our collaborative work we sought to formulate a conceptual scheme that could potentially be applied to circumstances and sites other than Britain and the US, where our work was concentrated. Thus, we were guided by a conviction that an important scholarly way forward is via comparative analysis of political communication systems in different countries (as argued in Chapters 5 and 6, though written fifteen years apart).

Third, there is a normative reason for, and a normative dimension to, the work assembled here. Throughout the years we continually stressed the deep-seated roots of the often lamented failures of political and communication practices to serve democracy well. The problems involved stemmed, in our view, not from the deficiencies of this particular person, of that group, or of the other given institution, but from the interplay of political institutions, media institutions and audiences. An implication is that (in Swanson's (1992b, p. 399) words): 'Attempts to reform political communication are unlikely to add up to anything more than rearranging the deck chairs on the *Titanic* unless they recognize the institutional groundings of objectionable practices.' This is not to advise scholars to withdraw from the struggle for communication forms that serve citizenship but to stress that proposed changes, to stand a chance of success, must have systemic relevance and be able to harness systemic support.

But if the normative impulse that animates these essays is valid, are the concepts that we fashioned in earlier years still relevant today, or are they time bound and therefore wholly or partially obsolete or in need of updating? Some of the evidence which formed the basis for certain of the older essays assembled here is, indeed, tied to its time and place, and may no longer reflect present-day conditions. In fact, it is quite sobering to consider how different – and not for the better – present-day circumstances for political communication are compared to twenty or even just ten years ago. Thus, for example, with hindsight and comparatively speaking, the 1970s appear to have been a period in which both the institutions of politics and the media were stable and generally enjoyed a greater measure of trust from the public than they do today. Their mutual relationship was less fraught with tension, eruptions of open conflict and a consequent legacy of mistrust. Television at that time was a limited-channel medium, and its dominance of the political communication scene was much less pronounced and visible than it is today. More generally, the civic culture in both Britain and the US appeared to have been in tolerable repair, less afflicted by the malaise of media 'feeding frenzies' (Sabato, 1991) and public alienation and indifference apparent today. These different conditions clearly shaped the theorizing and concept-formation which underlie these essays.

Awareness of these changes has confronted us with the question of whether our approach to the analysis of political communication systems required any conceptual modification. Readers will form their own judgements, but our answer to this rather vexing question is a mixed 'yes' and 'no'. In gist, we now consider that our past essays were strong on the analysis of structures, but weak in considering and dealing with the dynamics of change in political communication systems.

We have sought to correct this by including in this book two new essays. One is the aforementioned examination in Chapter 14 of the evolution of the British election communication system over the past quarter century. Our concluding chapter, however, addresses the dynamics of change at a more abstract level, opening with an analysis of some of the sources of instability that are built into the organization of political communication systems. More pertinently, that chapter goes on to argue that the deepening of the current crisis of civic communication can be best explained precisely in systemic terms, that is, in terms of developments in the relationships between politicians and journalists, between the institutions of politics and of the media, viewed in the context of the socio-political environment, i.e. in the context of the relationship of these institutions with an increasingly disaffected and fragmented audience/public/citizenry.

But above and beyond the reasons outlined above, the principles which guided our work – a holistic rather than fragmented approach to this field of study; the emphasis on comparative analysis; and an understanding of the evolution and change of political communication systems within a broader socio-political and cultural context – are already present, fully fleshed, in our 1977 statement. If nothing else, it is a testimony to the resilience of the concept whose career is traced in this book.

Part I

Structure

Chapter 2

Linkages between the mass media and politics[1]

INTRODUCTION

Assumptions about the political impact of the mass media have played a formative part in guiding the direction of mass communication research ever since its inception. In so far as the pioneer investigators accepted popular impressions of the media as omnipotent and capable of being employed for manipulative purposes, it was natural that much research attention should have been paid to communication influences on people's political opinions and attitudes. It is equally obvious why such a preoccupation with persuasive effects should have resulted in an imbalance of activity favouring studies of the audience at the expense of other elements in the communication process. Dramatic examples of seemingly successful uses of the mass media to propagate political beliefs and ideologies in World War I and the 1930s, plus the growth of political science interest in empirical analysis of voting behaviour, gave rise to and reinforced the conviction that the prime target for research should be processes of opinion and attitude change among individual receivers of mass-communicated messages.

The subsequent erosion of the myth of the media's irresistible powers of persuasion through the publication of contrary evidence had two related repercussions for the study of political communication. First, there was a marked broadening and diversification of the problems regarded as open to enquiry. Consequently, political communication provides a fertile field of study nowadays for researchers steeped in a wide range of disciplines and methodologies (see Swanson and Nimmo, 1990, for an overview). Second, in some cases those shifts of focus resulted in a virtual rejection of the audience as an object of research interest. This stemmed mainly from the assumption that the original seekers after persuasion effects had not only exhausted that particular seam of enquiry but had returned from their endeavours with precious little gold to show for their trouble.

The position taken in this essay is that the study of political communication could be enriched by adoption of a systems outlook. As conceived here, this is regarded not as competitive with other research approaches but as capable of incorporating them. Three benefits could ensue from attempts to place political communication phenomena in a systems framework. First, it links diverse bodies of evidence in broader analytical perspectives. Second, there would be an antidote against the tendency to under- or over-emphasize any single element of the political communication system (e.g. the audience). Third, by drawing attention to system factors which might have macro-level consequences that could be measured and compared, cross-national investigation would be facilitated.

THE ELEMENTS OF A POLITICAL COMMUNICATION SYSTEM

An underlying assumption of such an approach is that the main features of the political communication process may be regarded as if they formed a system, such that variation in one of its components would be associated with variation in the behaviour of its other components. In very broad terms, the main components of a political communication system may be located in:

1 Political institutions in their communication aspects.[2]
2 Media institutions in their political aspects.
3 Audience orientations to political communication.
4 Communication-relevant aspects of political culture.

Expressed somewhat differently, if we look at a political communication system, what we see is two sets of institutions – political and media organizations – which are involved in the course of message preparation in much 'horizontal' interaction with each other, while, on a 'vertical' axis, they are separately and jointly engaged in disseminating and processing information and ideas to and from the mass citizenry.

The interactions of the two kinds of institutions are to some extent conditioned by mutual power relationships. This presupposes that both have an independent power base in society, one source of which arises from their respective relations with the audience. The power of political institutions is inherent in their functions as articulators of interest and mobilizers of social power for purposes of political action. The independent power base of media institutions is perhaps less obvious and may even be denied by those who perceive them as essentially secondary bodies, entirely dependent on others for the news and opinions they pass on, and highly constrained in their operation by a number of political, economic, cultural and technological factors. Nevertheless, at least three sources of media power can be identified. These are structural, psychological and normative in origin.

The structural root of the power of the mass media springs from their unique capacity to deliver to the politician an audience which, in size and composition, is unavailable to him by any other means. Indeed, the historical significance of the growing role of mass communication in politics lies, among other things, in the resulting enlargement of the receiver base to such an extent that previous barriers to audience involvement (e.g. low level of education and weak political interest) have been largely overcome and the audience for political communication has become virtually coterminous with membership of society itself.

The psychological root of media power stems from the relations of credibility and trust that different media organizations have succeeded in developing (albeit to different degrees) with members of their audiences. This bond is based on the fulfilment of audience expectations and the validation of past trust relationships, which in turn are dependent on legitimized and institutionalized routines of information presentation evolved over time by the media.

It is the combined influence of these structural and psychological sources of strength that enable the media to interpose themselves between politicians and the audience and to 'intervene' in other political processes as well. This is expressed in the way in which they are capable of restructuring the timing and character of political events (conventions, demonstrations, leader appearances, etc.), defining crisis situations to which politicians are obliged to react, requiring comment on issues that media personnel have emphasized as important, injecting new personalities into the political dialogue (such as television interviewers) and stimulating the growth of new communication agencies (such as public relations firms, opinion-poll agencies, and political advertising and campaign management specialists).

Since such forms of intervention may be unwelcome to many politicians, the normative root of media power can be crucial at times of conflict. This springs from the respect that is accorded in competitive democracies to such tenets of liberal philosophy as freedom of expression and the need for specialized organs to safeguard citizens against possible abuses of political authority. This tends to legitimate the independent role of media organizations in the political field and to shelter them from overt attempts blatantly to bring them under political control.

It is not the argument here that political communication flows are merely the product of a naked power struggle waged between two sets of would-be communicators. On the contrary, the notion that such power-holders are bound together in a political communication system alerts us to the influence of other forces as well. One such influence arises from audience expectations, which it is the concern of both sorts of communicators to address effectively. In addition, a systems outlook implies that the interactions of the various actors occur within an overarching framework of organizing principles that are designed to regularize the relationships of media institutions to political institutions. The implications of those considerations are discussed more fully below.

ENTRY POINTS INTO THE SYSTEM

Any analysis of a system comprising a number of components linked by a network of mutual dependencies is faced with the need to identify a set of relevant conceptual perspectives and to select optimal entry points into the system. The following discussion proposes to proceed by selecting as points of departure those elements in each of the components of the political communication system which are most conducive to generating propositions offering a basis for both theoretical advance and empirical research. We look first at the audience, then at certain organizational characteristics of political and media institutions and finally at the political culture, as it is reflected in the principles which organize normative relationships between political and media institutions, which in turn have some consequences for relationships between these institutions and the audience.

Audience roles

The concept of audience roles has arisen from attempts to apply the 'uses and gratifications' approach to the study of voters' orientations to the political contents of the mass media. Evidence collected from this standpoint supports the implication that different receivers of political information are motivated by different expectations of it, develop different orientations towards it and may therefore be perceived as playing different roles in the political communication system. Investigating such orientations to political communications in Britain, Blumler (1973) has provisionally identified four such audience roles that might be applicable to the political communication systems of other competitive democracies. They include: the partisan, seeking a reinforcement of existing beliefs; the liberal citizen, seeking guidance in deciding how to vote; the monitor, seeking information about features of the political environment (such as party policies, current issues and the qualities of political leaders); and the spectator, seeking excitement and other affective satisfactions.

The notion of audience roles offers a point of departure for analysis of political communication systems in two respects. One use of the concept would enquire into the processes that lead people in different societies to take up one or more of the roles available to them. Supposing that the validity of a common repertoire of alternative role possibilities could be established for audience members in a designated set of competitive democracies, it would then be possible to identify some of the sociological and psychological correlates associated with the particular political communication roles that different people adopt and to compare their influence cross-nationally. Sociologically, such an analysis might focus, for example, on educational background (expected to differentiate monitors from spectators) or on early patterns of socialization to politics in the family and elsewhere. Psychologically, it might examine such variables as strength of partisan identity (expected to pinpoint the partisans at one pole and spectators at the other) and political cynicism (as a possible discriminant of spectators from the rest). The results might help to show how in the countries studied political culture impinges on political communication expectations at the audience level.

A second line of analysis would pursue the possibility that audience roles are matched by similar orientations among political and professional communicators. The underlying assumption here is that audience members and communicators are linked in a network of mutually shared expectancies (Tan, 1973). It does not follow that such a correspondence of roles will always be perfect. On the contrary, imperfections of feedback, differences of purpose, and especially constraints arising from the disparities of political stratification may all be productive of discrepancies between the orientations of the different participants in the political communication process. Nevertheless, the concept of a 'communication role' is at least as applicable to political communicators and to media personnel as it is to audience members. Moreover, the very notion of communication presupposes some degree of compatibility between the orientations of the originators and the receivers of messages. Table 1 presents a set of parallels that may be drawn between them.

Table 1 The complementarity of roles in a political communication system

Audience	Media personnel	Politicians
Partisan	Editorial guide	Gladiator
Liberal citizen	Moderator	Rational persuader
Monitor	Watchdog	Information provider
Spectator	Entertainer	Actor/performer

The utility of such a paradigm depends on its ability to stimulate speculation about the structure of a political communication system and to suggest hypotheses about linkages between the components of such a system. Attention to the role relationships indicated in Table 1 would open up at least three areas of exploration:

1 *System integration.* The degree of integration of a political communication system might be conceived in terms of the degree of correspondence between its constituent parts. Thus, a highly integrated system would be one with high inter-correlations between role orientations across levels, i.e. where all the participants in the communication process share

equivalent orientations and consequently speak on, or are tuned in to, similar wavelengths. Conversely, a system with a low level of integration would be one with low inter-correlations between parallel roles, reflecting a situation where the leading elements are at cross-purposes with each other, and in which a high degree of communication conflict across levels prevails.

2 *Inter-level distancing.* The relative distance between the audience and the media system, on the one hand, and between the electorate and the political system, on the other, might be measured by the degree to which audience roles correspond more closely with media personnel roles or with political leader roles. Closeness of correspondence might indicate the relative credibility of the media, and the trustworthiness of politicians, for the audience, while lack of correspondence might reflect a failure of one or the other set of communicators to address themselves relevantly to the needs of the audience.

3 *Cross-level influences.* The principles that normatively relate media organizations to political institutions in a particular society may help to shape the role definitions regarded as appropriate by those occupying different positions in the communication system. Various specific hypotheses may be derived from this possibility:

(a) Media systems with a high degree of political autonomy are likely to give professional communicators considerable freedom to adopt a variety of role orientations. This will leave audience role options wide open as well and tend to oblige political spokespersons to perform in multifunctional fashion. This might not be equally palatable to all politicians (some of whom might have a distaste for the actor/performer role, for example). In such systems, then, we might find more evidence of 'role distancing' among politicians and 'typecasting' forms of division of labour among journalists in the media.

(b) Where public-service-type goals prevail in media organizations, watchdog functions will be favoured by media professionals and audience members will be encouraged to assume the monitor role; this will exert pressure on politicians to give primacy to the information-provider role. On the other hand, more commercially oriented media might give greater prominence to entertainer roles because of assumptions about audience preferences for the spectator role. Conformity on the part of politicians would lead them to adopt actor/performer roles.

(c) Where political parties control the media, the gladiatorial role will be adopted more often by politicians while the role of editorial guide will be adopted by media personnel; this will exert pressure on audience members to assume the partisan role.

(d) Systems governed by more authoritative and paternalistic goals might have either of two consequences for audience members: audience roles could tend to follow those assumed by party and media communicators, involving a greater emphasis, then, on partisan and monitor roles; or audience expectations would be in conflict with the equivalent orientations of message senders, with resulting tendencies to avoid political information, distrust the media and feel alienated from politics.

Political institutions vs. media institutions: norms and structures

A second point of entry to the analysis of political communication systems springs initially from the necessary involvement of two kinds of actors – political spokespersons and media personnel – in recurrent patterns of interaction with each other. These can be seen as operating on two planes: of boundary maintenance between organizations, and of message production. In the first case, members of the top echelons of both organizations might maintain contacts aimed at regulating the relationships between the two, resolving conflicts where they arise and generally defining the boundaries between them and maintaining the smooth functioning of the system. But of course, second, the bulk of interaction between professional communicators and politicians is concerned (commonly at somewhat lower levels) more directly with political output as such. This takes place in both formal contexts – such as press conferences, briefings, interviews and so on – and informal ones – such as a confidential exchange of views over a drink. The products of these interactions include not only streams of specific messages – on problems of the day, policies evolved to deal with them, arguments for and against alternative positions, the personalities involved in controversy, etc. – but also (and more importantly) those more abiding ground rules that prescribe the standardized formats through which information is regularly presented to the public (Dearlove, 1974). The interacting parties on both planes are perpetually caught up in a tension between needs of mutual accommodation and various sources of conflict. Without minimal accommodation, little or no communication would take place, and nobody's purposes would be realized. Yet the conflicting functions, and independent power bases, of the two sides ensure that the terms of accommodation will continually be open to renewal and revision.

The conduct of the main participants in this relationship is often assessed from essentially one-sided standpoints: for example, that of the political activist who treats media output as a trivialized version of his own more lofty concerns (Crossman, 1968); or that of the journalist who regards politicians as inveterate corrupters of the independence of the press. A more analytical approach might aim instead to identify the sources of certain more or less constant influences on the behaviour of both interacting parties in so far as they subscribe to different codes of conduct and belong to different kinds of organization. Such constant factors may be found in two critical structural dimensions that influence the relationship between the parties concerned: the degree of professionalization characteristic of the personnel of media and political institutions; and the degree of bureaucratization characteristic of the two organizations.

Studies of mass media institutions have paid much attention to issues centring on the professionalization of staff communicators (Elliott, 1972; Kumar, 1975; Nayman, 1973; Tunstall, 1971). Although the degree to which media personnel exhibit all the characteristics usually ascribed to established professions might be debated, the influence of professional norms on their outlook is greater than in the case of politicians (Lattimore and Nayman, 1974). Some dimensions of this distinction may include the following:

1 *Bases of legitimacy.* These differ for the two sets of actors. Thus, whereas politicians derive their legitimacy from the authority of the causes they espouse, the degree of consensus among the interests they articulate and public acceptance of the procedures by which they have been chosen to represent such interests, media personnel are legitimated chiefly through their fidelity to professional codes.

2 *The service function.* The centrality of the service function in the behaviour of media professionals is reflected in the claim commonly made by them to be concerned primarily to serve the audience members' 'right to know', as distinct from the primary concern of the politician to persuade them in the cause of political and partisan goals.

3 *Autonomy.* The rewards that media personnel enjoy also derive partly from their professional autonomy. Such an emphasis might clash with the politician's often-held view of them as essentially middlemen in the political communication process. This potential conflict becomes yet more acute when politicians, who commonly are disposed towards more ideological criteria of political truth, are confronted with the tendency of media professionals to adhere to more empirical, sceptical (perhaps cynical) and many-sided descriptions of political reality. All this suggests an essential discrepancy between the codes of conduct accepted by partisan communicators and those that regulate the behaviour of professional communicators, irrespective of any higher-order principles that might be shared by both.

Another set of tensions stems from structural differences that obtain not between media professionals and politicians as members of different occupations but between the organizations to which they belong. Many mass media enterprises are formal institutions governed at some level of their organization by bureaucratic norms and procedures. Political parties, on the other hand, exist for long periods of time as relatively skeletal organizations, which are fully mobilized only periodically or in crisis situations. They are not designed to exert full bureaucratic control over politicians and cannot base their modes of operation on purely bureaucratic standards. One consequence of this is that, once appointed, media personnel enjoy relative security and need not be legitimated by the consent of others outside their own employing organization. The position of politicians, on the other hand, is essentially less secure, more bedevilled by uncertainty and more dependent on a continual renewal of the consent of their supporters. The vulnerability of the politician, in contrast to the bureaucratic security of the professional communicator, is illustrated by the highly visible and readily identified position of individual responsibility that the politician holds, as against the greater diffusion of responsibility that obtains in media organizations. To the politician, then, the protective bureaucratic shells of the media must seem intrinsically difficult to penetrate, provoking frustrations that may be less comprehensible and more irritating to individuals who do not usually operate in a bureaucratic environment and who could also resent bureaucratic challenges to the supremacy of their societal functions.

As has been noted before, the potential tensions inherent in these structural differences must be managed and contained, if the interests of both sides are to be accommodated. This suggests that one task in the analysis of political communication systems would involve an examination of the formal and informal mechanisms that span the boundaries between the two kinds of organizations. Apart from the evolution of basic ground rules that regulate the production and dissemination of political communication contents, these range from the establishment of specialized agencies (such as publicity and public relations departments) for coping with the demands of the other side, the development of formal and informal procedures for airing complaints, the setting up of various regulatory bodies, such as press councils, broadcasting councils, regulatory commissions and enquiry commissions that exist to relate the workings of the mass media to certain criteria of the public interest, or appointments that place individuals familiar with the values of one sphere in key positions in the organization of the other, to the ostensibly informal mixing of politicians and media personnel in social circles outside work.

Political culture as a source of regulating mechanisms

A final point of analytical departure arises from the fact that, apart from the procedures and mechanisms that are evolved by political and media institutions to govern the relationships between them, all political systems generate principles derived from the tenets of their political cultures, for regulating the political role of the mass media. Such organizing principles are vital, since the contributions of the mass media to the political process are too important to be left to chance. Thus, communication processes are involved in the legitimation of authority and serve functions of political articulation, mobilization and conflict-management. They set much of the agenda of political debate. They are partly responsible for determining which political demands in society will be aired, and which will be relatively muted. They affect the chances of governments and other political actors to secure essential supports. In short, they are so closely intertwined with political processes that they must be regulated in some appropriate and accepted way.

The manner of such attempted regulation is ultimately traceable to the influence of various tenets of political culture. The most basic one is, of course, the degree to which freedom of expression is cherished as a basic political value or, conversely, the degree to which restrictions on it are regarded as necessary and permissible for the sake of other political goals. Closely related is the value placed on ensuring the existence of outlets for voicing a variety of opinions and securing their ability to operate in a fashion unhampered by potential attempts of political actors to influence or dominate them. Political-cultural factors bearing on the structure of prevailing opinions may also play a part – for example: How far are the predominant positions polarized? To what extent do they tend to be expressed in ideological or pragmatic forms? And what is the manner of their relationship to underlying bases of social differentiation and cleavage? On another level one might identify the influence of assumptions about the suitability of market mechanisms for advancing society's communication goals: societies that share the basic tenets of freedom of political expression might differ in their conception of the desirability of subjecting communication outlets to economic constraints and to the pressures of a free market. Finally, political cultures may differ in the degree to which they value the political sphere itself as a dignified and important realm of activity, informed involvement in which deserves to be promoted.

Although all such tenets are relevant, no one-to-one relationship can be traced between any single strand of political culture and any specific principle designed to govern the role of the mass media in politics. In the end, the central issue in the relationship between media and political institutions revolves around the media's relative degree of autonomy and to what extent and by what means this is allowed to be constrained. Thus, it is the overall cultural 'mix' in a given society that will tend to fix the position of the media on the subordination–autonomy continuum and determine which constraints are permitted some degree of control over them. At least three main sources of constraints directly subordinating the media to political institutions may be identified: legal, normative and structural, respectively.

Legal constraints include all those rules and regulations defining the rights and obligations of media institutions that are ultimately enforceable by the executive and judicial arms of the state. They primarily define the area within which the media may exercise freedom of expression, circumscribed as the case may be by libel laws, legally protected rights of privacy, restrictions on national security grounds, the imposition of censorship on political comment, etc.

Normative constraints refer to expectations of political and public service by media organizations, for which they may be held socially accountable without falling under the direct control of either state or party machinery. They often arise from a conviction that the normal operation of the market mechanism is either insufficient to promote accepted communication goals or may work against them, and they typically invite attempts to ensure that the existing media disperse not merely entertaining fare but also a full and varied supply of political information and analysis suited to the needs of a conscientious citizenry. Some, by now classic, expressions of such 'social responsibility' doctrines, especially as they apply to the press, are to be found in the recommendations of the Commission on Freedom of the Press (1947) and in Siebert, Peterson and Schramm (1956) and Rivers and Schramm (1969).

Structural constraints concern the degree to which formal or semi-formal linkages may be forged between media institutions and political bodies. Thus, political parties, for example, may be involved in the organization of media enterprises through ownership, financial contributions or representation on policy-making bodies, or linkages may be established instead via a tradition of editorial support for the party's goals and policies. The phenomenon of press–party parallelism, comprehensively analysed by Seymour-Ure (1974), obviously belongs to this area of constraint.

Apart from these direct sources of political constraints, media organizations labour under a host of other constraints, some of which may be employed by political institutions in order to gain some measure of indirect control and influence over the media. Prominent among these are economic constraints. These apply not only to commercial media organizations (where advertising revenue might be regulated or taxed directly by the political authorities) but also to non-commercial media institutions whose cash inflows (be they licence fees, governmental or non-governmental subsidies) may be subjected to government approval or influence. Thus, the business and administrative personnel of media organizations, who are charged with their economic and financial viability and well-being, might be especially sensitive to external pressures affecting their organizations' finances, and consequently act as a potential channel for the introduction of political influence on their message outputs. Similarly, political control or regulation focused ostensibly on the technologies of mass communication (such as licensing the use of the airwaves, or control of the import or price of newsprint) may be used as a form of leverage to exert influence over media policies.

The two main media of political communication, broadcasting and the press, tend, for historical, economic and technological reasons, to be differently placed with respect to these constraints, and to exhibit different degrees of vulnerability to them. However, these differences are relative rather than absolute and some important similarities between them may, moreover, be identified. For example, although 'public service broadcasting' immediately comes to mind as an instance of normative constraint on broadcasting, it has a close analogue in the previously mentioned 'social responsibility theory of the press', with its attendant codes of journalistic practice and press councils set up to pronounce on instances of their infraction. Similarly, although 'parallelism' to political parties may seem more common to the press because of the relative multiplicity of outlets characteristic of that medium, in some countries at least separate broadcasting organizations have been instituted to follow political or other socio-cultural divisions (as in The Netherlands). In other countries representatives of political parties are admitted to membership of the governing bodies of broadcasting organizations on a pluralistic basis (e.g. Belgium).

Nevertheless, some crucial differences between these media still obtain. First, in many democratic countries newspapers have traditionally belonged in the private sector, whereas the dependence of broadcast transmission on scarce wavelengths immediately placed first radio and then television in the public domain. Many consequences have flowed from this distinction. Perhaps the most important one is the development of a regulatory licensing system for broadcasting, which was either totally absent or far looser in the case of the press. A related difference concerns the number of outlets, typically numerous in the case of the press in contrast to the relative paucity of broadcasting outlets, often resulting in the monopolistic or duopolistic position of many broadcasting institutions. Yet another difference might be identified in the relatively greater vulnerability of the press to market forces, from which broadcasting organizations have often been more sheltered (with the obvious exception of commercial broadcasting organizations). As a result of all these factors, the presumed power of broadcasting has been enhanced, and consequently means of controlling or neutralizing its potential rivalry to political institutions have had to be found. These have emerged in the form of norms requiring impartiality in the handling of controversial issues, non-editorializing, and the maintenance of a balance between the major political tendencies of the day.

Perhaps these inter-media contrasts are reflected in two main differences so far as the imposition of constraining principles of organization is concerned. First, it is far easier for newspapers to become involved in political controversy as participants rather than as mere referees; from this point of view, variations in media–party parallelism across countries and time periods, with possibly major consequences for audience behaviour and response, are more likely to be found in the press field than in broadcasting. Second, simply because broadcasting organizations are located in the public sector, they will tend, other factors being equal, to be situated nearer the subordination pole of the autonomy–subordination continuum than the press system of the same society is likely to be.

Since we conceive of communication processes as forming a system, variations in the regulatory connections between political and media institutions should have definite consequences for other components of the system, including content outputs and audience orientations thereto. Some examples of possible linkages of this kind are presented in the following hypotheses:

1 Party-tied media systems will produce a higher proportion of 'one-sided' political content, tending as a result to activate partisan role orientations among members of the audience as well as selective exposure mechanisms. They will also tend to produce dissensual rather than consensual issue agendas, giving rise in turn to a higher degree of conflict over issue priorities among electors dependent on the different media outlets.

2 The more subordinate the media system, the greater will be the degree of free access to communication outlets allowed for the statements and manifestos of party spokespeople as originally conceived. This may increase the frequency of partisan and monitor roles.

3 The greater the autonomy of the media system, the greater will be its tendency to generate 'balanced' political information contents (in ways which both reflect and protect its autonomous status). It will consequently perform primarily 'moderator' and 'watchdog' functions, which will tend to activate 'liberal citizen' and 'monitor' role orientations among its audience. Autonomous media systems are likely in turn to be found in two main variants.

(a) Commercially supported autonomous media systems might favour the presentation of political materials in terms of the conflicts and the strategies of political manoeuvring, focusing on personalities at the expense of issue coverage of the political scene. This will tend especially to precipitate and cater to a greater frequency of 'spectator' roles.

(b) Non-commercial and semi-commercial media systems that are normatively disposed to public service goals will produce higher proportions of issue-oriented political outputs and will tend especially to generate a higher incidence of 'monitor' role orientations among audience members.

CONCLUSION

The view of political communication presented in this essay draws upon the concept of a system as a set of input–output relationships that bind its constituent elements in a network of mutual dependencies. Such a model has both theoretical and empirical utilities. It should facilitate a comparative analysis of the political communication systems of different societies, and it has generated hypotheses on the basis of which a series of cross-national investigations could be launched.

Utilization of the main components of the system as analytical entry points provides, moreover, a set of complementary perspectives on the political communication process. From the standpoint of 'audience roles', this is seen in terms of mutual orientations to communication content that link (or fail to link) audience members with media personnel and political leaders. The structural/institutional perspective provides a view of the system in terms of conflicting goals and interests, ascribing these conflicts to structural differences between media and political institutions. Finally, the regulatory perspective focuses on the processes by which these conflicts are institutionalized and managed through the application of normative criteria, to which all participants subscribe to the extent that they share in and recognize the legitimacy of the political culture from which they derive. The model thus aims to take account of both consensus and conflict relationships in political communication transactions.

Chapter 3

Politicians and the press
An essay on role relationships[1]

This essay aims to conceptualize the relationship between mass media personnel and politicians in competitive democracies. It accordingly focuses on the political sub-area of the much wider field of mass media–source interactions in a liberal-democratic society. In such a society, the relations of media personnel to communication and information sources are (1) problematic, (2) pivotal and (3) exceptionally difficult to analyse.

They are *problematic* because they are not authoritatively prescribed in advance. Acceptance of the norm of editorial independence, plus the rarity of overt state control over media content, initially leaves the choice of sources in the hands of media professionals. In a liberal-democratic state, then, journalists are free to make their own arrangements with sources. As a result, they also zealously safeguard the near-sacred principle of confidentiality towards sources.

Media–source relations are *pivotal* in at least two senses. First, biography and observation confirm that such contacts typically absorb much of the energy, time and thought journalists devote to their work. Even though reporters are obliged by their essentially intermediate situation to face many ways at once, relating to such diverse reference groups as superiors, colleagues and audience images, reliable and well-placed sources are particularly preoccupying and formative. This is because 'the news is rooted not merely in organizational process and professional norms but in the action, inaction and talk of the elites who are the sources and subjects of most political stories' (Entman and Paletz, 1980).

Second, divergent interpretations of the media–source power balance lie at the heart of diametrically opposed views of the socio-political functions of mass communications. In this controversy we seemingly confront the equally plausible claims of Marx (or rather his latter-day disciples) and McLuhan. According to one paradigm, the mass media (even when formally independent and neutral) are essentially subordinate to society's institutionally dominant power-holders, treated as accredited witnesses whose opinions are regularly sought and whose interests and ideologies are systematically reinforced. According to a quite contrary thesis, however, the mass media are themselves power bastions, reality definers, and sites of professional cultures, with which other institutions must then come to terms. Exponents of the first perspective tend to deploy a terminology of source 'control and management of information', involving 'direct and indirect control and manipulation of the media' (Chibnall, 1977). Holders of the second view use a language of source adaptation instead, such that 'media ... are the dominant institutions of contemporary society ... to which other institutions [must] conform' (Altheide and Snow, 1979).

Media–source relations are *difficult to analyse* because their constituent elements are not easily isolated or disentangled. As Nimmo (1978) pointed out: 'Journalists do not gather news like a child plucking pansies from the meadow. Political news is the joint creation of the journalists who assemble and report events and other political communicators – politicians, professionals and spokespersons – who promote them.' Such a fusion occurs because each communicator is amply motivated to 'study' the other when pursuing his or her interests. Politicians are highly salient to reporters as staples of running stories, information resources for background insight, and even audiences for their output, providing knowledgeable feedback. At times they may also serve as validators of ambiguous political situations, the news status of which would otherwise be uncertain. But politicians must also tailor their activities to news media workways so as to make themselves more widely known; build up and sustain opinion constituencies; cultivate policy awareness and support; test public reactions to likely initiatives; and counter rivals' publicity efforts as well as damaging critical fire from other quarters.

Thus, the process whereby media constructions of political issues are shaped and produced is subtle and complex. It involves a close interaction between political advocates and media professionals, in the course of which the two sides may virtually be said to constitute a subtly composite unity. This is not to say that they merge to form a new unified whole in which their separate identities are lost. On the contrary, each side to some extent retains its separate purposes, its distance from the other, and occasionally even its oppositional stance towards the other. Nevertheless, the political messages which emanate from the dominant patterns of interaction between the two sides are in a sense traceable to a composite source. In fact, it would be extremely difficult to detect, within any given political message, the specific contribution to its shaping that was uniquely made by either side. They are inextricably intertwined.

The need to hone the conceptual tools we can apply to such relationships stems from policy concerns and theoretical puzzles alike. In the case of policy, the feasibility of promoting any desired political communication goal – whether it be building a more enlightened citizenry, reducing knowledge gaps, satisfying audience needs and expectations, or variegating the media issue-agenda – must largely depend on openings available in the predominant interaction patterns forged between prominent political actors and journalists. Similarly, the construction of adequate explanations of the production of political messages should be promising for the advancement of theory and for testing rival approaches. Moreover, identification of the main forces and mechanisms of interaction controlling these relationships should facilitate comparative political communication analysis, both across different societies and across different political situations and time periods within the same society.

THE AVAILABLE PARADIGMS

Analysis of the relationship between politicians as communicators and media personnel as observers of the political scene is in some conceptual disarray. Confusion arises because the models that are most often applied to it, the adversarial and exchange perspectives, share two fundamental defects. First, each is irretrievably partial in focus. Seeking to hit off its essence in some central flash of insight, neither can do justice to the inherent complexity of the relationship. Second, these views misleadingly pose as rivals in contention over the same ground – as if politician–journalist relations were most suitably to be treated as either adversarial or exchange-driven. Yet, at their most plausible, they are really applicable to different phenomena (instead of offering alternative interpretations of the same behaviours). Such a lack of comparability is further exacerbated by the fact that one of these positions, the adversarial, is permeated with prescriptive norms, for which there is no counterpart in the other.

The adversary model

The adversarial viewpoint is primarily ideological, prescribing how journalists *should* regard leading politicians and government figures. The relationship should pivot on a conflict of interest between themselves and politicians that is assumed to be abiding. Journalists should never be 'in the pockets' of the latter. They should warily scrutinize their conduct and rhetoric, supposing that the 'real story' could lie hidden below the source-constructed surface. How far journalists in different societies actually accept such a creed (which may reflect an American cultural bias) has not often been empirically examined, but most accounts support de Sola Pool's (1973) conclusion that 'it has a powerful pull on the journalist's imagination'. If so, its appeal springs from two roots: a view of political power and a sense of responsibility to audiences.

Thus, the adversarial ethic stems partly from the presupposition in liberal democratic theory of the self-serving propensities and potential fallibility of wielders of power. It follows that they should be carefully watched lest they abuse their powers, exceed their mandates, commit blunders they would prefer to conceal, and elevate themselves to positions of non-accountable authority. From this standpoint, it is natural to ascribe to the mass media the role of watchdog, protecting the public from the power of rulers, digging out evidence of abuse and error, and treating official information sources like Greeks bearing gifts. So far as members of the audience are concerned, they have needs and interests which, according to liberal theory, may well diverge from those of rulers. To pursue their goals effectively, they need access to trustworthy sources of information, which can tell them about developments in the wider political environment that may impinge on their fate. Such a surveillance service is then assigned to the mass media, which are expected independently to interpret environmental events according to their own lights and not just take on trust what interested parties say their policies are designed to achieve.

Despite its absorption into the professional ideology of many journalists, however, and the periodic eruption of stormy rows between politicians and reporters that appear to give it empirical credence, the adversarial perspective is open to serious objection on three grounds.

First, the adversarial ethic is extremely narrow; it cannot provide a comprehensive normative guide to journalists' behaviour towards their political sources and contacts. In itself, it includes, for example, no principles about the access rights of government spokespersons and critics; judiciousness; fairness; provision of an informed view of the problems and difficulties of government; or a readiness to give credit where it is due, in addition to publicizing mistakes and wrongdoing. Even William Rivers (1970), the most wholehearted academic exponent of 'the notion that there is an ideal relationship for government officials and journalists everywhere, and that ... relationship should be that of adversaries', was obliged, when developing that viewpoint in detail, to hedge it about with a whole host of reservations: asking, for example, 'How much adversarity is enough?'; seeking to 'define the limits of adversarity'; and declaring that an adversarial stance is not to be equated with a 'know-nothing belligerence towards government', with treatment of the President like 'public property' rather than as a 'public servant', with an indiscriminate 'manufacturing' of conflict in pursuit of 'adversarity with a vengeance', or with an 'escalation' of adversarity to such a pitch that 'the two institutions are driven to polar positions', ensuring that 'heat exceeds light'. The cumulative build-up of all these qualifications vividly demonstrates the impossibility of taking the adversarial ethic to its logical conclusion.

Second, regarded as an empirical account, the adversarial model is blind to certain essential features of journalists' daily relations with politicians. As Grossman and Rourke (1976) argued, it 'provides no mechanism for understanding the enormous amount of cooperation and even collaboration that takes place in the interaction between the press ... and the government'. But it is not only to be faulted for its inherently limited explanatory power. When coupled with its normative stance, forms of mutual assistance that may be indispensable to keep political messages flowing to the public in tolerably full supply are liable to be castigated as 'croneyism'.

Third, if it is true that the production of political messages is a joint enterprise, involving both sides in some degree of interaction (whether collaborative or complementary), mutually adversarial positions cannot be sustained for any length of time (except in a limited way and within clearly defined and mutually respected boundaries) without eroding the very basis of the relationship. Perpetual war, hostility, and obstruction would only impede each side from the effective pursuit of any constructive political communication task.

The exchange model

It is mainly in contrast to the adversary model that portrayals of inter-action between politicians and media representatives in terms of social exchange appear refreshingly realistic. For example, drawing on other investigators' studies of congressional press relations, Weaver and Wilhoit (1980) noted:

> In accepting and providing tips and leads, in willingness to float 'trial balloons' and accept leaks and in various arrangements of quid pro quo, reporters and Congressmen are often tacit, if not intentional, partners in the news ... 'You scratch my back and I'll scratch yours.'

In place of idealized visions of the journalistic St George tracking down the political dragon, then, this injects into the analysis the dimension of self-interest. Thus, exchange theory provides a plausible explanation of how the relationship is sustained through the many tensions and vicissi-tudes to which it is prone. A relationship persists, it implies, so long as its continuity and outcomes are perceived by the actors involved to serve their separate or joint interests. It thus overcomes a major weakness of the adversary model.

A closely argued application of the exchange model to the relationship between the American press and presidency has been provided by Gross-man and Rourke (1976). This hinges on the idea that 'reporters and officials have reason and resources to trade with each other, and that this interdependence is the key to understanding their interaction'. What politicians and reporters will agree to in striking bargains with each other, then, will depend on their respective calculations of advantage and disadvantage, including impressions 'of the resources, needs and likely actions of the other side', while from time to time they will also strive to alter the previous terms of trade in their favour.

The strengths of this approach are evident. First, it captures well the flavour of many moments when politicians and reporters decide to deal with each other. Though it suggests that much political reporting takes place because each side benefits from it, it need not imply that this is typically a matter of either actor being in the pocket of the other. It is compatible with the preservation of a certain distance and even an oppositional mentality in the relationship. The politician who survives an apparently tough encounter with an aggressive television interviewer may expect to gain more public credit than one who submits himself only to less challenging tests.

Second, this model seems more sensitive to the fluid nuances of the political advocate-professional communicator relationship than the adversarial view. Indeed, it has a built-in explanation for such fluctuations. When more co-operation between the two sides is observed, the reason must lie in the enlarged area of benefit that each expects to enjoy through collaboration with the other. If, on the other hand, co-operation declines and conflict increases, this is because the perceived benefits of withholding collaboration now outweigh the previous advantages of going along with what the other had proposed or was prepared to accept. Whichever way the relationship turns, the exchange model is capable of explaining it.

Third, as already pointed out, an exchange view explains how the relationship can be sustained amid the many tensions that inhere in it and disputes that punctuate it. This is precisely the issue on which the adversary model failed. It posits the relationship to be adversarial without suggesting a mechanism for sustaining it through all the built-in conflicts. But such a mechanism lies at the heart of the exchange model.

Despite these advantages, the exchange perspective also suffers from two defects which limit its explanatory power. First, it overly stresses the more personal, immediate, and non-formalized calculations made and bargains struck. In Grossman and Rourke's (1976) words: 'If we look at the process of exchange between executive officials and media representatives ... most striking is the informality of the relationship, the fact that it is based on unwritten rules, unnegotiated exchanges of commodities and mutual understandings.' But this begs the question of how the relationship is rendered predictable. The theory is vulnerable to the charge of being more concerned with *ad hoc* variations in the relationship than with its enduring regularities and structure. There is a more or less stable background of patterned assumptions and practices, within which journalist–politician exchanges take place, that are not them-selves entirely derivable from this version of exchange theory. Second, the exchange model fails to mention those norms that regulate the behaviour of individuals working in institutional settings, which define what is permissible and what is not in the terms of exchange they may offer or accept. Such norms may sometimes seem vague or porous, but they do exist and affect behaviour. For example, the self-images of media professionals include ideals of service to the audience, which set bounds to the forms of political coverage that they could even contemplate providing. Political commitments will similarly guide or limit officials' dealings with media representatives. Such normative influences on the chief producers of political communication may be taken for granted by exchange theory, but they cannot be explained by it.

Analytical dilemmas

It is as if the field of mutual interaction and influence between politicians and journalists has been illuminated from time to time by uncoordinated searchlights, each exposing a certain portion of the terrain to view without individually or jointly lighting up its entirety. Evidently we lack a more overarching framework that could transcend, while incorporating, the leading conceptual offerings so far favoured by outstanding analysts. The need for such an approach can be outlined from two standpoints.

First, there is the difficulty of meaningfully combining the available perspectives. Through what questions could they possibly be harnessed to each other? Should we ask how much 'exchange' or how much 'adversariness' a given relationship exhibits? Should we try to specify the conditions under which relationships might become more adversarial or more exchange-oriented? The project is futile – like enquiring when a certain tree might bear apples rather than oranges.

A second source of difficulty is the inescapable tension between the normative and operational levels of the relationships reviewed. On the one hand, the normative implications of liberal-democratic press theory prescribe an adversarial role for the media *vis-à-vis* the ruling institutions of society. But no lasting relationship can be built on such a basis in practice. On the other hand, theories which focus exclusively on operational interactions, attempting to explain how they work in practice, tend to ignore or minimize the role of normative ideologies and prescriptions in the outlook and conduct of those involved.

What seems to be required, then, is an approach that can take account of the complex cross-pressures which play on both parties to the relationship. On the normative plane, it would recognize the pull of norms and ideologies on actual behaviour. On the operational plane, it would start from the proposition that both sets of actors have a stake in maintaining the political communication process itself and that they typically appreciate the need to maintain a working relationship, to which each can settle.

Recognition of the tension between the normative and operational levels also sheds light on another characteristic feature of the relationship

– its instability and vulnerability. Sensitive observers of the media–government dance in liberal-democratic societies often comment on the 'delicacy' of the relationship, its fragility and proneness in moments of conflict to escalate into unanticipated confrontations. This reflects the fact that both sides are simultaneously exposed, on the one hand to the pull of ideologies which are often incompatible because they stem from different sources, and on the other hand to pressures to maintain in some repair the tissues of continuing interaction. At one level, the two sides are pulled apart in divergent directions. At another, they are hauled back together towards a joint or parallel course.

The inherently precarious and conflict-laden strains generated by such cross-pressures cannot provide a smooth basis for continually working together. What such a relationship requires is a measure of predictability and shared understandings, by recourse to which each side may reasonably try to anticipate the other's actions and reactions. To facilitate its continuity, that is, the relationship must, to some extent, be regularized and institutionalized.

AN EXPANDED FRAMEWORK

The production of political communications is inherently complex. When approached unilaterally, essential features tend to be distorted or ignored. Both in order to overcome the resulting theoretical problems and to structure empirical data derived from many observations of political communicators at work in Britain (see Part II of this book), we have developed an alternative analytical framework couched in the following summary terms: media-disseminated political communications derive from interactions between (1) two sets of mutually dependent and mutually adaptive actors, pursuing divergent (though overlapping) purposes, whose relationships with each other are typically (2) role-regulated, giving rise to (3) an emergent shared culture, specifying how they should behave towards each other, the ground rules of which are (4) open to contention and conflicting interpretation, entailing a potential for disruption, which is often (5) controlled by informal and/or formal mechanisms of conflict management. The following passages outline some implications of each of these elements in turn.

Dependence and adaptation

Political communication originates in mutual dependence within a framework of divergent though overlapping purposes. Each side of the politician–media professional partnership is striving to realize certain goals *vis-à-vis* the audience; yet it cannot pursue them without securing in some form the co-operation of the other side. Sometimes they share certain goals – for example, addressing, and sustaining credibility with, as large an audience as they can. Usually the actors' purposes are in some tension as well: journalists are primarily aiming to hold the attention of a target audience through some mixture of alerting, informing, and entertaining them; politicians are primarily trying to persuade audience members to adopt a certain view of themselves, or of their parties or factions, and of what they are trying to achieve in politics.

Whatever the exact mixture of goals, each side needs the other and must adapt its ways to theirs. Politicians need access to the communication channels that are controlled by the mass media, including the hopefully credible contexts of audience reception they offer. Consequently, they must adapt their messages to the demands of formats and genres devised inside such organizations and to their associated speech styles, story models and audience images. Likewise, journalists cannot perform their task of political scrutiny without access to politicians for information, news, interviews, action and comment: 'To be convincing purveyors of reality . . . journalists must get as close as they can to the sources of events' (Polsby, 1980).

Thus, each side of the prospective transaction is in a position to offer the other access to a resource it values. The mass media offer politicians access to an audience through a credible outlet, while politicians offer journalists information about a theatre of presumed relevance, significance, impact and spectacle for audience consumption. Because such resources are finite, however, rivals inside each camp compete more or less keenly for them, further strengthening the pressures promoting a mutual adaptation. The scope and terms of politicians' access to the media depend not only on conventional limitations of time and space but also on the 'threshold of tolerance' audiences may have towards political messages. So in competing for favourable attention in the preferred 'slots', politicians adjust to perceived media values and requirements. But politicians also command scarce resources. Not only is the amount of informational raw material they can supply limited; it may also vary in quality – for example, a strong leak on a headline development is worth more than a speculative rumour about a more technical issue from a lower-placed source. Politicians are therefore in a position, especially when newsworthy, to 'ration the goodies', use them as bargaining counters, and direct reporters' attention to their pet themes. 'Pack journalism', which stems from a subtle mixture of (1) uncertainty about what really counts as political news and (2) anxiety not to miss something the competition will be carrying, intensifies the ensuing adaptations.

Of course, many of these factors operate as variables, not constants. Politicians vary in their need for media publicity. Similarly, journalists will be more anxious to cover certain politicians and events than others. As some American studies have suggested (Ostroff, 1980; Clarke and Evans,

1980), the pressure on them to follow the top politicians and uncritically pass on their initiatives is greater in presidential campaigns than in state-level races. But despite such sources of variation, the forces of mutual dependence, competition and adaptation will tend most formatively to shape political communication about precisely those personalities and situations that receive the heaviest and most regular coverage in political news.

Role relationships

The recurrent interactions that result in political communication for public consumption are negotiated, not by unsocialized individuals, but by individuals in roles whose working relationships are consequently affected by normative and institutional commitments. In Chittick's (1970) definition: 'The term "role" refers ... to the socially prescribed behavior of a position holder .... Role theory posits that position holders will behave in accordance with both their own role expectations and those of counter position holders.' What theoretical advantages flow from treating political communicators as occupants of roles, the terms of which guide their own behaviour and shape their relationships with and expectations of their counterparts in the message production process? These may be outlined from three perspectives.

First, such an approach explains the behaviour of political communicators by locating them in their respective organizational settings, where their roles are chiefly defined and performed. In the case of political journalists, role-anchored guidelines serve many functions. They provide models of conduct to be observed when contacting politicians or appearing before the public as 'representatives' of their organizations, whose standards they are supposed to display (Kumar, 1975). They steer activity in countless daily routines. In an observation study of BBC current affairs producers at work during the British general election of 1966, for example, certain initiatives taken to improve their campaign coverage were traced to 'the internal role-definitions of their positions to which television journalists subscribe', including responsibilities 'to serve the audience adequately' and 'to the standards of their own profession' (Chapter 9 below). They are a source of support when conflict erupts. When, during the British general election of 1979, a BBC news executive dealt with various party complaints about unfairness, for example, he was observed to handle them confidently partly because he was an institutional figure. He could draw on corporation policy, professional standards, and past precedents both to justify what had been done and to suggest solutions to difficulties. So long as he was true to his role, he was protected.

In contrast to professional journalists, many practising politicians are only part-time communicators. Even so, their media arrangements are

often tended by full-time specialists with corresponding roles to match –
press officers, publicity aides, campaign managers, speech writers, and so
on. And when functioning as communicators, politicians also act out
certain role prescriptions themselves: 'representing' the interests of a
party, government or department of state; responding to the expectations
of political colleagues, with whom their reputations can be strengthened
or weakened by the quality of their public appearances; and addressing
the electoral audience in a certain style. In fact, there is often a close
connection between politicians' public images and their roles as communicators. Certainly impressions of politicians' qualities as communicators
have become increasingly important features of their public images in
recent years – and so, presumably, of their communication roles as well.

Second, a focus on roles as shapers and regulators of behaviour also
connects the interactions of media professionals and partisan advocates
to the surrounding socio-political culture. This helps to explain their
patterned continuity over time and their variety across diverse societies.
Thus, mass media structures, their organizational and professional ideologies, and their specific work practices are in every society specific to
and shaped by its culture. Likewise, the structure and operations of the
political institutions of society are products of the same cultural forces.
It is not surprising, therefore, that a high degree of fit should be found
between those institutions, which is reflected, at the interface between
media and political institutions, in a fit between the role-regulated
behaviours of the interacting communicators.

Several general features of such interaction are underlined by the
considerations spelled out above. For one thing, communication behaviour
is normatively prescribed, involving legitimated expectations and actions.
This suggests that the capacity of the participants to exchange resources
or exercise influence is constrained by the guidelines pertaining to the
roles they perform. Thus, political reporters cannot, without great risk,
offer politicians any type of news treatment that lies outside the authority
of their roles. Likewise, politicians will tend to avoid behaviour *vis-à-vis*
media personnel (such as blatant favours or explicit sanctions) that would
be construed as breaching their role prescriptions. Exchange and the
tussles of mutual influence are normatively bounded. In addition,
behaviour on both sides is conditioned by expectations of how each
will, because they should, behave towards the other. This has important
consequences for the structure of the interaction. It underlies and explains
the predictability of the behaviour patterns involved and the ability of
each side to count on much that the other will do so long as its expectations are met. It also helps to explain the note of outrage that is
sometimes sounded during adversarial episodes – reflecting the injured
party's conviction, not merely that its interests were damaged, but that
supposedly accepted moral boundaries had been overstepped. And it

explains the relative stability of structure of those many joint activities out of which political communication daily emerges.

Third, a reference to role conceptualization clarifies the partial plausibility of the adversary and exchange models and helps to reconcile their apparent opposition. On the one hand, exchange mechanisms are set in motion when performance of role obligations on either side requires the enlisting of co-operation from the other. On the other hand, adversarial relations are triggered when the role obligations of the two sides are such as to bring them into collision course with each other.

An emergent shared culture

Many British television journalists and party publicists, when interviewed by the authors afterwards about their roles in the country's general elections of February and October 1974, often emphasized the need for mutual trust in their relations with each other. A party press officer said: 'If I gave the media a bum steer over the significance of a speech about to be made by my Leader, they would no longer take my guidance so seriously in the future.' Another concluded a lengthy account of campaign exchanges by baldly asserting: 'Both sides are operating on the basis of news values.' Broadcasters also mentioned special efforts they had made to convince politicians they could be trusted to respect and apply shared norms.

This is not to imply that uncertainty could be eliminated from the relationship. Rather, the communicators can be viewed as playing a game with more or less agreed rules, in which one or another participant would sometimes make an unexpected move. Several party officials pictured their publicity initiatives as pieces of bait dangled before reporters. The journalistic fish might not bite, but if the anglers chose the right bait for the conditions, and the political weather did not suddenly change, they stood a good chance of making a catch. In the process, however, each side needed to count on the other's observance of certain rules of conduct to an extent sufficient to allow campaigners to frame their publicity strategies and to enable news executives to give assignments to reporters without risking a waste of precious resources.

All this reflects an underlying sociological imperative. In any continuing relationship based on mutual dependence and need, a culture, structuring all the areas of behaviour in which both sides regularly interact, tends to emerge. The norms of that culture then (1) regulate the relationship, (2) get embedded in behavioural routines which often assume the status of precedents to be followed in the future, (3) are points of reference when disputes arise over alleged failures to respect existing ground rules or demands to change them, and (4) revert to and become absorbed into the internal role definitions of the respective actors. This does not mean that all participants will embrace the operative norms equally enthusiastically or without reservation. Cultural differences will persist and be voiced as well. But a shared culture is continually re-established, even in the face of disagreement, because it is indispensable to undergird the relationship.

Such norms can govern a wide range of matters. For example, the emergent culture normally includes shared criteria of fairness – e.g. in British election campaigns the two major parties are usually reckoned to deserve equal amounts of air time, while smaller parties are allotted less time than the major ones. In other countries, quite different principles of fairness are applied – for example, absolutely equal treatment for all political parties regardless of size in Denmark.

A shared culture may also include certain criteria of objectivity. The many distancing devices, described by Tuchman (1972) as 'strategic ritual protecting newspapermen from the risks of their trade ... including critics', owe much of their defensive efficacy to their acceptance by politicians and other news sources as valid marks of an objective approach.

Role relationships are also regulated by criteria of behavioural propriety in interaction. Respect for embargoes, the anonymity of sources, and the confidences of 'off-the-record' disclosures come to mind here. In addition, certain boundaries distinguishing acceptable from impermissible areas of questioning may be well defined in one national news culture while following different lines in another.

In addition, and perhaps most significantly, interaction is regulated by a framework of news values that is to some extent shared, indicating both who and what will tend to be treated as newsworthy. As Elliott (1977) pointed out, 'Accepting some sources as official and reliable while questioning or ignoring others is an important part of journalistic routine', and those inside the charmed circle of access will expect its existing boundaries to be maintained more or less intact. Shared substantive definitions of news make it possible for each side to try to manipulate the situation to its own advantage. Politicians, for example, needing exposure but lacking control over it, can then so adjust their behaviour to strengthen their chance of winning the most favourable coverage possible in the prevailing news-based definition of the situation.

In all these spheres complex processes and calculations play on the emergence, entrenchment and revision of the ground rules. First, for each side there is often a mixture of benefit and cost in conforming to the prevailing pattern. Despite their highly privileged access rights, for example, top politicians may occasionally be on the receiving end of extremely unfavourable treatment, due to journalists' access to other news sources, a pile-up of incidents casting doubt on their competence and power to control events, or even the impact of being hoist with their own petard, when a statesman's verbal blunders are flung back into his face. The fact that politicians rarely object to such treatment suggests either that they accept the ruling news-value system or realize that complaining would be counter-productive. Likewise, in the course of covering election campaigns, television journalists sometimes criticize their own overly receptive response to visual events stage-managed by party Leaders. Yet they continue to present them, even after questioning their newsworthiness, partly because they cannot afford unilaterally to suspend a shared convention. Instead, they occasionally salve their reportorial consciences by clothing them in a sceptically toned commentary.

Second, the existing fabric of news values is not solely a media product, which is then imposed on and accepted by politicians as a *fait accompli*. Politicians' definitions of situations may not only differ from those of journalists; at times they may also contribute to what counts as political news. The history of election coverage in Britain includes several episodes of attempted news creativity by politicians. The first use of the 'walkabout' as a regular campaign device in the 1970 general election is a case in point. It originated in the need of the Labour Leader for a source of daily appearances in a campaign that he wished to play in low-key vein. Yet in later campaigns Leader walkabouts were screened almost daily in TV news. Broadcasters had come to accept them as a routine feature of their election coverage.

Third, an ever-evolving shared culture emerges from an ever tactically shifting process in which the principal actors strive to influence each other for their own benefit. As Polsby (1980) pointed out, journalistic professionalism demands that 'news media elites establish their own account of day-to-day reality, independent of that propounded by the politicians whom they cover'. In response, politicians can try either to exploit the dominant story lines or challenge their legitimacy. Rather more frequent recourse to the latter strategy has been encouraged in recent years by a growing awareness of the ultimate subjectivity of news judgements. Consequently, more and more groups may come to regard the news stories about themselves as wittingly or unwittingly politicized and therefore fit to be pressurized. The mass media respond by becoming more aware of these groups' sensitivities. At a given time, then, the dominant system of news values will in part reflect the outcomes of previous tugs of war between journalists and representatives of numerous sectional groups, including politicians.

Fourth, despite much argument and tactical struggle, the influence of forces promoting co-operation between the two sides can be detected in modern political communication systems as well. One is the presence inside media and political institutions of boundary roles, whose occupants are closely familiar with the values and practices of the other camp. The publicity advisers of politicians may convey to their masters an impression of the current news-value system as part of the natural order of things. Likewise, media organizations often appoint to their executive teams one or more individuals who are particularly sensitive to and *au fait* with leading politicians and their publicity problems. Both sides also seem to feel the need to be in a position, when engaged in or anticipating disputes, to appeal to principles that transcend their purely sectional interests. This strengthens the elements of shared culture by emphasizing their overarching standing. In our observation study of the British general election of 1966 (Chapter 9), for example, it was noted that 'the appeal of a political party to a principle of fairness which the producers themselves regarded as legitimate . . . helped to remind the broadcasters of considerations that had been overlooked in the hectic conditions of election programming'. For their part, media personnel also seem motivated to enter potentially tense situations with 'clean hands' – able to say, if a row were to erupt, that they at least had behaved properly and responsibly.

Underlying sources of conflict

However tightly woven, the web of mutual need and shared understandings cannot eliminate conflict. In the preceding discussion we have characterized politicians and journalists as locked into a complex set of transactions which, though mutually beneficial, also include potentials for disagreement and struggle. Underlying the resulting disputes are certain role-related, and therefore abiding, sources of conflict – ones that continually arise because they are part and parcel of a system of interacting role partners whose purposes to some extent diverge.

First, the participants' differing organizational and professional role commitments give rise to the *cui bono?* question of political communication: Who is supposed to be its main beneficiary? All commonly recognize that multiple purposes will be served, but their priorities are inevitably different. Politicians tend to regard the political communication process predominantly as an agency of persuasion, available to themselves (and their competitors) for mobilizing public support for their own causes and views, rather than as a channel for more detachedly educating and enlightening the electorate. When in power, they naturally tend to regard promotion of the national interest, as defined by their policies, as more important than the incessant search for their Achilles' heels and 'criticism for the sake of criticism'. For media professionals, the scales of ultimate aims are differently balanced. It is true that they often acknowledge politicians' special access rights, particularly at election time. Indeed, radical critics of mass communication have little difficulty in marshalling evidence intended to document media subservience and deference to those in power. Yet the principle of service to the audience is an integral part of the professional ideology of media personnel in liberal-democratic societies and is supposed to override the service proffered to other interests. Though in interaction they are often pulled very close to politicians' needs, journalists can never entirely forget their audience clients. The following musings by a BBC commentator on the coverage by British television of a recent round of political party conferences exemplify such a spirit (Dimbleby, 1980):

> Perhaps television has become too much at the service of the parties and their conferences.... The broadcaster is there, after all, at the service of the viewer, not the party. It would be a pity to confuse what the former wants with what the latter may choose to provide.

Second, different perceptions of the division of labour in the production of political messages generate the 'agenda-setting' question of political communication: Who should determine which definitions of political problems citizens will think and talk about most often? This arises because the reality-structuring role of the mass media is at one and the same time formative, ambiguous and doubtfully legitimate. That is, it often obliges politicians to discuss issues in terms they find irrelevant or repugnant; it is not always admitted that this is happening; and nobody 'elected' media people to play such a part. It is therefore sometimes perceived as an 'intervention' in the political arena itself, distorting its natural parameters, which presupposes in turn that the proper role of the media is one of reflecting and transmitting the statements, decisions and comings and goings of the 'primary' political actors.

Third, different ways of interpreting each other's roles give rise to a 'fixing-of-responsibility' question about political communication: Who is to blame when it goes wrong and proves unsatisfactory? Post-mortems after uninspiring election campaigns, for example, often show each side disclaiming responsibility and pointing the finger of censure at the other: journalists decry the politicians' evasive rhetoric; politicians deplore the journalists' reduction of their rivalry to a horse race. The origins of such a process are deep-seated and involve contradictions between three perceptual tendencies:

1 When presenting itself to others, each side depicts its role as in some sense sacred. The politician cloaks himself in a representative capacity. The journalist claims to enshrine freedom of expression and the public's right to know.
2 When reflexively contemplating its own role, each side takes full account of certain constraints that limit its ability to realize its more idealized goals. Indeed, each side often treats imperfections in the electoral audience – its ignorance, indulgence in fixed stereotypes, and lack of commitment to sustained intellectual effort – as explaining and justifying the compromises it must make when addressing ordinary people.
3 But when regarding the contributions to political communication of its

counterpart, each side lacks charity and is quick to point to the gap between its role performance and its role professions, interpreting this as evidence of inadequacy – or even hypocrisy.

Since the defects of political communication are plausibly and regularly blamed on the failures of the other partner to the process, neither assumes responsibility for putting them right, inadequacies persist without correction, and so the cycle of mutual criticism is perpetuated as well.

Conflict management

The preceding discussion has identified certain built-in sources of recurrent conflict. If our argument about the need to sustain the relationship is valid, then in any liberal-democratic society the political communication system will also include some mechanisms for managing conflict. In form, these will differ from one society to another, and their workings will not always be visible or openly discussed. In a sense they are delicate, for the co-operation required to smooth out conflict may seem at odds with the principle of media independence and its implication that political forces should not be in a position to dictate how journalists comment on political affairs. British arrangements are quite interesting in this connection, since they have moved quite far in the direction of institutionalizing conflict management. Consideration of some of the procedures that have been developed there highlights several functions that mechanisms of conflict management can perform for political communication systems.

First, there are numerous procedures for airing and dealing with complaints about the violation of ground rules. These may be hierarchically structured. In the case of the BBC, for example, aggrieved politicians with quite specific complaints may directly approach the editor of the offending programme. Complaints with broader implications may be channelled through a political party's broadcasting officer at national headquarters, or its Chief Whip in Parliament, to the chief assistant to the Director-General of the BBC. However, specially serious causes of concern might be personally raised by senior politicians with the Corporation's Director-General himself or with the Chairman of its Board of Governors. The loftier the channel through which the complaint flows, the more likely it is to trigger a semi-formal investigation and delivery of a verdict and reply in writing. But in all such exchanges the personalities and temperaments of the individuals handling the complaints are crucial. Those with a grievance to put like to feel that they are dealing with someone who is fair and sympathetic. Those receiving protests like to feel that they are dealing with a person of reason and common sense. A high valuation is often placed by those who are regularly involved in such transactions on attitudes that facilitate calm and accommodation:

moderation, avoidance of single-minded assertions of principle, readiness to compromise, sensitivity to the other side's flash points.

Second, forums may be created to review existing ground rules and consider proposals for modifying them. For example, the Committee on Political Broadcasting, representing the main political parties, the BBC and ITV, meets annually and in advance of every general election campaign to discuss the number, lengths, distribution and scheduling of party political broadcasts. In fact, suggested changes are usually aired first in informal soundings of everybody's views, aiming to hammer out disagreements well before any proposals are tabled at a formal committee meeting.

Third, institutions may be established to socialize the members of one side to the needs and demands of the other. An example is the Lobby Committee in the precincts of Parliament, which, though staffed by journalists, ensures the conformity of their accredited colleagues to certain rules of behaviour that are regarded as quid pro quos for privileged access to Ministers and MPs.

Fourth, forums of consultation may be created to secure the continuing co-operation of one of the sides in a joint task. One example is the D-Notice Committee, which involves newspaper editors in a voluntary censorship of specified forms of security-sensitive information. Another is the aforementioned Committee on Political Broadcasting, at the pre-election meetings of which broadcasters outline their campaign programming plans, both as a courtesy to the politicians who will be affected by them and to allow objections to be raised in advance that could be highly disruptive if they were to erupt while the campaign was already in hectic flood.

THE SYSTEMATIZATION OF POLITICAL COMMUNICATION: CONSEQUENCES AND POLICY IMPLICATIONS

This essay has outlined some ways of approaching the communication élites whose joint activities yield political news and comment for the masses. It interprets their relationship as one that typically develops through patterned interactions, which are shaped and constrained in turn by requirements seated in their roles as political advocates and mass media professionals. They badly need each other's services and dependability, but as a result of their conflicting purposes, roles and definitions of politics, they are periodically buffeted by upsets and strains. Yet even such conflicts often bind as well as divide them, since key figures inside each camp tend to acquire stakes in workable conflict management.

What principal consequences flow from such a system for the production of political messages in competitive democracies? The answers are not all reassuring:

1 The system gives a rather privileged position in political communication output to the views of already established power holders. Of course, many others get a say as well, but only the activities and statements of those in well-entrenched positions tend regularly to be relayed to electoral audiences as a matter of course. Sometimes the news-value justification for such near-automatic access is not easy to spot: it is as if the comments of the most highly accredited witnesses are worth transmitting, not for what they have said but for what they are.

2 The other side of the coin is that leading politicians get their say almost entirely through formats devised and controlled by journalists. Such a 'subordination' is the price they pay for their privileged access position. This *is* a price, because it denies them direct access to the mass audience, except in circumscribed ghettos (party broadcasts) or paid advertisements. Thus, the system has more or less settled for the reduction of political messages to the demands of journalism, with its emphasis on the dramatic, the concrete, the personalizable and the arresting – and with its turbulent and episodic view of the flow of civic affairs.

3 Meanwhile, the needs of the audience may be relegated to a back seat in the political communication bus. This is because, in their preoccupation with a complex of conflicting interests, mutual dependencies, and problems of second-guessing each other, the two main sets of communicators may well lose sight of the ordinary voter's concerns and come to behave largely in those ways that seem likely to forge the most convenient accommodation to the other side's behaviour (Blumler, 1977). Fortunately, potentially strong antidotes to such a tendency can be found in the journalistic ethic of audience service. Yet even this may be impoverished in application by the hold of sharply stereotypical impressions of what the average audience member is like as a news-processing animal. And if prevailing audience images fail to do justice to genuine kernels of concern among members of the public to make some sense of their political environment, then communication dictated by such images could ultimately prove frustrating to its would-be receivers because of not seeming to them to provide anything worth heeding.

4 Finally, much of a society's political news 'conveys an impression of eternal recurrence' (Rock, 1973). Although a strain towards the ritualization of political communication (such that 'new political situations . . . fall quickly into old symbolic molds'; Bennett, 1980) has many sources, one of its roots may be traceable to the inherent caution of interdependent communicators. This is not to imply that innovatory impulses are often stifled at birth; but that they may have to fight a steep uphill battle even to stand a chance of being tried. This is essentially because pressures to maintain the stability of the working relationship between

'partisans' and 'professionals' militate against the purposive introduction of new political communication forms. Thus, innovatory communication proposals often start life with three strikes against them. First, a new departure may not get off the ground because it is in somebody's interest not to co-operate – as with the fate of numerous attempts to stage party Leader debates on British television at election time. Second, an innovation may be risky because of the uncertainty it would generate. Third, some innovations may offend, because they seem to violate shared cultural norms and established precedents.

Such formidable blockages to innovation are worrying, not because novelty should be valued for its own sake, but because freshness of approach is indispensable when tackling the inherently difficult tasks of making political information palatable and political argument comprehensible to large masses of voters.

Chapter 4

The orientations of journalists to social and political institutions[1]

The idea that the mass media play a pivotal part in the nexus of power relations in society is by now largely accepted by most communication researchers, irrespective of theoretical differences. Nevertheless, analysis of the linkages between media organizations and other power-wielding institutions in society is still segmented and incomplete. Individual scholars have variously examined media relations to markets and business institutions, as in the political economy perspective (Murdock and Golding, 1977); to parties and political institutions (Seymour-Ure, 1974); and to a host of pressure groups, such as trade unions (Glasgow University Media Group, 1976), the women's movement (Tuchman, Kaplan and Benet, 1978), the environmental lobby (Greenberg, 1975) and social reformers (Goldenberg, 1975; Gitlin, 1980). Lacking, however, has been a more enveloping scheme, stretching across several power domains, and designed to explain differences in the orientations of the mass media to a range of diverse social groups and organizations.

This essay proposes an approach to the development of such a scheme. The empirical data on which it is based emerged from a case study of the launching of the sound broadcasting of Parliament in Britain in 1978. In the course of that inquiry, much evidence was gathered from different sorts of news and current affairs broadcasters about their attitudes towards coverage of Parliament, once the possibility of directly broadcasting its proceedings had been created. Generalizing from that study, and from the different viewpoints disclosed by it, we have sought to develop a conceptual framework, within which media portrayals of a variety of social and political institutions might be theorized.

MASS MEDIA RELATIONSHIPS TO NEWS SOURCES

In their daily routines, journalists engage with social and political institutions predominantly as potential sources of news. As Roshco (1975) has pointed out, 'The sociology of news must ... be concerned with the basis for establishing reporter–source relationships as well as with the nature and consequences of subsequent interactions.' Yet our ability to analyse the structure of media–source relationships has been hampered by the absence of a fully considered analytical scheme. Several signs of such neglect are noticeable.

First, as deployed in the literature, the very notion of a 'source' is ambiguous. The term has been applied both to the organizations and groups, which often feature as subjects of news reports, and to the individuals, whose location within such institutions enables them to serve as informants about decisions and events which they have made or witnessed. Such a distinction already alerts us to a possible duality of journalistic response to sources: as subjects they will be judged for their newsworthiness, but as informants they will be assessed for their authority and credibility.

Second, although differential access to the news may be a key mechanism in public opinion formation (for example, through agenda setting and status conferral), little attempt has been made systematically to specify the range of factors that could account for the varying treatment that diverse sources enjoy or suffer at the hands of news workers. In trying to explain the differences of news visibility between groups or individuals, different analysts tend to latch on to different single mechanisms, ignoring other potential influences. Media professionals, for example, usually refer to news values to explain why, say, presidents and prime ministers get more attention than miners and garbage collectors (except, of course, when the latter go on strike!). In offering such explanations, media professionals appear to be oblivious to the origins of news value judgements, tending to see them as inherent in the events or individuals they cover, rather than tracing them to their own collective professional assumptions and rules of thumb. Some scholars have suggested that the personal predilections of reporters towards 'the issues involved in the group's activities' may influence their contacts with and stories about their sources (Goldenberg, 1975). Critical researchers tend to argue that a permeation of ideological influences ensures a reproduction in the news of differential power relations in society at large (Hall, 1982). Yet another line of explanation attributes the greater ability of certain sources to attract favourable coverage to the more powerful controls and sanctions which they can exert – for example, the denial of information, advertising and other 'goods' valued by the news organization (Tunstall, 1971). Little attention has been paid, however, to how these different explanatory mechanisms might be related to each other – whether as competing alternatives, as mutually complementary, or as diverse influences cutting across each other in a more complex field of forces.

Third, the presumed uniformity of journalists' orientations to a given institutional source has rarely been questioned and probed. Do all media professionals, who are able to take or influence decisions about the reporting of a source's affairs, approach them in a more or less uniform manner? If so, how is such presumed uniformity achieved? To answer such questions, it is necessary to identify those roles in news organizations whose incumbents might react differentially to the source concerned and are in a position to affect its coverage. In the literature, this problem has mainly been addressed through a dichotomous distinction between specialist and generalist reporters or between news-gatherers and news-processors, depicting the former as more open to co-optation by source perspectives and interests than the latter.

Finally, in certain studies of news-making too narrow a view is taken of the journalistic role in relation to those of sources. Journalists are sometimes depicted as individuals whose relations with their contacts are shaped by calculations of utility or preference, reflecting their professional goals (Grossman and Rourke, 1976) or their political and ideological inclinations (Noelle-Neumann, 1980). Omitted from such explanations are interpretations that take more broadly into account both the institutional structures in which media professionals are employed, and the socio-political cultures which may impinge on and shape their representations of social institutions, issues and actors.

In short, media–source relations may be even more complex than most analysts have so far imagined. Such was certainly an implication of our own attempt to understand the attitudes of British broadcasters to a central political institution in British society – Parliament – at a time when their access to its proceedings had significantly changed.

AN ENQUIRY INTO THE BROADCASTING OF PARLIAMENT

Parliament has long been a major site of information about political processes in Britain and hence a prominent topic of mass media coverage. Most decisions of government are announced there. Daily opportunities to elicit government reactions to breaking news stories and unfolding events are ever present in Questions to the Prime Minister and to other departmental Ministers. Parliament is also the prime forum in which party differences over issues of the day are ventilated. The prestigious lobby of Westminster correspondents is based there. The main conventions and routines of reporting from Westminster are consequently long established and firmly rooted.

For many years, however, British broadcasters had felt hamstrung in their ability to present Parliament to the viewing and listening public. As long as the tools of their trade – microphones and cameras – were excluded from Westminster, the coverage and colour they could provide was diminished and thwarted. Perhaps this situation also symbolized the restrictions of access and secrecy, under which the media laboured more generally, when trying to record the activities and decisions of the British Government and bureaucracy. The introduction of the sound broadcasting of Parliament in 1978 was therefore perceived as something of a victory in the continuing struggle over media rights to collect and publish political information. Even such a minor victory was bound to be regarded as inaugurating a new departure in the communication of parliamentary affairs to the public and was initially greeted with some enthusiasm. The key change here was the possibility of direct coverage. For the first time members of the broadcast audience could listen to MPs' contributions to debates, either live and *in extenso* or in an edited form afterwards. Hopes ran high.

This innovation in political communication was sufficiently important and problematic to merit an investigation of the consequences and problems it would bring in its wake. A 'systematic' perspective was adopted, involving (a) observation of the production process at Westminster and in national and local radio newsrooms, (b) interviews with many broadcasters, including policy-makers and executives, those directly involved in reporting from Parliament (such as Westminster correspondents) and those who, as controllers of radio channels, managers of local stations and editors of News and Current Affairs programmes, were mainly schedulers or transmitters of parliamentary items, (c) a content analysis of parliamentary reporting in a wide range of radio and television News and Current Affairs programmes during a single parliamentary session, and (d) a study of audience responses to extracts of parliamentary proceedings presented in a variety of ways. This essay is based largely on our interviews with and observations of parliamentary broadcasters.

BROADCASTERS' ORIENTATIONS TO PARLIAMENT: LAYERS AND LEVELS

When examining the interview material, we were impressed with the exceptionally varied sets of attitudes that broadcasters had displayed towards Parliament – or rather towards parliamentary proceedings as a source of programme material. Broadcasters' reactions to parliamentary events, and the recorded actuality of such events, appeared complex and multi-layered. In our attempt to structure their responses, three underlying dimensions of broadcaster orientation were identified.

First, broadcasters could regard Parliament simply as an important and rich source of information about politics in Britain: what the issues of the day are and how they are debated by the main parties, factions and their leaders; the policies that governments announce for coping with current problems and how these are received by the same forces; and as the arena in which fluctuating power relationships are mirrored and played out and the demands and viewpoints of key subgroups of society confront each other and are resolved. At this level, broadcasters may be said to relate to Parliament as media professionals, regarding it primarily as a source of materials for selection and processing as news values dictate.

Holders of such an attitude tended to minimize the innovatory potential of recorded parliamentary material and often expressed modest expectations about its impact on public awareness. They were far more interested in the availability of short extracts for incorporation into news reports than in the transmission of entire debates. They appeared to regard Commons sound, then, as just another 'tool' in their professional kit, to be used mainly to illustrate and enliven their usual ways of presenting news from Parliament. In their eyes, parliamentary tape was rather like another wire service that could supplement, without radically altering, their customary approaches to political coverage. As a local radio station news editor told us at an early stage:

> We will cover exactly the same stories as before, but we will have a new tool at our disposal. It's just a new source of material for us. The use of actuality will make the news 'better radio' because it will be first-hand. It's far better to have Jill Knight actually speaking in the House rather than a repeat of what she said. However, the main point remains: What's the best way to do a story? . . . We should apply the same news values to this material as we apply to all other material.

Second, and overlaying this professional approach, there was the fact that, constitutionally, broadcasting organizations are ultimately accountable to Parliament. This is the central feature of the relationship of broadcasting to the state in Britain, distinguishing it on the one hand from those broadcasting systems which are directly subordinate to state organs or have party political appointees inside their governing bodies, and on the other hand from those in which a diluted line of political accountability is channelled through a relatively weak regulatory agency. Of course broadcasting organizations everywhere are exposed to pressures and influences from a whole range of powerful bodies in society, such as political parties, industrial interests and civic groups. But the further element of constitutional subordination in their relationship to Parliament obliges British broadcasters to bear in mind the acceptability of how they work and what they produce to those who are ultimately in a position to determine their organizational futures. The need to ensure and demonstrate that their uses of recorded extracts from parliamentary debates will be 'responsible' reflects this unique relationship – the influence of which was probably reinforced by the establishment of a House of Commons Select Committee on Sound Broadcasting to monitor and report on the service.

Third, we identified yet another extra-professional layer to the relationship, which stemmed from the symbolic position that Parliament occupies in society, standing as the presumed institutional embodiment of the central values of British democracy. At this level, partly out of civic commitment to the national political system, and partly because in their eyes the values that British broadcasting stands for flow integrally from the values of 'parliamentary democracy', some broadcasters tended to treat the institutional symbol of that system with a certain deference and respect – as if imbued with a degree of sacredness.

Holders of such an attitude were inclined to assess the sound broadcasting innovation for its prospects of acquainting the audience more fully with what Parliament represented in the British system. As one correspondent put it:

> The broadcasting of Parliament provides a great opportunity for us. Most people have never been to Parliament and have not seen how intimate a place it is. They should get a feel of the peculiar quality of the House of Commons and of MPs themselves and realise that they are Members of something a bit different and special.

The fact that broadcasters could relate to Parliament along these different dimensions implies that they were caught up in a web of tensions emanating from the different, and sometimes incompatible, claims on their loyalties of professional norms, embedded in the first layer of the relationship, and of the extra-professional values and considerations represented by the other layers. Professionally, Parliament was viewed primarily as a source of raw material for the journalistic mill. But the extra-professional attitudes implied that Parliament was entitled to treatment in a manner that would uphold its symbolic value in the political system and not undermine its dignity. At this stage, it is worth noting a similar distinction that emerged from a previous study of broadcasters' attitudes towards coverage of an election campaign. Like Parliament, election campaigns symbolize the values of a democratic political system and can therefore provoke equivalent contrasts of perspective among broadcasters involved in their coverage. In that study (see Chapter 9 below), Blumler distinguished between 'sacerdotal' and 'pragmatic' responses to the claims of campaign reports for inclusion in the nightly current affairs programme, *24 Hours*. So-called 'sacerdotalists' largely comprised those political specialists and commentators who considered that campaign developments deserved a regular and prominent airing almost as an inherent right and regardless of news-value calculations. 'Pragmatists', on the other hand, were those editors and producers who regarded themselves as having a wider programme brief to tend, were keen to cover non-election stories when news values justified their inclusion and aimed to serve an audience, many members of which, they argued, were less than fully interested in election news as such.

BROADCASTERS' ORGANIZATIONAL ROLES AND ATTITUDES TO PARLIAMENT

The preceding discussion has depicted broadcasters as swayed by different sentiments towards Parliament. It is reasonable to assume, however, that they do not perform their duties under a continual buffeting of cross-pressures. Rather will each broadcaster resolve these attitudinal conflicts for himself or herself in a relatively consistent manner.

Elsewhere (see Chapter 3), we have proposed the notion of 'role relationships' as a tool for analysing complex interactions between mass media professionals and politicians in the production of political messages. This implies that the behaviour of people in roles is prescribed by the requirements of such roles and is guided by the socially defined expectations which govern them. Two advantages of analysing the behaviour of broadcasters (as well as politicians) in such terms were identified by us. First, 'Such an approach draws attention to influences on political communicators that derive from their respective organisational settings, in which their roles are largely defined and performed'. In other words, broadcasters are anchored in a framework of tasks assigned to them by their organizations, and their reactions to other political institutions and communicators will stem in large part from their occupancy of defined positions in the organizational hierarchy. Second, 'A focus on roles as regulators of behaviour also links . . . media professionals . . . back to the surrounding political culture of the society concerned'. This helps to explain the continuity of professional behaviour over time, as well as the diversity of patterns of professional behaviour when viewed across different societies. Thus, the relationship of British broadcasters to Parliament is largely specific to the British political system, which has shaped both the place of Parliament in British society and the purposes and structure of British broadcasting itself.

For our present purpose, adoption of a 'role perspective' has the further advantage of sensitizing us to the multiplicity of broadcasters' roles that may have a bearing on how Westminster materials will be used. Up to this point, we have referred to the broadcasters as if they comprised an undifferentiated group, all enmeshed in the tensions arising from conflicting orientations to Parliament. But this appeared not to be the case. Interviews with many broadcasters, involved in different capacities in the processing of parliamentary material, suggested that their outlook on the institution and on the value, in broadcasting terms, of its proceedings as captured by the microphones in the Chambers, varied according to the roles they occupied in their organizations.

At least three groups of broadcaster roles appeared distinguishable by this evidence: first, there were the editors, correspondents and commentators who worked at Westminster. These individuals were closest to the institution of Parliament both geographically – working as they did in 'the belly of the beast' – and socially – through frequent and often intensive interactions with MPs. Of course, their professional identities and reputations were also bound up with the number and prominence of the parliamentary stories that were eventually broadcast.

Second, there were the journalists, editors, managers and channel controllers who were positioned on what might be described (from this standpoint) as the periphery of the broadcasting organizations, working with the various local radio stations and networked news and current affairs programmes, into the output of which parliamentary items were often inserted. Such broadcasters were more remote from Parliament than their Westminster colleagues, not only geographically and culturally but also occupationally. They were less exposed to the 'culture of Parliament', and parliamentary proceedings comprised but one among a quite wide range of news sources and broadcastable material with which they had to concern themselves.

Third, there were the higher executives and policy-makers in the broadcasting organizations. Although such individuals were not directly involved in processing parliamentary material, they had an overall responsibility to ensure that the broadcasting of Parliament was seen by the main clients that their institutions had to satisfy – principally MPs and audience members – as in some sense a 'success'.

So far as we could tell, the differing attitudes to Parliament that had been identified were not distributed at random across broadcasting staffs. There was a tendency for broadcasters in certain roles to adopt one set of attitudes, while incumbents of others exhibited different orientations. This is not to claim that we can precisely measure the strength of this association, for the distinctions proposed here have emerged from an analysis of originally unstructured interview material. Nevertheless, important differences across broadcasters did seem to emerge from the evidence, drawing attention to three main lines of linkage between their organizational roles and their attitudes to Parliament.

First, the outlook characterized as 'professional', that is to say, relating to Parliament primarily as a source of political information and stories, seemed far more prevalent among those broadcasters who worked on the 'periphery' of the system – that is, for the local radio stations and the networked News and Current Affairs programmes which present parliamentary items as part of a wider service to listeners and viewers. More distanced from Parliament, these individuals worked closely on the interface between the broadcasting organization and the mass audience. Not surprisingly, a central preoccupation was winning and keeping the loyalties of their listeners and viewers, in whose hierarchy of interests parliamentary material was assumed to occupy a relatively low place. As one newsman in a local station described his audience:

They're not interested unless it is something that affects them. The example I would give here is the Budget, because taxes affect them – taxes on cigarettes, sweets and drink. But the general run of parliamentary business is of no relevance to them.

The second orientation, according to which Parliament was perceived as the sovereign authority to which broadcasting was ultimately accountable, appeared to be more salient to broadcasting executives and policy-makers. A prime task of this echelon is to represent the organization to their 'political masters' and to cultivate as positive and conflict-free a relationship with them as possible. It followed that among the reference groups to whom they would turn when assessing the success or failure of the sound broadcasting of Parliament, MPs would be central. This is not to imply that interviewed executives often expressed such views to us in unqualified form. Nevertheless, other broadcasters sometimes perceived them as if naturally motivated by such impulses:

> The service we provide for BBC central management in using parliamentary material and maintaining contact with the MPs, they see as a purely political function. They are only too pleased that there are these nice chaps ... who are talking to MPs and actually know them. After all, we must not forget the licence fee and the importance of keeping Parliament sweet. We act as lobbyists on behalf of the BBC, and that is how we are seen.

Third, the more 'sacerdotal' orientation to emerge from the interview material was expressed most often by parliamentary correspondents stationed at Westminster. A number of factors – including the fact that they worked and had their offices in the Palace of Westminster, their dependence on daily access to MPs to do their job and their total immersion in the affairs of Parliament – all probably conspired to encourage a view of Parliament, not only as an information source, but also as a keystone of the British political system and the repository of its core values. These broadcasters were often depicted by their colleagues as not only being carriers of Westminster values, but also as less likely, for example, to provide a stringent commentary on certain parliamentary developments than would their less inhibited colleagues in the written press.

Varying attitudes to Parliament, however, were not purely differentiated by organizational role. Broadcasters who perform different roles are naturally dependent on each other and on the organizational structure as a whole in carrying out their tasks. For example, the parliamentary correspondent at Westminster is in daily contact with editors and producers on the periphery and is thus thoroughly accustomed to fashioning his or her output in approaches, lengths and styles that will suit the needs of the programmes in which the items are to be slotted. In addition, they realize that they stand in the front line of their organization's relationships with Ministers, Opposition spokesmen and MPs generally, having to defend or justify reports that may from time to time be criticized. Similarly, many producers and editors on the periphery will have become accustomed to the regular receipt of parliamentary stories, impregnated with a Westminster viewpoint, as a sheer fact of programming life. Like other members of the organization, they too must appreciate the desirability of keeping on tolerably good terms with Parliament. And for their part, the higher executives are aware of the need to support the professional troops in the field, on whose commitment and dedication the regular production of attractive programming depends. Thus, the three sets of broadcasters, though differently preoccupied and oriented, were also aware that they belonged to the same organization, sharing certain corporate interests, which the policies and practices of parliamentary broadcasting should, so far as possible, promote.

JOURNALISTS' ORIENTATIONS TO POLITICAL INSTITUTIONS

We now turn to the larger issue to which this essay is addressed, namely, media professionals' orientations to the broad range of social institutions and organizations whose activities they follow and report. What might we learn from this case study of parliamentary broadcasting about the structuring and application of such attitudes? Are the sensitivities to cross-cutting, sometimes contradictory, loyalties specific to the reporting of the British Parliament? Or do similarly conflicting orientations shape their reactions to other organizations and groups as well? Can the framework outlined in this study extend our understanding of the place of the mass media in the web of power relationships in society?

Two opposed explanatory frameworks are often pitted against each other in interpretations of newspeople's relations to prominent power groupings in society: the more conventional journalistic paradigm (Hackett, 1984) and the critical approach. The former stipulates that media professionalism requires an 'above the battle', objective and impartial stance towards the objects of media coverage. Media professionals are expected to ignore or subordinate all loyalties implicit in their other roles, such as support for a given partisan position or preference for the interests and causes of other groups in society. The main exception is support for the core values of society, as in the familiar BBC dictum that as between democracy and totalitarianism, impartiality is inconceivable. The critical alternative rejects this position as an expression of a professional ideology, which obscures and provides a 'cover-up' for the true loyalties of media professionals to the prevailing status quo. Allegiance to the core values of society translates, in this view, into propagation of a 'dominant ideology'.

We perceive difficulties in both perspectives. However convincing in suggesting reasons why journalism reproduces and reinforces the contours of social power, the critical approach is too dismissive of the attempt by media professionals to apply universalistic criteria to the social and political actors whose affairs they report. Consequently, they cannot explain the many instances when even highly prestigious institutions and personalities attract negative news coverage.

For their part, many journalists in Western media systems would probably regard the evidence in the parliamentary broadcasting case study as highlighting little more than a minor exception to their usual rules. And one sees what they could mean. There does seem to be a tendency for reporters to apply similar yardsticks to all groups and institutions, whenever they are embroiled in episodes of conflict, drama, failure, hypocrisy and scandal that can be related in news-story form. Yet that is not all that is involved in news-making. Media organizations develop and express distinctive policies, which are reflected not only in their editorial positions, but also in their reporting perspectives. Much news has a normative function as well as an informative one, relating reported events, explicitly or by implication, back to issues in which societal values are at stake (Lazarsfeld and Merton, 1957; Alexander, 1981). Moreover, certain groups persistently attract certain forms of coverage in the media, whether positive or pejorative. The structured and internally consistent treatment of, say, the recipients of welfare (Golding and Middleton, 1982), soccer hooligans and other perpetrators of deviant behaviour cannot be plausibly explained as an outcome of the application of news values alone.

We therefore contend that journalists react to all social groups and institutions, not only via news-value criteria, but also according to the degree of respect (or lack of it) to which they are regarded as entitled by the dominant value system. The utility of this perspective for theorizing and analysing media relationships with other social institutions is reflected in the following five major implications which flow from it.

First, it might be possible to arrange all social institutions and groups on a continuum, according to the degree to which their representation in the media betrays a more sacerdotal or more pragmatic orientation by those assigned to report their activities. The monarchy, for example, has probably received more sacerdotal treatment in the British media than have most other social institutions. This is not to deny that the Royal Family may occasionally be subjected to more 'professional' coverage, as exemplified in attempts by the press to intrude into the privacy of its members. But such behaviour is episodic, normally confined to the more 'popular' end of the British press and is sometimes frowned upon, even censured, by other sectors of the media. A similarly sacerdotal treatment may be accorded the Church, though again more pragmatic perspectives may be applied when members of the clergy express unorthodox views, engage in political controversy, or indulge in 'unseemly' conduct. Slightly lower down the sacerdotal ladder, we may find the central institutions of the state and government, including Parliament. It should be emphasized that their status does not preclude a critical, even hostile, media stance towards the policies and personalities of such institutions. But the treatment meted out to policies and personalities should be distinguished from a more sacerdotal orientation towards institutions *qua* institutions, which in this case will often attract the respect to which they are entitled by virtue of their symbolic embodiment of the value system of society. Then perhaps there are a number of 'half-way' institutions, recognized as part of the legitimate fabric of society, often entitled to voice their views on current issues, yet mainly reported in pragmatic terms. In Britain, perhaps the trade unions are an outstanding example of this mid-point category. Finally, some groups seem to occupy the other end of the reporting spectrum. Every society has its pet villains – those groups and organizations which are most remote from, indeed stand in opposition to, the central values of society. In Britain, this role has been assumed in recent years by certain deviant groups, such as 'welfare spongers' (Golding and Middleton, 1982), 'muggers' (Hall *et al.*, 1978), teenage hooligans (Cohen and Young, 1973) and IRA 'terrorists'.

Second, as the above examples suggest, journalism is inherently, not just incidentally, a several-sided enterprise. Media coverage of a given institution will reflect the interaction between two sets of influences – its more or less abiding sacerdotal standing in the scale of social values and its momentary weight on news-value scales.

The validity of such a dualistic perspective is strengthened by its compatibility with other tensions in which journalism is enmeshed. One arises from the intermediary position of the news media in society, dependent on sources yet professionally committed to cater for presumed audience needs and interests. Exposed to pressures from both sides, then, journalists will naturally respond, more or less sacerdotally, to differences of prestige and power among source institutions and, via news-value calculations, according to what they think audiences will find most exciting and significant.

The field of forces within which journalists operate contains another source of potential tension – that between their professional loyalties and their need to sustain a continuing relationship with their sources. On the one hand, they look to their own colleagues for daily stimulus on the job, confirmation of their news-value decisions and an affirmation of their professional standing. On the other hand, they enter into 'role relationships' with their prime news sources, building up a shared 'emergent culture' with them, including various mutually accepted ground rules and criteria of publicity appropriateness and fairness. It stands to reason that in such relationships, the more esteemed sources will be able to exert greater 'clout'.

This dualistic view of journalism may help to clarify its much-disputed relationship to the socio-political status quo. Does it tend to uphold or to undermine, legitimize or discredit the dominant institutions and ideology of society? In our view, the least simplistic answer is that it performs both functions in different ways and at different times. Both potentially and in practice mass media workways have both legitimizing and disruptive implications for the social order. They are involved in processes of both social control and social change.

Third, the sacerdotal orientation could be said to prescribe that some institutions should be reported by the media according to what those institutions regard as their inherent deserts and not merely according to what they do and how that chimes with conventional news values. It follows that the more sacerdotal the media's orientation towards a given institution, the more likely it is that that institution will be represented through its own perspective, that is, in ways which reflect its own view of its purposes, values, activities and relations to society. Perhaps this proposition sheds fresh light on those intensifying conflicts that have recently erupted in many Western societies between the mass media and a host of aggrieved parties, such as trade unions, spokespersons of ethnic minorities, women's liberation and many others. The root of such conflicts may be traced to a desire on the part of the groups concerned for a more sacerdotal treatment of their affairs by reporters, who, faced with criticism, may resist such demands by refusing to acknowledge that they are involved in the sacerdotal game at all, claiming instead to be impartially guided by news values. Such conflicts are peculiarly intractable, because the grounds to which the contesting parties appeal are radically different without always being openly professed.

Fourth, the outlook advanced here may clarify the sources of cross-national similarities and differences in how journalists present the news. In Western societies, news values as such tend to be transculturally uniform. But it is primarily due to the specificity of cultural factors, entailing different rankings of social institutions in different countries (for example, Congress is probably lower in the American pecking order than Parliament in the British hierarchy of institutional prestige), that news output can seem quite divergent and varied when compared across a number of different societies.

Finally, this framework alerts us to the fact, little explored so far in the literature, that media institutions themselves may be on the receiving end as well as on the originating end of the orientations discussed in this essay. If, as we believe, all social institutions evoke in the members of society a varying mixture of sacerdotal and pragmatic attitudes, then the news media are no exception. They too are regarded by their audiences, and more importantly by their sources, in a mixture of lights, combining sacerdotal respect for the principle of freedom of expression with a pragmatic recognition that the media can distort and trivialize and may be harnessed to the service of particular interests. Important consequences for the political functioning of the media in society could flow from how this balance is struck. The readiness of the leaders of powerful institutions uninhibitedly to indulge in news management practices may turn on it. The course of the previously mentioned conflicts between media professionals and groups wanting to be represented in the press and broadcasting 'through their own eyes' may be affected by it. And ultimately, it may determine society's response to the claims of the news media to the respect, independence and other privileges to which they feel they are entitled by virtue of their own embodiment of certain sacerdotal values.

Chapter 5

Towards a comparative framework for political communication research[1]

Writing in 1975, nobody could claim to be able to paint an assured portrait of the field of investigation to be discussed in this essay. It is not merely that few political communication studies have yet been mounted with a comparative focus. More to the point, there is neither a settled view of what such studies should be concerned with, nor even a firmly crystallized set of alternative options for research between which scholars of diverse philosophic persuasions could choose.

The obstacles impeding such a development reflect imperfections to some extent endemic to all branches of social science: poor measurement; primitive theory. In principle, at least, measurement problems could be tackled with an expectation of success if scholars in different societies could reach some agreement over the topics and relationships they wished to examine in concert. Theoretical clarification is logically prior.

The lack of sustained discussion of theoretical issues pertaining to comparative political communication study is therefore deplorable. The resulting vacuum has tended to be filled by both improvisation ('I did so-and-so in my own country with interesting results, so will someone else-where please replicate my work') and randomness ('Let's see what turns up when 39 predictor variables are regressed onto four mass communi-cation variables in 115 countries'). Unfortunately, work of this kind is inimical to progressive continuity. It trades in no predefined problems, the resolution of which would open up yet other issues for scrutiny. It lights no torch that can be handed on from one investigator to the next.

Other difficulties arise from the diffuse yet problematic place of com-munication in politics. On the one hand, all political life implies some form of communication activity. If politics is about power, the holder's possession of and readiness to exercise it must in some manner be con-veyed to those expected to respond to it. If politics is about participation, this consists in itself of 'the means by which the interests, desires and demands of the ordinary citizen are communicated to rulers' (Verba, Nie and Kim, 1971). If politics is about the legitimation of supreme authority, then the values and procedural norms of regimes have to be symbolically expressed, and the acts of government have to be justified in broad popular terms. And if politics is about choice, then information flows clarifying alternative policy options must circulate to those concerned with decisions, whether as their shapers or as consumers of their consequences. Communication, then, is so ubiquitously embedded in politics that a bewildering embarrassment of riches confronts the would-be cross-national researcher. Objects of investigation must somehow be selected, and the principle of parsimony requires an economical yet productive choice. But what exactly would it repay researchers to concentrate their comparative attention on?

A PROPOSED POINT OF DEPARTURE

Before canvassing various ways of organizing a comparative research effort, we should ask some prior questions: Why bother to study political communication cross-nationally? What has this line of research to offer that no other approach could provide?

The answers to these questions provide a point of departure for generating a conceptual framework in which a series of comparative political communication studies could be anchored. It is true that many political communication processes could be fruitfully studied in all their concrete detail in single-country research, and the projection of such work across national lines might dramatically expand 'the range of variation in the national setting from which the ... researcher draws his cases' (Frey, 1970). But thus conceived, comparative research would pose no new questions for investigators to answer, only extend the data base for tackling old ones. Yet there is one highly important question on which single-country research, however comprehensive or sophisticated, can shed virtually no illumination: *how does the articulation of a country's mass media institutions to its political institutions affect the processing of political communication content and the impact of such content on the orientations to politics of audience members?*

Clearly the relationship of mass media institutions to political institutions is assumed in all states to have consequences of major import and is never left to chance. All political systems must one way or another regulate the performance of media institutions in the political field. In part this is because the mass media, through their relations with the audience, have access to a potentially independent power base in society. Partly it is because the media 'play a constitutional and political role in society' (Hirsch and Gordon, 1975). That is, they set much of the agenda of political debate. They help to determine which political demands will be aired, and consequently have a chance of being satisfied, and which others will be relatively muted. They affect the chances of governments and other political actors to secure essential supports. And they present a broader or narrower band of opinion about how the issues of the day should be tackled, structuring the options between which voters may choose. Consequently, care is taken in all states to identify those political agencies to which the media will be accountable and specify the terms of their brief; to clarify the rights and obligations falling on both political and media personnel in the communication sphere; and to define and safeguard whatever freedoms are thought to belong to it. The universality of the assumption of a public stake in how the media operate politically is demonstrated by the fact that even regimes rooted in the most liberal traditions have found it necessary to monitor the adequacy of press performance and to recommend remedies for any identified shortcomings.

Yet the consequences that flow from the regulatory arrangements made on the interface of political organization and media organization cannot be measured without introducing some comparative element. This is because in a single country at a given moment there can be no variation at this high structural level. It is true that such a comparison can be effected longitudinally over time within one country's borders where changes in the linkages of the media to politics have occurred during a particular historical period (for an example, see Chapter 14). But historical research in a single country is unlikely to encounter the same range of variation that can be found by cutting across national boundaries. Cross-national comparisons are essential to any attempt to probe and understand the effects of different ways of controlling the mass media politically; and a central ingredient in any framework for comparative political communication analysis must be a set of dimensions specifying how the linkages between political and mass media organizations may vary in different societies.

Two questions therefore arise for conceptual attention. First, what are the main varieties of linkage by which political and media institutions and personnel may be connected? Second, what consequences are likely to flow from variations in how the mass media are politically regulated?

POLITICAL AND MEDIA STRUCTURES: FOUR DIMENSIONS OF LINKAGE

Our first theoretical task is to conceive a set of dimensions along which the connections between media institutions and political institutions may vary. Since the purpose of such a scheme is to facilitate and guide cross-national research, its elements should (a) together cover the most important features of any country's political communication structure and (b) be such as to tap and explain differences in the political performance of media systems under highly varying structural conditions. Accordingly, we propose a framework, consisting of four dimensions, by reference to which political communication arrangements of different states could be profiled, and their further consequences for the production, reception and wider repercussions of political messages could be hypothetically specified: (1) degree of state control over mass media organizations; (2) degree of mass media partisanship; (3) degree of media-political élite integration; (4) the nature of the legitimizing creed of media institutions.

Degree of state control

Despite the seeming familiarity of the dimension of degree of state control over media organization, its conceptualization bristles with many awkward difficulties. First, while media systems can be subjectively characterized as more or less subordinate to government control, even informed judges may be guided by different criteria or be misled by appearances. Are there any manifestations of media subordination, then, that could be translated into a more objectively compiled set of indicators? Second, the notion of 'state control' itself is quite wide-ranging: its expressions are legion and its targets myriad. What specific forms of control, then, most merit inclusion in a measure of media subjection to (or autonomy from) the state? Third, we need to avoid the trap of conceptualizing freedom of communication in exclusively dichotomous terms – as if it prevailed in certain societies and was absent in others without susceptibility to significant gradation in either camp. Such a distinction is not entirely false, as Siebert, Peterson and Schramm (1956) realized when differentiating liberal from authoritarian theories of the press. Communication will certainly assume a different role in those societies where (a) political organization is essentially monopolistic, (b) political truth is believed to inhere in the tenets of some authoritative doctrine as interpreted by a ruling party and (c) the mass media are primarily expected to uphold such a unitary conception of political truth, from those societies in which (a) diverse political organizations compete with each other for popular support, (b) the legitimating creed of the state transcends all existing political formations (none is assumed perfectly to embody it) and (c) the mass media are expected, individually or in concert, to transmit a variety of political standpoints. In the first case political control of the media will seem natural and legitimate, and in the second its imposition will always require a special justification. Nevertheless, even in the first situation professional communicators may enjoy more or less latitude to cover political affairs according to their own lights, while in the second freedom of communication may be limited by a more tightly or loosely woven web of restrictions.

Some of these difficulties may be eased by dimensionalizing in terms of the commonly exercised rights of governments (or agencies responsive to their wills) to intervene in the affairs of the mass media so as to regulate their communication performance. This formulation directs attention to certain concrete areas where such rights of intervention may exist and where the resulting degree of state control could be fairly readily measured as if at high, intermediate or low levels. In particular three such areas may be singled out on the grounds (1) that when rulers strive to bend the media to their wills their efforts are most commonly directed to these fields and (2) that in less controlled systems media professionals jealously guard their independence in precisely these respects. They are: control over the appointment of media personnel; control over the financing of media enterprises; and control over media content.

Control over appointments can be a powerful instrument of subordination by ensuring a stationing of politically reliable individuals inside the media instead of obliging rulers to depend on the problematic impact of external pressures and sanctions on the behaviour of communication staffs. This form of control mixes two elements: a right of political appointment; and a belief that political criteria are relevant to the selection of media personnel. At one extreme all appointments could be based on the political credentials of the candidates. Or recruitment might be restricted to candidates who had first undergone approved training and socialization procedures including some element of political indoctrination. Or media personnel might have to be licensed, thereby giving the licensing authority a power to grant or withhold permission to work in the communication sector. Such comprehensive devices are unlikely to be found in systems sensitive to the creed of freedom of expression, where a more limited political control may focus on appointments to top positions in media organizations. A good example of low control of this kind may be found in the British system of public service broadcasting, where the Prime Minister merely appoints the governors of broadcasting authorities, and where no stipulation reserves these posts for politically affiliated individuals. In contrast, there is a stronger right of state intervention in certain continental European systems, either because the government may appoint to executive posts (e.g. Director-Generals) as well as to supervisory boards, or because many board places are specifically set aside for politicians.

On the principle that he who pays the piper calls the tune – or at any rate is less likely to have to listen to uncongenial and discordant tunes – control over media finance may also be a powerful vehicle of state subordination. Such a form of control will function differently according to the sources from which media organizations draw their revenues. Those organizations which depend entirely or in great part on directly provided government funds are clearly most open to direct political control. Even where the media derive their income from their own clientele, however, whether on the basis of sales (as in the press), of a licence fee (as in some broadcasting systems) or of advertising (both press and broadcasting), governments may institutionalize their rights of intervention either by subjecting these sources of income to government approval (e.g. when licence fees are raised) or by special taxes (e.g. a levy on advertising revenue). Media operating in such conditions usually prefer them to the tighter financial controls perceived to inhere in government funding *per se*. The degree of financial subordination involved in these arrangements may depend less on the size of the funds available for subsidy, however, than on how they are allocated – whether by discretionary decision, enabling administrators to discriminate between different media outlets, or by more automatically applicable objective criteria. Thus, media systems in different countries may be placed on a continuum according to the proximity of their revenue sources to the government, the degree to which governments maintain legal holds over non-governmental sources of revenue, and the degree of discretion enjoyed by a political authority in allocating funds at its disposal.

The existence of political control over media content is more important for its indirect repercussions on the work of professional communicators than for instances of its direct exercise. For one thing a need to apply the control by censoring some media article in advance of its appearance, or by subsequently punishing its authors and publishers, is a sign that the system has in a sense failed. For another, little theoretical order could possibly be superimposed on the many discrete and variable grounds by which content regulation may be justified in different regimes.[2] Content control is theoretically interesting primarily in its role as a sanction, capable through its background presence of influencing the behaviour and attitudes of communicators in advance of, or while preparing, media output. If so, what might matter in placing political communication systems on a continuum from high to low control of this kind would be (a) the overall range of content that may be subject to regulation, (b) the degree of specificity inherent in such regulation (more specific injunctions entailing less latitude) and (c) how far the control system is operated directly by the political authorities themselves or by intermediary bodies, such as quasi-judicial regulatory agencies or communication councils.

Degree of mass media partisanship

Our second main dimension of political communication structure focuses on the degree of partisan commitment exhibited by mass media outlets. Although the manifestations of media partisanship are not so complex as in the case of state control, they are also not quite so straightforward as might seem at first sight to be the case. Seymour-Ure's (1974) notion of 'press–party parallelism' rests on three criteria: party involvement in mass media ownership and management; the editorial policies of newspapers; and the party affiliations of readers. We would eliminate the last criterion from a structurally focused definition of media partisanship, however, since it is an important empirical question how far party linkages of an organizational and editorial kind give rise to selective audience patronage patterns along party lines.

Nevertheless, the determinants of media partisanship are indeed multiple. They include any organizational connections to political parties, the stability and intensity of editorial commitments, and presence or absence of legal restraints on the rights of the media to back individual parties. In combination these would allow for five levels of media partisanship. The highest degree of partisan involvement exists when the parties are directly associated with the running of media enterprises via ownership, provision of financial subsidy or membership on management and editorial boards. Some examples of highly partisan systems in this sense may be found in Scandinavia, where there is a strong party press, and in Holland, where TV and radio programming are to some extent the responsibility of separate, politically affiliated broadcasting bodies. Next, there is a condition of voluntary fixed partisanship, where, short of any structural connection of the parties to the media, a party may count on the unconditional and unswerving loyalty of a particular organ – as in the support invariably given the Conservatives by the *Daily Telegraph* in Britain. A third level reflects a more qualified brand of partisanship, where a medium may usually back a favoured party but where the support tends to be conditioned by the expression of numerous qualifications, hesitations and references to party shortcomings as well as by a readiness to see some merit in the policies of opposing parties (including even an occasional refusal to proffer the customary election endorsement). Fourth, there is an *ad hoc* and in a sense unpredictable form of partisanship, where the political stance of a medium is determined afresh according to the merits of the case perceived as decisive each time a need to declare a preference arises. Finally, there is a condition of non-partisanship in which a communication outlet may not take sides and strives at all cost to maintain its political neutrality, as exemplified by those broadcasting organizations that are obliged by law or charter to refrain from openly supporting any political position.

Degree of media–political élite integration

The two dimensions outlined so far apply mainly to certain formal arrangements through which political influence over the media may be channelled. However, much of the mutual responsiveness to each other of the personnel working in these spheres may be due to less formal aspects of the relationship between them. Hence, there is a need for an additional dimension, focusing on the degree of integration between media élites and political élites, and serving to identify and highlight some of the informal mechanisms through which flows of influence, in both directions, may be managed.

The main concern here is the degree of political affinity and social-cultural proximity that obtains between these two sets of structurally differentiated élites. Clearly in most political systems media organizations are to some degree structurally differentiated from political institutions. This structural gap may nevertheless be bridged in various ways. First, members of media élites may be recruited from or socialized into the same social and cultural backgrounds that characterize members of political élites and thus come to share similar interests and uphold similar values. Second, there may be an overlap of personnel. Many media élite members may either support particular parties and even undertake activity on their behalf or alternatively think of themselves as lukewarm adherents or as 'independents'. Contrariwise, some legislators may be drawn from the ranks of ex-journalists. Moreover, as the persuasion process becomes more intense and specialized, 'boundary' agencies may be formed both in political institutions (press officers) and the media (public relations or liaison officers), staffed by individuals with experience in the other domain. Finally, outside the specifically vocational contexts where politicians and professional communicators meet, members of media and political élites may engage in more or less informal interaction with each other, perhaps belonging to the same clubs, mixing in the same circles and generally seeing each other more or less often for diffuse social purposes. Such contacts may promote a growth of mutual under-standing among individuals in these different élites, rendering them more responsive to each other's views and problems.

The nature of the legitimizing creed of media institutions

A central mechanism that may act as a check against the formal and informal tendencies to subordinate media performance to politicians' goals may be found in the occupational creeds embraced by members of media professions. Essentially media professionalism implies a distancing of the reporter, commentator, producer or media executive from the pressures of external interests and a fidelity to the internally generated norms of the profession itself. Creeds promoting such an insulation may be compounded in varying mixes of such elements as: belief in the primacy of service to the audience member (over and above any duties owed to organized political authority); emphasis on the need to master certain specialist communication skills before audiences can be addressed effectively; belief in the watchdog function of journalism and the need for media personnel to adopt an adversarial stance in their relations with politicians; and commitment to such universalistic criteria of political truth as impartiality and objectivity, at the expense of tenets of party doctrine. In short, communication systems may be classified according to the degree to which the legitimizing creed underlying them expects media personnel to pay allegiance and give service to some hegemonic or party-determined ideology or conversely gives pride of place to 'professional rationality' and requires media professionals to behave as if above the political battle.

POLITICAL COMMUNICATION STRUCTURES AND THEIR CONSEQUENCES: THREE AREAS OF EFFECT

How exactly do the political communication arrangements outlined above matter? Where should we look for evidence of their impact on media reporting of political events and how citizens react to such coverage? Our next theoretical task is to elucidate some of the consequences that might flow from variations in the structural linkages between the mass media and politics. We have striven to define below a limited set of dimensions capable of accommodating a large number of related consequences. In conceiving them we have focused on phenomena that (a) should be sensitive to structurally derived influences, (b) might be amenable to cross-national comparison and (c) would represent some of the most deep-seated perspectives likely to underlie the political outlook and behaviour of citizens when responding to political communications.

In sum, three dimensions of the effects of political communication arrangements seem to meet these conditions. They are: (1) the valuation of politics as such; (2) degree of partisan commitment; (3) degree of consensus over society's agenda of political issues. Each of these dimensions has been so conceived as to embrace consequences at both the medium level and the audience level. At medium level they will be visible in both the ground rules that professionals are expected to comply with when processing political outputs, as well as in the amount and direction of media contents that are devoted to political affairs. At audience level these consequences will be manifested in the orientations of individuals to political communication and in their attitudes to closely related features of the political system. Thus, our overall theoretical framework proceeds from the structural linkages of media institutions to the political system, via the performance of media institutions as reflected in the ground rules governing the production of political output and consequent variations of content patterning, to the attitudinal and behavioural linkages of individual citizens to their political systems.

The valuation of politics as such

Politics is a field of activity that can attract or repel, engage people or turn them off, be thought worthy of respect or be treated with indifference and contempt. The precariousness of its attraction renders it vulnerable to various influences, among them some that stem from the perceptions that people form of the connections between communication sources and political institutions. This dimension of politicization runs like a vertical thread through all the ranks and levels of the political communication system. Media personnel may enthuse about their political duties or approach them in a perfunctory spirit. Media organizations may employ a larger or smaller team of specialist political correspondents. Their ground rules may reflect either a 'sacerdotal' or a 'pragmatic' attitude to the claims of political items, in the former case regarding political coverage as an intrinsically important service that must be provided as of right, and in the latter insisting that political material should fight its way into print and programmes on its news-value merits alone. Media organs may devote a larger or smaller proportion of their space and time to the airing of political questions. The content they do provide may concentrate on explaining and interpreting the substantive issues of politics, or treat them instead as mere counters in a power game to be followed for the drama and spectacle that its ups and downs afford (Weaver, 1973). Similarly, audience members may be more or less politicized. They may be more or less interested in political affairs, find political decisions more or less relevant to their personal lives, be better or less well informed, feel a keener or lesser sense of duty to be involved, and be prepared to participate more or less actively in their country's political processes. They may also assume different roles in the political communication system, adopting that of a 'monitor', for example, if looking primarily for cognitive insights into developments, or that of a spectator, if interested more in the 'thrills and spills' connected with the fluctuating fortunes of actors performing in the political arena (Blumler, 1973). Finally, people may repose a higher or lower degree of trust in the authenticity of political messages and in the integrity of their sources.

But how might structural differences in the linkages of the media to political institutions affect the valuations placed on politics as such? Different answers to this question may be generated in the form of opposed hypotheses.

On the one hand, there is a 'subordination-promotes-politicization' hypothesis. This reflects the outlook of politicians who are suspicious of the incorrigibly 'trivializing' tendencies of independent media professionals when presenting political news and views. In their eyes subordination should serve to check these tendencies and help to bring political communication processing, content provision and audience outlook in line with the high regard and respectful attention that this supremely important sphere of life deserves. According to this standpoint, then, more subordination will yield more political content of an essentially serious kind that will be followed more avidly, with a monitor's concern to become well-informed, by members of the audience.

On the other hand, there is an 'autonomy-promotes-politicization' hypothesis. Reflecting the outlook of professional communicators who stress the need for their own intermediary intervention before messages will be meaningful and credible to audiences, this view regards subordination in all its forms as counter-productive to politicization. In subordinate systems political intervention will be seen by media personnel and audience members alike as mechanisms designed to control and limit comment on behalf of 'external' elements. Consequently trust will be impaired, leading to a loss of attention and a reduction of respect for what goes on in the political arena. Conversely, less restrictive arrangements may encourage media personnel to exercise independence and initiative in covering political affairs, and audience members to show more interest in politics and to pay more attention to materials about it.

It is clear, then, that subordination of the media can be hypothesized to have consequences of more or less politicization according to one's philosophic taste.

Degree of partisan commitment

A second major area of structurally derived effects focuses on identifications with the main contestants in the political arena. The converse of partisan commitment is not political apathy, or dismissal of all politics as uninteresting and political communication as untrustworthy, but rather an attitude of political open-mindedness and a disposition to accord an equal hearing to all viewpoints. The hypothetical derivation of consequences in this area from linkages of the mass media to the political system is rather straightforward. We may postulate a hand-in-glove relationship between the range and intensity of party ties to the media at the structural level and degree of partisan commitment at other levels.

Manifestations of media partisanship may be found, first of all, in the various ground rules that guide the production of political material. Thus, those media that are committed to non-partisanship may operate ground rules that lean over backwards to guarantee a balanced coverage of all political parties. Alternatively, in media under more partisan influences, the ground rules may include formulae intended to justify a favoured treatment of certain positions. Structural differences may also be reflected in patterns of media content itself – for example, in the inclusion of varying amounts of committed editorial comment; in the provision of one-sided or more balanced platforms for the statements and views of different party politicians; and in the headlining and angling of news reports themselves. At the audience level, we may or may not find that party-linked media attract followings that are predominantly determined by the party affiliations of readers, listeners and viewers. And, more subtly, individual audience members may either follow politics in an open-minded, non-committed fashion, looking for materials that may help them provisionally to make up their own minds on the points at issue between the competing parties, adopting the role, then, of 'vote-guidance seekers'; or they may be aiming more single-mindedly to bolster an already established partisan commitment, taking up the role, so to speak, of 'reinforcement seekers' (Blumler, 1973).

The dimension underlying these various ramifications is reminiscent of Parsons and Shils' (1951) pattern variable of universalism–particularism. People and institutions may be oriented to political conflict either in terms of their affiliations to particular parties, in which case the key values being upheld would include loyalty, a forthright readiness to take sides and steadfastness of commitment; or with reference to such more abstract, universal and in a sense disembodied principles as impartiality, fairness, objectivity and measured choice. It is intriguing to note the possible bearing of this distinction on the phenomenon of increasing electoral volatility. Some part of this development may be traceable to the increasing intervention in politics of the essentially non-partisan and highly universalistic medium of television. This underlines the importance of clarifying the part played by the universalistic or particularistic orientations of different communication outlets in steering audience members towards one or the other of these polar attitudes.

The structure of the political agenda

A third area where the political connections of the mass media might have measurable consequences concerns the main issues forming the political agenda of a society at a particular time. What we have in mind here is related to, but not identical with, the numerous 'agenda-setting' studies that have played such an important part in the study of political communication effects but which, because of their preoccupation with specific agenda items, might at first sight seem unsuited to cross-national comparisons. By shifting the focus of attention away from the determination of individual issue concerns and towards the overall shape of the agenda placed before the public, however, the area becomes more amenable to comparative research.

Questions can be raised about the main sources of issue inputs. Are they dictated chiefly by political leaders or do they stem from the perspectives of media professionals (see also Chapter 7)? In more autonomous systems, media ground rules may encourage journalists to inject their own view of the issues that count into the political debate; in more subordinate systems, professional self-restraint may be more the order of the day. As far as media content is concerned, the political affiliations of media outlets may affect the degree of consensus they reach in terms of the issues that are emphasized most frequently and prominently. Here we can postulate the emergence of a high degree of consensus in situations where the media tend to give play to various issues on the basis of standardized and widely shared criteria of news value. Hence, in relatively autonomous systems the application of professional criteria to the selection and presentation of political issues could result in a consensual view of the political agenda. In single-party systems this might lead to a high degree of consensus among the different media, albeit based on political rather than news-value judgements. In party-linked multi-party systems we might expect the media to put forward more divergent views about the items that belong on the national agenda. Finally, at the audience level, we would expect a reproduction of these same patterns – citizen consensus over issues being higher in both autonomous and single-party subordinate systems and lower in highly partisan systems with little state control.

RIVAL PERSPECTIVES

The philosophical orientation underlying this essay should by now be clear. It treats seriously certain distinctions that adherents of other philosophic positions tend to dismiss as relatively insignificant. It supposes that media systems may be classified as more or less subordinate to, or autonomous from, the political institutions of society; that such structural differences give rise to a differential processing of political material and manner of presenting political ideas, issues and events to the public; and that political communication processes in different societies, as initiated or mediated by more or less autonomous media, will have differential consequences for the linkages between individual citizens and their political systems.

Disagreement with this viewpoint comes in several shapes and sizes. Some analysts have maintained that the media in all societies play an essentially passive role, and hence are bound to be subservient to the political order:

> Essentially the mass media do not produce anything original; their normal function is to transmit news. At certain moments of history the mass media may be able to influence the timing of political events, but in the long run the media must adapt to the institutions which are its information sources; they are thus likely to reproduce certain features of the political order.
>
> (Hoyer, Hadenius and Weibull, 1975)

Others regard the mass media as transmitters of a hegemonically shaped consensus of social and political values:

The mass media cannot ensure complete conservative attunement; nothing can. But they can and do contribute to the fostering of a climate of conformity, not by the total suppression of dissent, but by the presentation of views which fall outside the consensus as curious heresies, or, even more effectively, by treating them as irrelevant eccentricities, which serious and reasonable people may dismiss as of no consequence.

(Miliband, 1969)

Yet others will suspect that we have concentrated our attention on a 'merely formal autonomy' of media institutions 'from the state and government' (Hall, 1974) and indeed that media production is always and everywhere subject to control: 'There is no such thing as unmanipulated writing, filming or broadcasting. The question is, therefore, not whether the media are manipulated but who manipulates them' (Garnham, 1973).

The essence of our response to these rival perspectives takes two forms. First, they pay less than sufficient regard to the relationship that the mass media can enter into with their audiences – a relationship that provides them with a potentially independent power base in society, which explains in turn the insistent but varying attempts of many political authorities to control their operations. We have therefore treated the extent to which variations in such forms of control are productive of major consequences at other levels as an empirical question, to which the answers are not predetermined. When they emerge, they might even support the scepticism expressed in the rival perspectives quoted above.

Second, we are aware of a failure of many members of these other camps to suggest how the accuracy of their picture of the place of the media in politics might be tested. If the focus of analysis is shifted towards the inescapably political character of the mass media and their inevitable dependence on the distribution of external power forces, then we must apparently view the media as if in a fixed and unvarying relationship to the world of politics. It is difficult to see how such a perspective could be effectively substituted for our own as a methodological corner-stone of comparative political communication analysis.

Chapter 6

Comparative research
The extending frontier[1]

In our 1975 essay on comparative political communication research (see Chapter 5), we depicted a field in its infancy that lacked 'a settled view of what such studies should be concerned with' as well as a theoretical focus and an empirical track record.

Looking back at the progress made over the last decade and a half, we are struck by the growth, changing face, even emergent identity, of this creature as it appears today. The results of a number of scientifically motivated comparative research efforts have by now seen the light of published day. Although, taken as a whole, their fruits may still appear patchy, quite a few have demonstrated the theoretical fertility and empirical utility of macro-comparative approaches to political communication analysis. It is as if comparative research has progressed from infancy to – if not yet full adulthood – at least late adolescence.

Comparative analysis can now be regarded as *indispensable*, in the sense that without it certain very important questions and phenomena of political communication will simply not be addressed; highly *demanding*, in the sense that it poses exceptional difficulties of conceptualization, implementation and sheer practicalities of fieldwork organization and collaboration; but particularly *rewarding*, for when such work is well done its outcomes can be most interesting and illuminating. It may not be too strong even to suggest that much of the future promise of political communication scholarship lies with comparative research, an extending frontier of the field that deserves yet more intensive cultivation.

On what grounds do we make such a claim? Before outlining them, a prior and deceptively simple-seeming question must be tackled: How should we define the comparative approach to political communication scholarship? After all, all scientifically geared research is inherently comparative. What distinguishes comparative work as a more specialized activity? It is not, or should not be, just a matter of fielding common instruments in as many societies as possible and seeing what emerges. Nor is it even a matter of simply trying to ascertain how selected phenomena compare and contrast in different countries. It is rather (or should be) a matter of trying to take account of potentially varying macro-social system-level characteristics and influences on significant political communication phenomena.

In our 1975 essay we argued that the significance of such an approach stems from its ability to address a core question that cannot possibly be answered in a single-country study, namely, 'How does the articulation of a country's mass media institutions to its political institutions affect the processing of political communication content and the impact of such content on the orientations to politics of audience members?' On that point, our view has not materially changed. Comparative political communication research, we would argue today, is based on the assumption that different parameters of political systems, that is, different features of the structures, norms and values of political systems, will differentially promote or constrain political communication roles and behaviours within those systems. Moreover, it highlights the formative influence of the political system on political communication processes as conducted through the media.

However, three caveats to this position should be noted. First, it accepts a somewhat bounded notion of 'the political', focusing on politics as the activity of those institutions in society – governments, legislatures, executive bureaucracies – commonly regarded as its specifically political institutions. A much broader definition of politics, regarding all activities and all communications that bear upon the question of power in society as political, would of course be possible. Such a broad definition would regard almost the entire range of media content as political messages. A difficulty with such an outlook for political communication researchers, however, is the loss of any specificity of their field. It is for the sake of maintaining the consensual boundaries of the field, rather than for any theoretical reasons, that we will largely work with the narrow definition of 'the political' in this essay.

Second, our view of the manner in which media institutions are articulated to the political system does not imply a one-way relationship. Media linkages to political institutions involve a set of interdependencies in which formative influences flow both ways. Media institutions are, of course, dependent on political and other social institutions in varying ways, which take on different forms in different societies. Yet at the same time it is important to recognize that in all societies media institutions enjoy at least some measure of independent power, varying according to the specific characteristics of the political systems in which they operate (McLeod and Blumler, 1987). Even in societies in which the media are typically regarded as highly subordinate to the political system, some measure of an independent power base may be identified for them, resulting in some political and societal dependence on the media. Indeed, in certain societies developments in the media sphere *per se* have a quite formative impact *on* the political sphere.

Third, what we called the 'articulation' of political and media institutions to each other should not be interpreted as referring narrowly only to linkages between organizations (Senate to NBC; BBC to Parliament; the Conservative Party to the *Daily Telegraph*). For us, the articulating relationships between political and media institutions that are to be studied comparatively include both structural and cultural components.

WHY GO COMPARATIVE?

Four types of reasons for regarding comparative work as potentially highly productive may be mentioned.

Conceptual/methodological advantages

1 *The most immediate and obvious advantage to be derived from comparative research has to do with the expansion of the data base*, which in turn facilitates more solidly established generalizations. In this respect, comparative work has a still underutilized potential for clarifying, modifying, and amplifying established political communication theories. Its role from this standpoint is to provide multiple tests in diverse social settings of the validity of such theories, aiming especially to identify the system circumstances in which they apply. Some obvious candidates for such a theory-centric approach would include mass media agenda-setting, which could be a peculiarly American phenomenon (because its news media system seems ideally organized to facilitate it, as with 22-minute news bulletins, hierarchically ordering items from top to bottom); the 'spiral of silence' (which could be a peculiarly German phenomenon); or the cultivation effects of heavy TV viewing, some of which could be peculiar to highly commercialized broadcasting systems. It should be evident, however, that such a clarification cannot be derived from a mere *aggregation* of single-country studies, but only from a considered conceptual approach, in which evidence from different systems is gathered and compared within a preformed theoretical framework.

2 *Comparative research is an essential antidote to naïve universalism*, or the tendency implicitly to presume that political communication research findings from one society (normally one's own!) are applicable everywhere. Thus, although many theoretical propositions about the social and political functions of the mass media are couched in universal terms, the evidence adduced in support of them is almost always culture-specific. It may be true, for example, that the mass media set voters' issue agendas, erode trust in leaders and the legitimacy of institutions, foster spectator orientations, tell people what it is safe to talk about, depict the urban

world as a mean, violent and unsafe place, and simplify and intensify conflicts while projecting them as essentially soluble. But the unvarying validity of such propositions would really be quite staggering, given the many different cultural, stratification, political and media systems to which they would have to apply across the globe.

3 *Comparative analysis can serve as an effective antidote to unwitting parochialism*. It not only makes us aware of *other* systems, it can help us to understand *our own* better by placing its characteristic features and practices against those of others. A revealing example can be found in Ranney's (1983) references to 'the abundant flow of political information regularly turned out by national newscasts' on American television and 'the national networks' tendency to broadcast a great deal of political information', thereby even telling us 'more than we want to know'. Based on evidence that network newscasts have a higher proportion of political stories than local news programmes and than front pages of American national newspapers, these claims are entirely single-system tied. They look very different, however, in a cross-national context. For example, when comparing British and American television news coverage of the 1983 and 1984 election campaigns in those countries, Semetko *et al.* (1991) found that the BBC presented many more election stories on its main evening news bulletin in three and a half weeks than NBC, CBS or ABC did in over two months, taking up a much larger proportion of programme time each night as well, and leading the news with a campaign report on three-quarters of the nights in question (compared with only one-quarter in the US case). Viewed comparatively, Ranney's abundance is suddenly transformed into something like poverty.

4 *One of the more significant payoffs of the comparative approach lies in its capacity to render the invisible visible*. It draws our attention to imperatives and constraints built into the very structure of political communication arrangements, which, though influential, may be taken for granted and difficult to detect when the focus is on only one national case.

Globalization of the media

Perhaps the most compelling argument for comparative research today stems from a predominant development of the current media scene: the dramatic globalization of the flow of political messages. Brought about by the stunningly rapid deployment of new communication technologies, the global diffusion of political information has rendered thoroughly porous the boundaries of all national communication systems. Of course, this is just part of a broader 'globalization of networks of all kinds that has taken place during the last decade' (Wakeman, 1988), including international banking, the sway of multinational corporations, the spread of cross-national pressure groups, political movements and sectarian allegiances, the increasing role of English as the dominant international tongue, and the diffusion of worldwide entertainment habits and fashioning of fare deliberately designed to capture the international market. In the light of the apparently unstoppable momentum of such trends, reliance on purely single-country scholarship seems almost perversely provincial.

One consequence of media globalization is the diffusion of methods and techniques of conducting competitive political communication campaigns. Here, American-style 'video politics' seems to have emerged as something of a role model for political communicators in other liberal democracies. Some of the key features of political communication in the United States – such as the establishment of television as the primary site on which election campaigns are conducted; a preoccupation with 'image-making' as a crucial political activity; the tailoring of activity by politicians to fit in with, and hence be picked up by, the media; evolving styles and ground rules of supposedly effective political advertising – all these have become an American political export around the world.

A concomitant trend may be the globalization of media professionalism. The export of professional ideologies from the media in Western countries to Third World media organizations (Golding, 1977) has, of course, preceded the emergence of a more global media system. But the availability of transnational communication channels and the subsequent establishment of linkages, exchanges and dependencies between news and broadcasting organizations in different countries has undoubtedly accelerated this process. Whether it has reached the point of becoming a global profession – resembling in its universality a classic profession such as medicine – is a question that is now highly relevant for comparative communication analysis.

What are the implications of these developments for political communication research? Clearly, no country is an island any more, at least so far as its communication system is concerned. National communication systems may even be viewed as subsystems linked together in a global one. Consequently, no nationally bounded study can do justice to 'external' influences on its communication structures, nor can it fully explain its functioning. A comparative analysis, on the other hand, should be able to reveal both the characteristics of the national 'subsystems', the similarities and differences between the different components of the global system, and the linkages and relationships that are binding such units into a more constituent whole.

Our argument is not that every place in the world is gradually becoming more like every other place – as if reinstating the premise of naïve universalism from the global, rather than a parochially national, angle. Rather, we discern in globalization a potential for certain politico-communication processes to transcend national boundaries *in varying degrees*, depending in great part on differences in certain structural and cultural features of the societies they are reaching and permeating. Systematically comparative research is best placed to identify the main common and differentiating patterns that are emerging in this fluid scene.

Spurs to creative imagination

A third type of incentive to engage in comparative research concerns the capacity of this mode of enquiry to trigger the creative imagination of researchers, to open hidden conceptual doors, to spur improvisation of new modes of analysis. The added value of comparative analysis over the single-country study could be illustrated by a number of works published in the 1980s. We briefly describe two such examples below:

1 *A comparative study of British and German journalists.* Köcher (1986) sought to examine role perceptions, professional motivations, and evaluations of the norm of objectivity among British and German journalists. The rationale for the study related to the tendency among communication researchers to view journalism as a 'pan-cultural profession', due to the prevalence among journalists of defining their task as that of providing information, and the 'increasing similarity of the technical conditions of production and the international network of mass communication'. However, the researcher identified extensive differences between journalists in Britain and Germany:

> German journalism follows the traditional role of a species of political and intellectual career, which tends to place a lot of value on opinion, and less on news. British journalism, in contrast, particularly sees itself in the role of transmitter of facts, a neutral reporter of current affairs.

The author sought to capture these differences through the metaphors of 'bloodhounds' (for British journalists) versus 'missionaries' (for German journalists). It is highly unlikely that such a revealing portrait could have emerged from two separate single-country studies. A comparative approach, in which significant differences are found under a layer of apparent similarities between the practice of journalism in two societies (e.g. belief in the freedom of the press), has created a picture in which the whole is greater than the sum of the parts.

2 *A comparative study of American and Italian television news.* Hallin and Mancini (1984) approached the comparative analysis of American and Italian television news from the perspective of the 'construction of meaning' and sought to relate it to certain questions of media content and performance and larger issues of social and political organization and cultural context. American news, they argued, is patterned to be thematic

and interpretive, while political news in Italy is fragmented and less consciously symbolic. These differences are considered to reflect different definitions of the public sphere and the stances that journalists in the two countries adopt *vis-à-vis* that sphere. Again, the study illustrates how a comparative approach, by heightening our awareness of differences between the coverage of political news in two countries, enriches our sense of how differences in the structures of political systems – in societies that otherwise share a commitment to democratic rule – can lead to major differences of roles in politics for the news systems studied.

Policy Relevance

The results of comparative research can also offer normative and policy clarification, informing evaluations of, and proposals for change in, communication arrangements. The rapid development and diffusion of new communication technologies and the continual flux of social and political conditions have rendered the making of national communication policies in most societies around the world an ongoing and seemingly endless process. A voluminous literature (not limited to academic work) and a vast store of experience of policy-making has by now accumulated. Much of this literature and experience is limited, however, to single countries, with relatively few attempts to deploy policy experience in one country in the service of policy formulations in others. Efforts to profile the incidence of policy problems across national communication systems, and the manner in which they have been tackled, could constitute a genuine contribution by the research community to policy-making processes in different societies. Researchers with a comparative bent of mind would seem uniquely qualified to perform such a service.

THEORETICAL PROSPECTS

Apart from the advantages of comparative research discussed above, perhaps the most significant question is whether this mode of investigation can lead to important theoretical advances. For two broad reasons, our answer is affirmative.

First, most of our leading communication theories have been framed at national system levels. The predominance of American work in the field, at least until a decade or so ago, even encouraged researchers in other countries to shape their studies along theoretical models of communication processes in American society. The emergence of work by European scholars during the last two decades, based on alternative theoretical models, has significantly challenged such past American dominance. Nevertheless, the theoretical bases of mass communication research still largely reflect perspectives and problems that originated in Western societies. Today, however, the mass communication research community is becoming more global. The time has come, therefore, to strive to replace such Western dominance with theories of a more global applicability. The admittedly long road towards such a goal is through comparative research. This work could hold a dual theoretical promise: on the one hand, it could serve to test the extent and the conditions of the validity and applicability of Western-based theories for the study of communication processes in non-Western societies. On the other hand, it could prompt the formulation of theories based on experiences and issues in non-Western societies, which in turn could be tested for their applicability to Western societies. Only in this way can we hope to develop theories with a wider global application.

Second, the argument above holds with even greater force for the development of theories of political communication as such. Because of their sensitivity to a large number of political and other societal circumstances and influences, systems of political communication are highly specific to their time and place. Theorizing only on the basis of such specific experiences, however, can be highly constrained. To become more theoretically valuable, they should be liberated from their constraining specificities. A comparative examination of the organization and consequences of different political communication systems offers at least the possibility of working towards that goal.

SOME CHALLENGES AND PROBLEMS

Many of the advantages and benefits of comparative research should be clear by now. Nevertheless, pursuit of such a task confronts researchers with a number of challenges, problems and potential pitfalls. To be forewarned is to be prepared.

Perhaps the most common danger in designing comparative research is that of conceptual parochialism. Ironically, that is precisely the problem that comparative research should be designed to rectify. It is the difficulty that all researchers, irrespective of background, have in extricating themselves from their geographic or intellectual origins and viewing the world as others might see it. Because, for example, mass communication research was pioneered by American scholars, American models of communication and society have dominated the field for many years. Now that the field has reached a level of maturity, characterized not only by 'paradigm dialogue' but also by a greater awareness among researchers of work done in different countries and on different continents, the challenge of overcoming parochialism can at last be faced. Comparative researchers should be well placed to develop more far-reaching perspectives on political communication.

The other predominant challenge is methodological. The problem of

measurement in cross-national or cross-cultural research is often compli-
cated by the incommensurability of notionally identical measures. Some
examples are obvious: measures of the supply of political messages or
audience exposure to them make little sense if taken out of the context
of the communication conditions prevailing in different societies. The
problem is then how to standardize such measures given their different
meaning and significance in different societies. Comparative researchers
must often seek to establish *equivalences* and not necessarily search for
identical measures. Another methodological issue has to do with the
typically small number of cases available for comparative purposes. Given
that the unit of analysis in cross-national research is a country, a society,
a media system, or a broadcasting organization, the possible number of
cases on which a feasible study could be based is inevitably very limited.
For example, an effort to study comparatively the role of television in
the 1979 European Community elections was based on nine national
cases (Blumler, 1983). Clearly, one solution to this problem is to base the
research on a case-study approach. However, that approach negates
the idea of a truly comparative effort, in which the same dimensions in
different systems are examined comparatively. Comparative researchers
must, therefore, accept this limitation and should not necessarily attempt
to deploy statistical modes of analysis that would be more appropriate
in, say, survey research.

Finally, comparative research always involves a certain loss of the
diverse cultural complexity and richness of detail that can be elaborated
in single-country studies. Such a cost is inevitable where procedures are
undertaken, as comparative analysis requires, to convert societies into
dimensions, limited in number, that lend themselves to comparison. For
that reason, comparative research will never replace, and could never
substitute for, in-depth studies of the communication systems of single
societies. Political communication research needs to advance on both
fronts, with single-case studies feeding into comparative analysis, and a
comparative approach contributing to specification of system features that
could then be further explored in greater detail in single-case studies.

IN COMPARATIVE SPIRIT

Evidently, many exciting opportunities, mixed with daunting challenges,
beckon the would-be comparativist. If the former are not seized and the
latter not faced, research will not be able to do justice to essential features
of political communication itself: its emergence from varyingly patterned
relationships between powerful media and political institutions and its
increasing tendency to spill over national boundaries. How, then, should
comparative researchers proceed? The following suggestions are offered

not in an attempt to set an agenda but in the spirit of sharing with colleagues our thoughts about future work:

1 *Let all comparative flowers bloom.* There is, of course, no single comparative theory that can be outlined, accepted, and critiqued. Rather, there are many different varieties of comparative theorizing, depending on researchers' priorities, interests, conceptual predilections, and theoretical attachments. From this standpoint, comparative work is best seen as a strategy for extending knowledge in two respects – in level (from the micro-individual towards the macro-societal) and in scope (extending the number of sites to which theoretical propositions might apply and in which they might be tested). Operationally, too, comparative research can fruitfully draw on a multiplicity of methods. The literature gives examples of interesting insights drawn from work based, respectively, on comparative mass surveys, élite surveys, content analyses, focus group discussions, and ethnographic/participant observation attachments. In certain cases the use of more than one such method in combination has enabled investigators to span several levels of the system compared.

2 *Give up global typologizing of media systems* (à la Siebert, Peterson and Schramm's *Four Theories of the Press*, 1956). Such gross categories ignore a host of theoretically important variations between different national communication system types. As Köcher (1986) concluded from her comparison of British and German journalists, 'Even in countries with freedom of the press, journalism can develop in completely different directions, dependent on the political, legal and historical settings.'

3 *Take heart from the variety of 'dependent variables' that have provided interesting foci for attempted comparative analyses.* The availability of many different points of entry may help investigators to disentangle system-level influences on political communication arrangements in different societies. Those variables already tackled and reported in the literature include audience political communication gratifications and roles; media 'effects' on audience members (e.g. on political information levels, issue saliences, mobilization and turnout); journalists' political roles and degrees of intervention in the political process; message characteristics (e.g. campaign agendas, the formal and thematic structures of political messages, and news stories); and contributions to policies for the introduction of new media forms. Some of these variables have been more fully explored than others. Other possibilities await our attention.

4 *Be creative in the fashioning of 'independent variables'.* We note some promising ones below.

(a) *'Party logic' and 'media logic'.* Adapting the work of Altheide and Snow (1979), Mazzoleni (1987) distinguished what he termed 'two basic patterns of message production': party logic, or the structural and cultural assets that govern the communications enacted by major political parties; and media logic, or the sets of values and formats on which news organizations rely to ensure presentations compatible with their scheduling needs, professional standards, ways of gaining and holding attention, and images of the audience. Though utilized by Mazzoleni to examine the impact of major changes in how Italian elections are waged through the media, stemming from the secularization of politics, the crisis of the mass party, and the commercialization of broadcasting, the distinction is amenable to cross-national as well as cross-temporal analyses of political communication systems.

(b) *The strength and consequent influence of political party systems.* Thus Hallin and Mancini (1984) suggest that the public sphere may be differently structured in different societies. In Italy it is filled with all sorts of institutions that dominate the political discourse, whereas in the United States it is comparatively 'empty'. This, in turn, explains why the role of television journalists in the former is relatively passive, whereas in the latter they assume a more active interpretive role. Blumler and Semetko (1987) suggest that there are variations in the specificity of the definition of spokesmanship roles in national political systems, and that these are translated into varying degrees of politicians' access rights to media attention. In parliamentary systems, they suggest, 'where the media are accustomed faithfully to reporting the pronouncements of Government Ministers and their Opposition Shadows, there may be less onus on candidates to fight their way into election news reports with carefully crafted media events'. But in other systems 'politicians may have to work harder, keeping journalists' news values in mind, at getting the publicity they desire' (Blumler and Semetko, 1987).

(c) *Economic and financial variables.* The place of media systems in the economic marketplace, structures of ownership and control, and the intensity of competition for audience patronage deserve greater comparative attention than they have received thus far. Blumler and Gurevitch (1991), for example, suggest that marked differences between the ways television journalists were organized to report national election campaigns in Britain and the United States, and how they interpreted their journalistic roles, could be explained in part by the distinction between a public service television system and a more fully commercialized one:

All recognize that television is an inherently limited tool of political enlightenment, but when something as important as an election comes along, policy makers [in a public service framework] can afford to try to push back some of the constraints that those [in a commercial system] must observe for fear of ultimately incurring a financial penalty. Scheduling, the amount of time allowed for election news, the terms of its competition with other stories, the commitment to issue analysis – all were affected as a result.

(Blumler and Gurevitch, 1991, pp. 59–60)

(d) *Variations in political culture*. Many such variations are clearly relevant to comparative analysis of political communication performance. Political cultures in all societies prescribe and define the roles, 'purposes', and functions of the media as well as the ways in which the media will portray different social institutions. For example, Blumler and Gurevitch have proposed (see Chapter 4) that variations in the treatment by the media of different social institutions and groups could reflect, in part, the deference to which such institutions are presumed to be entitled by virtue of their place in a society's hierarchy of social values (such as the treatment of the US Congress versus the British Parliament in the media of the respective countries). In short, researchers should be alert to the different ways in which the media in diverse national cultures will resonate to political communications emanating from different groups and institutions.

(e) *Grasp from a **synchronic** standpoint that political communication takes place everywhere under key 'system conditions' that may be specified and compared for different societies*. To illustrate through an example, the special shape and flavour of American political communication might be captured through such system conditions as the conceptualization of political competition as a game, akin to baseball or football, explaining why it is so often *reported* as a game; the relatively inchoate and weak political system from which it springs, including a low cultural valuation of 'politics and politicians as such', affording more scope, then, for journalistic agenda setting and the imposing of more strict news-value filters for politicians' messages to fit; a relatively strong media system, constitutionally honoured and privileged, and governed by a professional culture of independence, autonomy and adversarialism; the pervasive professionalism of political message making, pressure group advocacy, and campaign activity; and the thorough dependence of the main media outlets for political communication on conformity to imperatives of the economic marketplace.

(f) *From a **diachronic** perspective, strive to fashion concepts and strategies for understanding political communication system change*. Blumler (1990), for example, has proposed a definition of a broader set of political communication processes at work in the post-1960s world of competitive democracies, within which enquiries of many kinds, including comparative analyses, could be situated. Its point of departure is the fluidity and fickleness of public opinion, the lack of stabilizing political and demographic props, and the correspondingly greater significance of short-term information flows. All of these point to what Seymour-Ure (1987) has termed 'the growing intrusiveness of media' in politics, resulting in a perception, shared by many influence-seeking political actors, of the greater centrality of the mass media to the conduct of political conflict and its outcomes. This has propelled emergence of a 'modern publicity process', defined as involving 'a competitive struggle to influence and control popular perceptions of key political events and issues through the mass media'. Important subprocesses unleashed in its wake include: a high prioritization of media strategies and tactics among would-be political influentials; 'source professionalization' (or the extensive reliance of political actors on publicity advisers, public relations experts and campaign consultants); intensification of conflict between politicians and journalists; increased uneasiness among journalists about their own roles in political communication, given their vulnerability to news management; and an increased circulation of negative messages about political actors, policies and decisions.

This process is more advanced in some societies than in others, however, depending on how relations between their media systems, political and economic structures, and national cultures are organized. For example, in the United States the modern publicity process would appear to have moved very close to the heart of national politics, almost as if the two were synonymous. In other countries it may not dominate the political arena to quite the same extent. British politicians, for example, may often flirt with it, be drawn to it, and at times even heartily embrace it, but, in a 'safe sex' spirit, they hesitate to go all the way to full consummation with it. If so, it is probably due to the less than wholeheartedly populist political culture in that country, to the strength of its parliamentary institutions, to the more sacerdotal orientation to the political sphere of its primary media organizations, and, more generally, to elements of subordination of the British media system to the political system.

(g) *Seek potentially productive collaborative alliances*, for example with researchers working in political communication systems undergoing revealing and exciting processes of change. This is precisely the case with Europe east of the Elbe at present, where, as Jakubowicz (1989) vividly shows, long-thwarted communication scholars have at last found new empirical and normative missions, while working on the interface between profound impulses of societal change toward openness and diversity, on the one hand, and a traditionally fossilized and straitjacketed media system, on the other. West and East alike could learn much from joint efforts to explore how democracy is faring in polities that are becoming, despite such different points of departure, ever more media-centric.

A FINAL WORD

Comparative research in political communication presents challenges as well as problems and some hidden risks. We have attempted to outline some of these in this chapter. Researchers embarking on this road should, therefore, be well armed, conceptually and methodologically, and should possess 'deep' knowledge of the societies they intend to examine. That may be a tall order, but ultimately it is a road that must be travelled, for it represents the field's extending and extendable frontier.

Chapter 7

The formation of campaign agendas in the United States and Britain

This chapter outlines a comparative cross-national perspective on the role of the media in the formation of election campaign agendas. It draws from the introductory and concluding chapters of *The Formation of Campaign Agendas: A Comparative Analysis of Party and Media Roles in Recent American and British Elections.*[1] The body of that book presented the findings of a comparative investigation, based on content analysis and newsroom observation, of influences on campaign agendas in mass media coverage of the British general election of 1983 and the US presidential election of 1984. The first section below lays out a rationale and framework for research of this kind, while the second section summarizes what was learned from this two-nation enquiry into the formation of election campaign agendas.

CONCEPTUAL FRAMEWORK

This comparative study has two points of departure. First, it conceives of the notion of agenda setting not in the 'classical' (McCombs and Shaw, 1972) focus on the impact of the media on the perception of political agendas by members of the audience (McCombs, 1981) but rather in terms of the relative contributions of the media and political candidates and parties to the shaping of campaign agendas as they evolve during an election period. It harks back to the call by Tichenor (1982) to examine the *discretionary* power of the media in the agenda-setting process. Second, it aims to contribute to our understanding of the media's role in the formation of election campaign agendas by adopting a comparative perspective. Essentially, our argument is that the contribution of the media in this respect is shaped by the political culture and structure of the society in which the media operate and is bounded by the parameters through which a given political culture defines the 'permissible' interventionary function of the media, as well as the constraints that a political structure imposes on the performance of such a function. Thus, the nature of the media's contribution to election campaigns can best be highlighted through comparative analysis, from which similarities as well as the unique features of the operation of the media in different societies will emerge.

Comparative research on the structure and contents of election campaigns appears to be rather rare. Perhaps because the concept of agenda setting has its origins primarily in American research, and therefore carried with it the functionalist and liberal-pluralist theoretical connotations of much American mass communication research, its travel across the Atlantic has not been especially successful or significant. Many European researchers have been guided by, and preoccupied with, a view of the media as an ideological agency in society, occupying and servicing the ideological mainstream and therefore essentially subservient to the 'primary definers' of political positions. In this view, the notion of agenda setting as described by McCombs and Shaw (1972) ignores the crucial (and assumed to be subordinate) relationships of the media to a society's centres of political power.

Despite the predominant concern of American researchers to examine the agenda-setting powers of the media *vis-à-vis* members of the audience, calls have been sounded from time to time to consider their role in a wider institutional context. In addition to Tichenor (1982), Becker, McCombs and McLeod (1975) have suggested that forces in the environment of the media that trigger their agenda-setting activities might be studied. Gandy (1982) has sought to go *Beyond Agenda Setting* in considering the 'information subsidies' by which powerful would-be newsmakers encourage the mass media to accept their versions of public affairs. It was probably only a matter of time before the obvious question that is implicit in these calls – namely, 'If the media set the agenda, who sets the agenda for the agenda setters?' – was to emerge. This question extricated the concept of agenda setting from the realm of media effects and relocated it in the web of relationships between media and political institutions. It thus opened up new questions about the role of the mass media in defining social issues and, in the specific case of election campaigns, in their contribution to the formation of campaign agendas. It also gave a new lease of life to the notion of agenda setting, by broadening the field of its potential applicability and rescuing it from its rather limited focus on media–audience relationships.

The discretionary power of the media

Our concern, then, is with the discretionary power of the media – that is, with the extent to which the media are capable of playing a formative role in shaping the agenda of election campaigns, and with the forces that enable them to play such a role or limit their performance of it. We take it as given that the proposition that the media merely reflect or mirror an agenda constructed by political spokespersons is bankrupt. Such a position obscures the intricate ways in which political messages emerge as the joint product of an interactive process involving political communicators and media professionals.

An awareness of the active role that the media play in constructing the coverage of election campaigns is by now not only commonplace among political communication researchers but seems to be also shared by some media professionals. There are, however, some signs of Anglo-American differences in journalistic attitudes towards the notion that the media may play an independent part in political agenda setting. Thus, CBS correspondent Leslie Stahl has stated: 'We didn't want their campaign to dictate our agenda' (cited in Robinson and Sheehan, 1983). Stahl's statement seems to run counter to the still entrenched tendency among professional newspeople to argue that their role is confined to 'telling the story as it is'. But it reflects the centrality of the value of independence and autonomy in the professional ideology of American newspeople and insists on the discretionary power of television correspondents to tell the campaign story not as the politicians wish it to be presented, but as the reporters see it.

Compare this with an example of a British journalist's views on this issue. Brian Wenham, Head of BBC Current Affairs in the late 1970s, explained to one of us the rather static and truly mirroring character of the BBC's coverage of the annual conferences of the major political parties in Britain by stating that they were 'the events of the political parties' and that the BBC had no business interfering with or reshaping their representation on the screen. This should not be taken as indicative of a more supine position by the BBC towards the British parties. But it reflects the differences between the approach of British and American newspeople to the coverage of political events and, by implication, the differences between the professional philosophies of television producers and reporters in Britain and the United States.

Factors impinging on the media's discretionary power

What, then, are the forces that might impinge on the discretionary power of the media *vis-à-vis* political institutions, candidates and parties? In the following discussion we attempt to identify some of the factors (or variables) that might be relevant to an understanding of the exercise of that power by the media, and that could explain the variability of its exercise in American and British election campaigns.

1 *The position of politics and of politicians in society*

The 'valuation of politics as such' might vary in different societies, with important consequences for the political communication process. As we have explained elsewhere (see Chapter 5), since 'politics is a field of activity that can attract or repel, engage people or turn them off, be thought worthy of respect or be treated with indifference and contempt, . . . the precariousness of its attraction renders it vulnerable to various influences'. For our purposes we need to consider whether 'the valuation of politics as such' is different in the two societies compared here, and in which ways these differences might affect the campaigns' coverage and thus impinge on the media's discretionary power.

We propose that there are clear differences between the United States and Britain in this regard. Whether because of the greater 'openness' of the American political system compared to the British, or because of the high visibility of the links between American politicians and money, with its potentially corruptible effects (for which there is ample evidence), or perhaps because of the apparently pragmatic character of American politics, public perceptions of American politicians seem to be characterized more by suspicion of political activity and of those who engage in it than by respect for it. Conversely, the more structured character of the British party system, the clearer ideological character of these parties and the consequent higher degree of politicization of British society as a whole, might give political activity in Britain a relatively higher status. These differences, we suggest, could be reflected in the orientation of media professionals towards politicians and their campaigning activities, and could impact on the attitudes towards politics implicit in their reporting of the campaign.

2 *Newspeople's orientations towards politics and politicians*

As suggested earlier, general societal valuations of politics as a worthy and significant activity, or as suspect and self-serving, may be mirrored in media reporting of this activity. The labels 'pragmatic' and 'sacerdotal' have been used to describe the poles of that dimension (see Chapter 4). A pragmatic orientation implies that the treatment of politicians' activities will be based on journalists' assessments of their intrinsic newsworthiness and that consequently the prominence given to stories reporting these activities, the amount of time or space allocated to them, as well as other aspects of the way they are treated will be determined by strict consideration of news values. A sacerdotal orientation, on the other hand, impels newspeople to treat these activities with the respect due to them as inherently significant and important, deserving consideration beyond that prescribed by the application of news values alone. Thus, we suggest that coverage of an American presidential campaign in US media would tend towards the pragmatic end of the continuum, whereas coverage of a British election campaign in British media would be characterized by a more sacerdotal orientation. In practical terms, a sacerdotal orientation would be exhibited in the degree to which political candidates would be given greater space in news reports to state their positions in their own words. Conversely, if the pragmatic orientation prevails, candidates' statements and activities will more likely be used as 'raw material' in the construction of reporters' stories.

3 *Degree of professionalization of election campaigns*

One of the more significant developments in the evolution of election campaigns in recent years has been the emergence of specialists as a dominant force in shaping the course and contents of campaigns. We refer specifically to the variety of communication and media specialists, public relations experts, pollsters, and campaign managers who seem to have an increasingly powerful voice in the selection and packaging of campaign issues, and in managing the conduct of political candidates in such ways as to achieve the 'best picture' on television. The notion that the evening television news programmes constitute the prime area on which election campaigns are fought has accelerated this trend. Although this is true to a large extent both of the United States and of Britain, it would appear that developments in that direction have gone further in the United States than in Britain. This might be so not only because the United States has always been in the forefront of the application of public relations techniques to the field of politics, but also because any restraining or countervailing forces, such as a sacerdotal orientation towards politics which could have slowed down the full-fledged emergence of 'political marketing', are probably weaker in that country.

What consequences, then, for the discretionary power of the media in the agenda-setting process might flow from the full flowering of political marketing? We would hypothesize that under such circumstances any lingering sentiments among newspeople that political candidates should be treated sacerdotally would be further eroded. A campaign that is being perceived as being stage-managed by PR experts and marketing professionals is likely to encourage disdainful attitudes among newspeople. The outcome might be a tendency among them to exercise greater discretionary power. On the other hand, campaign speeches that are judged by journalists truly to reflect a candidate's own political philosophy are perhaps more likely to command greater fidelity by newspeople to the candidate's own words.

4 *Variation of media competition*

One of the main consequences of competition, in politics as in commerce, is assumed to be a heightened sensitivity to the demands and wishes of the public. A political system structured along ideologically defined party lines also defines more sharply the constituencies to which different candidates will appeal. On the other hand, a system in which ideological differences are less sharply etched encourages candidates to be 'all things to all people'.

Competition among media organizations might have similar consequences. Thus, we might hypothesize that where competition for audiences is tougher, there will be a greater tendency to tailor the contents of news stories to presumed audience tastes and preferences. The lesser the competitive pressures, the less would media organizations feel the pressure to capture and maximize audience members' attention and the more attuned they would be to politicians' needs.

Competitive pressures on the media vary both between countries and between different media. The British press, like the British party system, is structured along fairly well-defined constituencies, or audiences. Thus, the so-called 'quality press' hardly engages in competition with the tabloid newspapers, and the readership of the quality newspapers is itself segmented along clearly defined socio-economic and political lines. At the same time, competition among the tabloid newspapers is quite fierce. Competitive pressures on the press in the United States are much weaker, by comparison, primarily because the American press is structured largely along local and regional, rather than national lines, and because many American newspapers now enjoy a monopoly or near-monopoly position in their cities or towns.

The competitive situation of television in both countries is somewhat different. To begin with, due to the massified character of the television audience, the segmentation of the audience is hardly apparent. Competition for the audience is thus the predominant characteristic of American television. Because large audiences determine the financial lifeblood of the US networks, their dependence on and sensitivity to apparent audience tastes is all-encompassing. The television networks in Britain are, of course, also locked into competition for audiences, but because their financial underpinnings are still quite different, the pressures exerted by that competition are less powerful than those to which the American networks are subjected.

The overall picture on this dimension is thus rather complex, with a variety of forces pulling in different directions. We nevertheless hypothesize that the American news organizations – but primarily television – would be comparatively more audience oriented than their British counterparts. The implications for hypothesizing about their relative inclination to exercise discretionary power are fairly straightforward. High levels of competitive pressures are likely to render the media more audience oriented and therefore more likely to exercise discretionary powers *vis-à-vis* the politicians. Lesser concern with competition could shift media orientations toward greater sensitivity to political candidates and could result in reduced tendencies toward discretionary reporting.

An interim summary

The British and the American political communication systems exhibit different characteristics, both in the structure and the culture of the political systems in the two countries and in the structure and professional culture of their respective media systems. The two dimensions are, of course, closely interrelated because the structures of media organizations and their roles in the political communication process are, in every society, shaped by the political system. At the same time, the specific ways in which media organizations perform and contribute to the political communication process cannot be fully deduced from the general characteristics of the political system. Media organizations in liberal democratic societies are confronted with some options and choices in their relationship with the political system, and the choices they make clearly affect, in turn, some features of the political system. At the very least, their choices can have a formative effect on the behaviour of politicians. The relationship between the two sets of institutions is transactional rather than deterministic.

Many features of that transactional relationship appear in sharp relief during periods of heightened political communication activity, such as election campaigns. A cross-national comparative study of the performance of the media during these periods thus offers opportunities for identifying the roles and the contributions of the media to the political communication process that might not be clearly visible in studies of a single country or of a single campaign.

We should also note, however, that the framework outlined above refers to traditionally significant features of political communication systems which may be undergoing gradual change. Observers of the political communication scene in Britain have in recent years noted trends that point towards an evolution of British election campaigns in an 'American' direction. Thus, the British media seem to become gradually more competitive; election campaigns are clearly affected by tendencies towards greater professionalization; and the political culture generally is becoming more 'pragmatic' (see also Chapter 14 below). Clearly, these are long-range processes, the evidence for which is too complex (and mixed) to be detailed in this work. However, if these trends should hold and persist into the future, the differences between the political communication systems in the two countries could gradually weaken, thus increasing the similarities in the performance of the media and in the roles they play in structuring the political and campaign agendas in these two societies.

WHAT HAVE WE LEARNED ABOUT AGENDA SETTING?

Our focus on the discretionary power of the media to play a more or less interventionary role in the structuring of campaign agendas led to a reconsideration of the notion of agenda setting. It now seems to us that agenda-setting theory and research require attention and development from two main angles. One concerns perspectives on the process itself; the other concerns the sources that feed it in different systemic conditions.

First, academic researchers need to appreciate more fully a basic truth about the formation of campaign agendas, which most practitioners (politicians and journalists alike) have entirely absorbed by now – namely, that the process is a deeply political one, as is the role of the media in it. Agenda-setting terminology is not well placed to alert us to this. It tends to reduce the process to a semi-mechanical practice, connoting a sedate ordering of items for sequential consideration before the real business of debate and decision taking over them begins.

In election communication, however, the reality is quite different. Once a campaign is announced (or approaches), a common element in both the United States and Britain is the unleashing in earnest of an implacably competitive struggle to control the mass media agenda, a struggle that pits, not only candidates and parties in contention for agenda domination, but also political campaign managements against news organization teams. Awareness of their involvement in such a struggle is a leitmotif of our observations of NBC and BBC journalists, expressed variously as a 'tug of war', a desire not to give electioneering politicians a 'free ride', and a concern to show that they were not completely in the pockets of the candidates and political parties.

The root of this process is, of course, the fact that (apart from advertisements and party broadcasts) journalists command the gates of access for political messages to reach the electoral audience, including powers not only of selection but also of contextualizing commentary, packaging, and event definition. To would-be wooers of increasingly volatile voters, breaking through those gates with one's preferred message as intact as possible is quite vital. Interpreting the ensuing struggle as 'political' is useful in highlighting an advantage that politicians bring to it. They have no difficulty or inhibition about treating message projection as a process of exerting leverage, pressure and manipulation. After all, they regularly play games of that kind in all their other activities. For media personnel this does present a problem, however, because it highlights their involvement in a political process, despite their claims to be outsiders and their protestations that they are merely observing and reporting campaign events through the self-denying norms of objectivity and impartiality.

Indeed, the tensions inherent in their position may be seen in the near-consensual view expressed by television newspeople in the American presidential election of 1988, that campaign managers and their media 'mavens' had discovered and exploited the medium's Achilles' heel, namely the predictability of the journalists' news judgements, and their inability to resist 'good pictures'. Consequently, many of them felt that they had ended up being the 'losers' in that campaign, acknowledging thereby that they are indeed involved in a struggle over the agenda. The resulting frustration probably helps to explain their readiness, when politicians seem to have put one over on them, to 'disdain' the news they are presenting by drawing attention to its deliberately crafted and manipulative origins.

Agenda setting, then, should be conceived as a dynamic process, not a settled procedure. Regarded as a struggle for control, it will take place differently in different societies, depending on differences of political systems, the positions of the media within those systems and internal differences of media organization. Because, however, both sides deploy significant resources in the struggle, and because the outcome matters greatly to each, for self-identity as well as for more pragmatic reasons, even those who gain an upper hand at one election moment cannot confidently count on retention of their superiority at the next.

Another major implication of this analysis is that future studies should not take mass media agenda setting for granted (as in much of the past literature). That is, media agendas should not be regarded as solely determined by journalists and news organizations. Nor should they be regarded as primarily determined by political parties and candidates during election campaigns. Instead there are a number of differentiating influences that affect how much discretion both journalists and politicians have in setting campaign agendas, and these influences must be considered in drawing conclusions about how much either journalists or politicians contribute to campaign agendas.

At the system level, such influences include:

1 The strength of the political party system – with a stronger party system generally associated with less discretion on the part of journalists to set the campaign agenda and more opportunity for politicians to do so.
2 Public service versus commercial media systems – with commercial systems associated with stronger inclination by journalists to set political agendas and not merely reflect party and candidate agendas, but with less space into which to squeeze their contributions.
3 Differing levels of competition for media audiences – with more competition being associated with more attention to perceived audience interests and less attention to politicians' agendas by journalists.
4 Differing degrees of professionalization of the campaign – with more professional management of political campaigns being associated with less discretion for journalists to set the agenda and with a growth of cynicism and scepticism about the legitimacy of the election communication process generally.
5 Cultural differences – with more respect for politics being associated with a greater willingness on the part of journalists to let the political parties and candidates have more discretion in setting the campaign agenda and less emphasis on the election as a game or a horse race at the expense of substantive issues.

These system-level or macro influences are not the only ones affecting the agenda-setting process. There are also more specific, or micro-level, conditions that enhance and limit the discretionary power of journalists and politicians to set campaign agendas, including:

1 The partisan or ideological leanings of specific media organizations. Even though this influence is more obvious in editorials, feature columns and commentaries, there is some evidence that it can affect specific subject and theme agendas in news coverage.
2 The status of the candidate. An incumbent president or prime minister is usually in a better position to influence the campaign agenda than a challenger. Even in a system historically endowed with third parties, like that in Britain, their agenda-setting powers are limited.
3 Journalistic norms of balance and objectivity. These are most likely directly to affect the amount of coverage of each party and the number of sources cited from the different campaigns rather than their issue agendas, although covering candidates with balance and objectivity may have some effect on which issues are emphasized.
4 The size of the news slot. Most newspapers have far more space for news of a campaign than do television news programmes, and full-size broadsheets have more space than tabloids. More space permits more issues to be covered in greater detail and has the potential to broaden the agenda.
5 Journalists' notions of what roles are most appropriate (e.g. prudential, reactive, conventionally journalistic, analytical; or neutral transmitter, interpreter, adversary) when covering a campaign. Our studies suggest that the roles of analyst or interpreter and adversary are likely to be associated with more endeavour by journalists to shape the campaign agenda by initiating stories and raising questions that politicians might prefer not to address.

Taken together, these influences suggest that the formation of the campaign agenda is a complex process that varies from one culture and one election to another. Scholars of media agenda setting need to take these factors into account when theorizing about the process, even if their primary interest is in relationships between media and public agendas as has been the case for most research on this topic in the United States.

Whether or not the media are actively setting agendas or simply passing on the agendas of powerful news sources (to think of the extremes) very much depends on the influences itemized above. In the case of Britain it is difficult to speak of the media *setting* agendas, whereas even in the US case it is clear that the major news media do not have unlimited discretion to set campaign agendas. Perhaps a more accurate term for the role of the news media in recent American campaigns might be *agenda shaping*, whereas some portion of their contribution to British campaigns might be termed *agenda amplifying*. Indeed, future studies of the formation of media and public agendas might wish to conceive of a continuum from 'agenda setting' to 'agenda reflecting' with 'agenda shaping' and 'agenda amplifying' falling in between the two extremes.

The preceding discussion should also alert us to the possibility that the agenda-setting approach in its conventional form may miss out on important aspects of the role of the media in election campaigns. How plausible is the argument that the media, and especially television, indeed play only a relatively marginal 'agenda-shaping' or 'agenda-amplifying' role in political campaigns? Reflecting on that question, we would suggest that such a marginalized view of media power may result from a tendency to focus on agenda setting as a matter of the selection and prioritization of news items, while ignoring the role of the media in *framing* election stories and thus defining and constructing their meaning. In other words, a limitation of agenda-setting research is its emphasis on the *what* (i.e. what stories are selected and which priorities guide the selection and placement of news items) rather than on the *how* (the manner in which stories are framed and how close the media's frames are to the frames of the candidates and their campaign managers).

This suggests that in future studies we may need to shift the focus away from the traditional emphases of the agenda-setting approach to one that looks in more detail at the *processes of meaning production* that take place within and between media and political organizations. Such a process of framing campaign events takes place independently of the degree of discretion that media professionals in different societies exercise in reflecting, amplifying, shaping, or setting political news agendas.

Chapter 8

Political communication systems and democratic values[1]

This chapter deals with the tensions and disparities between the ostensibly democratic ideals that the mass media are supposed to serve and the communication structures and practices that actually prevail. We argue that these disparities undermine the capacity of the system to serve those democratic ideals. Our diagnosis rests on some broad assumptions which are stated, elaborated and illustrated in the following sections.

DEMOCRATIC EXPECTATIONS OF MEDIA PERFORMANCE

Democracy is a highly exacting creed in its expectations of the mass media. It requires that the media perform and provide a number of functions and services for the political system. Among the more significant are:

Surveillance of the sociopolitical environment, reporting developments likely to impinge, positively or negatively, on the welfare of citizens.

Meaningful agenda setting, identifying the key issues of the day, including the forces that have formed and may resolve them.

Platforms for an intelligible and illuminating advocacy by politicians and spokespersons of other cause and interest groups.

Dialogue across a diverse range of views, as well as between power holders (actual and prospective) and mass publics.

Mechanisms for holding officials to account for how they have exercised power.

Incentives for citizens to learn, choose and become involved, rather than merely to follow and kibitz over the political process.

A principled resistance to the efforts of forces outside the media to subvert their independence, integrity and ability to serve the audience.

A sense of respect for the audience member, as potentially concerned and able to make sense of his or her political environment.

But it is no easy matter to achieve and serve these goals. At least four kinds of obstacles hinder their attainment.

First, conflicts among democratic values themselves may necessitate trade-offs and compromises in the organization and performance of the media. There are tensions, for example, between the principle of editorial autonomy and the ideal of offering individuals and groups wide-ranging access to the media. The aim of serving the public by catering to its immediate tastes and interests is likely to conflict with the aim of providing what the public *needs* to know. Media organizations are also confronted by the conflict between a majoritarian concentration on mainstream opinions and interests and the rights of dissident and marginal views to be heard.

Second, authoritative political communicators often appear to exist in an élite world of their own, distanced from the circumstances and perspectives of ordinary people. In fact, political communication could virtually be defined as the transmission of messages and pressures to and from individuals who are demonstrably unequal: the highly informed and the abysmally ignorant; the highly powerful and the pitifully powerless; the highly involved and the blissfully indifferent. Thus, the very structure of political communication involves a division between movers and shakers at the top and bystanders below, imposing limits on the participatory energy the system can generate.

Third, not all in the audience for political communication are political animals, nor are they obliged to be. On the one hand, a viable democracy presupposes an engaged citizenry; on the other hand, one of the freedoms the members of a liberal society enjoy is to define for themselves their stance towards the political system, including the right to be politically apathetic. As a result, political messages are doubly vulnerable. For one thing, they must jostle and compete for limited time and space with other, often more entertaining and beguiling, kinds of contents. They are not guaranteed a favoured share of our attentions. For another, their ultimate dependence on winning and holding the attentions of a heterogeneous audience can inhibit the media from committing themselves wholeheartedly to the democratic task.

Fourth, the media can pursue democratic values only in ways that are compatible with the socio-political and economic environment in which they operate. Political communication arrangements follow the contours of and derive their resources from the society of which they are a part. Even when formally autonomous and sheltered by sacrosanct constitutional guarantees of a free press, they are part and parcel of the larger social system, performing functions for it and impelled to respond to predominant drives within it. In the United States, for example, media organizations are large business enterprises and first and foremost must survive (and if possible prosper) in a highly competitive marketplace.

Their pursuit of their democratic role is inexorably shaped by that overriding economic goal. Politically, too, media institutions are linked inextricably to the governing institutions of society, not least because of their mutual dependence as suppliers of raw materials (government to media) and channels of publicity (media to government).

SOME REDEEMING FEATURES

However constraining such pressures and problems, symbolically at least, journalism in Western liberal democracies does reflect the influence of democratic values.

For example, the news media provide a daily parade of political disagreement and conflict. In that way what appears regularly in the news is a standing refutation of the anti-democratic notion that there is some single valid social purpose for pursuit through politics and some single group which is entitled to monopolize power because it alone knows what that purpose is and how best to realize it. In addition, the existence of a free press enshrines the democratic concept of the political accountability of power holders to ordinary citizens. Much of what the press reports in political affairs can be thought of as designed to encourage audience members to judge how what the government has been doing relates to their interests, problems and concerns. Similarly, a free press can be said to embody the notion of citizen autonomy. It implicitly stands for the assumption that readers, viewers and listeners are offered material on the basis of which they can make up their own minds about who the 'good guys' and 'bad guys' in politics are.

Beyond what it represents symbolically, the press in a democratic society can be seen as performing an indispensable bridging function in democratic politics. Inevitably, an enormous gulf stretches between the political world and people's perceptions of it. Although political decisions may affect people's lives in many ways, from *their* perspective the political world often seems remote, confusing and boring. What the press does, it might be argued, is to bring developments in this distant and difficult arena within the reach of the average person in terms that he or she can understand. Viewed in this light, certain features of political reporting may be regarded as enticements to become involved in political questions, ways of interesting the public in affairs for which they might feel little prior enthusiasm. So the crowd-pulling appeal of journalism, the tendency to dramatize, the projection of hard-hitting conflict, the use of sporting analogies to awaken a horse-race-like excitement, are on this view inducements to become interested in and aware of political matters. Even the media's proclivity towards the dramatic may be applauded in this spirit. A dramatic story can be treated as a peg for more information about the wider political context in which it occurred.

Even the much criticized tendency of the press to trade in simple stereotypes can be viewed in this light. As Winfried Schulz (1983) has put it, 'In order to make politics comprehensible to the citizen, it must first be reduced by journalists to a few simple structural patterns.' Personalization, the penchant for clear-cut issues, the tendency to reduce most political conflicts to only two sides of the argument – all might be thought of as aids to popular understanding.

Yet such a positive evaluation ignores three problems. First, surveys of what audience members actually glean from the news show that it is a highly inefficient mechanism for conveying information (cf. Robinson and Levy, 1986). Second, there are few signs that media personnel seriously try to verify for themselves how much information and insight their audiences get out of news reports, with a prospect of changing their news-telling ways accordingly. Third, with many journalistic practices the means seem to have become the end. An election campaign is predominantly treated *as* (not like) a horse race. Journalists and their audiences are more often stalled on the bridge than transported to a more enlightened land beyond it!

SYSTEMIC CONSTRAINTS

Allegations that news organizations fail to serve democracy well are not unique to the United States. Even in democracies whose structures and institutions appear to be less dominated by a capitalist spirit, and where large and impressive public service broadcasting organizations have long existed and enjoyed much esteem, similar complaints have been voiced by academics and pressure groups alike. In our view, the incidence and the obduracy of these problems can be traced to the fact that in large, complex, industrialized societies, political messages emanate from more or less rigidly structured and enduring political communication systems.

The notion of a political communication *system* is intended to highlight the interdependence of key communicators within it, the reciprocal nature of their relationship with each other and with the audience, and a crystallization of communication norms, roles, genres, formats, traditions and practices that tend to persist over time. Presumably the 'system' character of political communication arrangements confers predictability and familiarity on the otherwise hectic, volatile and uncertain climate of the modern publicity process. Officials, opinion leaders and journalists can form some sense of the ground rules and behaviours which they can count on their counterparts to observe. Audience members also learn what to expect and how to respond accordingly. Nevertheless, built-in system constraints tend to block and thwart the realization of democratic values. We will consider the role of such constraints at four different levels of the political communication system: the societal level; the inter-institutional level; the intra-institutional level; and the audience level.

The societal level

We have already suggested that the production and dissemination of political messages occur within a web of economic, political and cultural subsystems, which incline the media to select certain issues rather than others as subjects for public attention; to frame their stories according to favoured scenarios; and to give the views of certain groups and individuals privileged treatment and heightened exposure. Such pressures need not be applied overtly or deliberately. Indeed, our emphasis on political communication as a systemic product reflects our view that the reciprocal flow of influence between the media and other social institutions is a more or less 'natural' and mutually accepted phenomenon, tending to reproduce the power relations and reciprocal dependencies that obtain between them. And it is the varying linkages between such institutions, including closer relations and more powerful dependencies in some cases and more remote links and lesser dependencies in others, which may result in various constraints on 'communications for democracy'.

We can examine media linkages to the *economic* environment via the structure of ownership and control and via the dynamics of supply and demand in a commercial marketplace. Researchers have paid some attention to the former, where current trends point to an increased concentration of ownership in fewer hands, as well as a process of conglomeration, placing media organizations within larger corporate structures controlled by non-media interests Murdock, 1982; Bagidikian, 1987) The implications of such ownership patterns for media 'bias' towards certain opinions and interests are not clear-cut. Owners of media outlets may leave editors free to follow their own political and professional leanings; yet the potential for influencing editorial policy is clearly present. The Conservative bias of the Fleet Street press in Britain is now blatant and open, while Rupert Murdoch has exercised control with a vengeance over the editorial policies of certain newspapers he has acquired. In American television in the late 1980s, waves of mergers and take-overs brought new actors – such as Capital Cities and General Electric – into the media arena, thus giving even greater weight to financial 'bottom line' considerations.

Market mechanisms may threaten democratic aspirations when two or more media organizations compete for a large and heterogeneous mass audience. Such circumstances have generated pressures towards the 'tabloidization' of much information programming on American television, shifting its style from the serious and extended to the entertaining and arresting. They also impose format rigidities on public affairs coverage.

(Even in election campaigns, the nightly news shows on American network television cannot be extended beyond their 22-minute ration; nor can their commercials be re-timed to create room for longer and more coherent reports.)

Of course *political* constraints on the media can take different forms, ranging from direct political controls, through overt pressures to promote or suppress specific contents, to strategies for steering journalists towards favoured stories and away from less favoured ones, to a more subtle reliance on informal channels and contacts. One form of highly significant political 'control', however, is less often noticed. Powerful institutions in society *are* powerful at least in part because they can plausibly claim authority over the definition of the issues falling in their spheres. This is not to imply that critics are silenced, but that they often have to make their case on grounds not of their own choosing. Thus, in the US, the Treasury and the Federal Reserve Bank are regarded as the authorities to turn to on the state of the economy; the Pentagon is defined as the authoritative voice on defence and military matters; the police pronounce on issues of law and order; and the President is the 'primary definer' of what constitutes the 'national interest'. Not surprisingly, when journalists seek an authoritative perspective on a certain field of issues, they turn to those officials who are defined by their positions as authoritative sources. Media professionals do not see this practice as a violation of the canon of objectivity, since the sources are consulted precisely for their presumed expertise and not merely as proponents of a certain point of view. Alternative definitions of social issues are then disadvantaged – either not represented at all, given short shrift, or labelled as 'interested' and 'biased'.

Social systems also structure a pecking order of status and prestige, giving those higher up the ladder a better chance of having their affairs reported in line with their own perspectives. Thus, certain institutions are commonly accorded respect, even reverence, in the news. Some enjoy benign neglect. Some evoke a mixture of symbolic deference and pragmatic exploitation. Some mainly suffer the slings and arrows of straight news-values fortunes. Some can get attention only if they stir up trouble. In Chapter 4 we have outlined a conceptual framework for analysing news personnel's orientations towards social institutions, based on a continuum between more sacerdotal and more pragmatic approaches to institutional reporting. We argue there that social institutions that are regarded as the symbolic embodiment of the core values of their society tend to elicit portrayals of their activities as if 'through their own eyes'. Conversely, the treatment of institutions, groups and individuals that represent less central values, or dissident and deviant values, is likely to be guided more strictly by journalists' news values.

The inter-institutional level

In modern political communication systems mediated political messages are a subtly composite product, reflecting the contributions and interactions of two different types of communicators: advocates and journalists. Each side is striving to realize different goals *vis-à-vis* the audience; yet it cannot normally pursue these without securing the co-operation of the other side. Politicians need access to the communication channels operated by media organizations; and they must adjust their messages to the demands of formats and genres that have been devised inside such organizations. At the same time journalists cannot perform their task of political reporting without access to politicians for interviews, news and comment. Thus, while they may have different goals, if they are to proceed at all, they must work through and with the other side. And from this interwoven process three problems of democratic communication arise.

First, there is a potential for blurring institutional functions which ideally ought to be kept distinct. For their part, politicians start to think, speak and behave like journalists, as, for example, when politicians' statements are couched in one-liners designed to ease the work of newspaper headline writers and to give television reporters pithy 10-second sound bites. For their part, journalists, despite their professional values, may be reduced to virtual channels of propaganda. This poses a dilemma for the media. When politicians can predict confidently which events and comments will ring reportorial bells, media professionals are deprived of opportunities to exercise their own judgement. Yet the routines that open the media to such manipulation cannot be discarded or overhauled without much disruption and cost. Thus, reform of the political communication process is seriously hampered by professionally rooted inertia in the media and by the cosiness of the relationship between journalists and politicians, which appears to accommodate both sides, notwithstanding its occasional rough edges and adversarial explosions.

Second, striking strategic developments have occurred in recent years on the advocates' side of the political communication process. Because politicians and other would-be opinion moulders are competing fiercely for exposure in the media; and because in order to achieve this they must tailor their messages to the requirements of journalists' formats, news values and work habits; and because this is thought to demand anticipatory planning, fast footwork, and a range of specialist skills – for all these reasons, a significant degree of 'source professionaliztion' has emerged. By this we mean the ever deeper and more extensive involvement in political message-making of publicity advisers, public relations experts, campaign management consultants, and the like.

Such 'source professionals' are not only far-sighted, assiduous and gifted at fashioning messages for media consumption. They immerse journalists in what appears to be an increasingly manipulative opinion environment. Perceiving themselves to be 'professionals' rather than 'advocates', source professionals regard news-making as a power struggle, rather than a process of issue clarification. Consequently, they introduce into the political communication process a potentially corrosive and disturbing set of assumptions. They tend to be sceptical about such notions as the free marketplace of ideas; the autonomy of the press to set its own agenda; or any obligation on the press and politicians to cater to the conscientious, information-seeking citizen (thought to be a fiction, since most people's responses to politics are said to stem from a medley of emotions, impressions, sentiments, wishful feelings, valued symbols, hopes and fears, plus a lacing of direct personal experience).

Third, faced with such developments, journalists become uneasy and concerned to reassert their autonomy. One device they have developed for this purpose has been termed 'disdaining the news' (Levy, 1981). This involves attempts by reporters to distance themselves from the propagandistic features of an event by 'exposing' it as contrived and suggesting to their audience that it should be taken with a grain of salt. As an NBC reporter told us during the 1984 presidential election campaign:

> There is a naïveté of people out there. They see a one-minute to two-minute story, cutting from one election scene to another and can be taken in by them .... Many television news stories can give a false sense of what the event is like. So if viewers are helped to recognize by a story of this kind that they're being manipulated, they can then analyse the situation and understand it even better. If that is the way politicians want to run their campaign, then that is also the way in which we should report it.

Clearly such an approach has a potential for cultivating political cynicism and mistrust among viewers and further undermining the contributions of the media to the democratic process.

The intra-organizational level

Significant constraints on the portrayal of social and political issues in the media also stem from factors internal to the organization of journalism, including relations between news media outlets and the values and ideologies that guide media professionals in their work.

In liberal-democratic societies, the relationship between media organizations is characterized primarily by competition to maximize audiences, to be first with the news, or to scoop one's rivals in other ways. Thus, although competition for audience patronage is related directly to the media's economic goals, it is also rooted deeply in the professional culture of Western journalism. This diverts attention away from the aim of serving the audience towards the democratically irrelevant goal of beating the competition.

Competition is only one force shaping the behaviour of journalists. Professional values, such as objectivity, impartiality, fairness, and an ability to recognize the newsworthiness of an event, also serve as influential guidelines for framing stories. At one level, such norms provide safeguards essential to a democratic media system. They prescribe that reporters should stand above the political battle, serve the audience rather than politicians with partisan axes to grind, and do so with due regard for all the interests at stake in an issue. But at another level, the routinized application of such values can have distorting consequences. Many writers have pointed out, for example, that the neutral stance enjoined by the values of objectivity and impartiality can lend implicit support to the more powerful institutions and groups in society and for the social order from which they benefit (Hall *et al.*, 1978). Instead of promoting a 'marketplace of ideas', in which all viewpoints are given adequate play, media neutrality tends to privilege dominant, mainstream positions.

Adherence to professional definitions of news values may also act as a powerful force for conformity, for arriving, that is, at a common answer to the question: What is the most significant news today? Widely shared and professionally endorsed definitions of news values may force journalists' hands in other ways. For example, during our 1984 observation study at NBC, one reporter, assigned to cover Geraldine Ferraro, the Vice-Presidential candidate, described to us how within 30 seconds of her selection by Mondale as his running mate she was type-cast by news editors and producers as 'the first woman Vice-Presidential candidate' (Semetko *et al.*, 1991, Chapter 4). His own wish to report her in terms, say, of the compatibility of her campaign utterances with her voting record in the House of Representatives was rejected by editors as not part of 'the Ferraro story', and a later attempt to place the same item ran into the obstacle that by then the dominant theme of 'the Ferraro story' had become her response to the issue of her family finances. Revealed here is how widely shared news values can severely constrain the range of options within which reporters themselves can deal with political issues and leaders. Clearly, such tendencies constrict the potential of the media to serve as a genuine 'marketplace of ideas' or to transcend the boundaries of the social and political mainstream.

Thus, the principal mass media openings for political information are moulded into standardized formats and conventions, which control what journalists can do in conveying ideas to the audience, while at the same time reflecting how much time and space media organizations consider they can afford to devote to the examination of social and political issues. Although they are the major channels of political communication, the mass media dance to other tunes than those of democratic communication alone. Through their acceptance of the imperatives of competition, and in their adherence to a self-generated and self-imposed set of professional standards, they shape their contributions to the political process in ways that may well fall short of the democratic ideals they claim to serve.

The audience level

What role does the audience play in a democratic media system? Ideally, its needs and interests should be uppermost. In practice, the media promptly heed any sign of decided audience dislike or rejection of certain ways of addressing it – if, that is, the media's competitive goals are perceived to be at risk as a result. In that sense, the audience holds a sort of reserve veto power.

Such sensitivity to audience attitudes may be interpreted as reflecting the media's democratic impulses. Nevertheless, there are systemic reasons why the audience for political communication is vulnerable to neglect and misrepresentation. Of the three main elements in a political communication system – politicians, journalists and audience members – it is the audience which, though most numerous, is least powerful, because least organized. Amidst their preoccupations with the intricacies, problems, calculations and subtleties of coping with each other, politicians and journalists are liable to lose sight of the ordinary voter's concerns and instead to attempt to accommodate each other. Thus, audiences are 'known' to the media primarily as statistical aggregates produced by ratings services and market researchers, and the media's orientations to their audiences are therefore dominated by numbers. Three problems arise from these circumstances.

First, research suggests strongly that if useful information is to be effectively conveyed to people through the mass media, a *sine qua non* is sensitivity to what the audience wants or needs to know (Nowak, 1977; Robinson and Levy, 1986). The system does not foster such sensitivity.

Second, an audience known mainly through numbers is open to over-simplification, stereotyping, even contempt. This is illustrated by the comment to us of an NBC news executive in 1984: 'The only thing that viewers want to know about this election is who is going to win.'

Third, this statement (taken in conjunction with other similarly pithy maxims about audience propensities that gain currency in the lore of media executives) illustrates a feature of widely held audience images which contributes to the entrenchment of the system. Authoritative communicators tend to dismiss the audience *as if it were capable only of absorbing that which the system supplies.* A deeply conservative view of the audience is thus propagated, one that reinforces the communicators' own identities and interests, and preserves the communication status quo.

OPPORTUNITIES FOR REFORM

System-based constraints on the workings of the mass media, such as those highlighted here, must be sobering to democrats, because they are so resistant to change; yet within current political communication arrangements there are certain 'chinks', which may open up some opportunities for reform.

First, it should be asked whether there are any advocates for democratic political communication. A first look suggests not. Instead (as we have already suggested), when preparing speeches, media events, and political stories, major political communicators (whether journalists or politicians) are not normally moved by abstractly conceived principles, such as the promotion of an informed citizenry. Rather, they are constrained by more or less abiding pressures, traditions and relationships, embedded in the fabric of the system in which they are placed, to communicate in ways that do not necessarily promote democratic goals. Nevertheless, the elements of an advocacy group for democratic political communication can be found among some academics concerned with democratic policy issues, media critics, foundations and various civic groups, plus a handful of media professionals who occasionally rise above the daily pressures of their job to consider its broader issues and consequences. Yet such a constituency cannot claim to have any organized support at present. Our own experience in Britain suggests that academic advocacy for change, even when it is welcomed and supported in principle, can quickly wither on the vine (or gather dust on the shelf), when entrusted to politicians and media organizations for implementation (Blumler, Gurevitch and Ives, 1978).

The constituency needs, then, to be expanded and bolstered. Where might such support come from? The most important source could be journalists themselves. Western journalism is experiencing a crisis of legitimacy at present. In part this springs from the increasing inability of many groups with a stake in civic affairs to recognize themselves in the stereotyped portraits of their activities in the major media; in part from a sense that the authority and veracity of media coverage are questioned by many ordinary audience members. And in part it stems from the academic critique of the conventional journalistic view of the nature of news. Rather than regarding news (as journalists typically do) as a selection of the significant and interesting happenings of the day, these critics have depicted news personnel as active constructors of social reality (Tuchman, 1978; Fishman, 1980; Bennett, 1982), with the resulting implication that it might be permissible after all to blame the messenger for the message. This crisis may be resolved only by defining certain purposes for media organizations, above and beyond their survival, which the media are expected to serve and which do not entail their subordination to dominant particular interests. This conclusion points to a need to formulate notions of democratic media purposes, from which fresh statements of the purposes and standards of journalism could be drawn. For journalists, then, a way out of the toils could be a stronger and deeper commitment to democratic service.

In addition, pressures for change may come from the present inadequacy of political journalism. If 'journalism steered by news values' converts so readily into 'news management for politicians', something will have to be done from within to put this right. Again a need to rethink the journalistic role arises. Too often the alternative to the conventional journalistic role of 'gatekeeper' has been posited as one of an 'advocate' on behalf of deprived groups and neglected issues (Janowitz, 1975). Other possibilities exist and should be explored, including the role of 'democratic midwife'.

Additional pressures for reform may come from outside the media as well. Evidence suggests that various groups in society are targeting the media as sources of distorted portrayals of their aims and activities. Although some of these complaints are *parti pris*, the media may be obliged to respond in a self-critical but principled spirit. After all, they are notorious for their sensitivity to shifting public currents and moods: this too is part of the climate of democracy.

A final chink may be found in the largely ignored potential among audience orientations to political communication. Research into the ways in which audience members 'use' and relate to political content in the media reveals a rich mixture of varying expectations, needs, concerns and resistances (Blumler and McQuail, 1968; McLeod and Becker, 1981). This is not to claim that the average audience member is a highly politicized person constantly longing for reasoned political argument and enlightenment on complex issues. But more serious forms of political discourse and coverage could strike neglected chords and would find an audience ready and willing to attend to them. In the long run such coverage might even awaken dormant interests in some audience members and hence expand the circle of politically aware citizens.

Part II

Development

Chapter 9

Producers' attitudes towards television coverage of an election campaign (UK election 1966)[1]

Voters depend heavily on the mass media, and increasingly on television, for their perceptions of the significant political issues and personalities of the day. Even though initial predispositions help to filter what electors notice, the sheer visibility of issues and events, as determined by media prominence, must also fill out their maps of the political scene. Since (as Campbell *et al.* (1960) have pointed out) 'the decisions of those who control communication are partial determinants of public awareness . . . more information is needed about them'. The focus of this attempt to collect such information is a set of attitudes which apparently influenced the approach of certain BBC producers to their task of reporting the British General Election of 1966.

This study was made possible by a generous invitation which was extended to the first author by the BBC in late February 1966 to attach himself for the period of the forthcoming campaign to the Current Affairs Group (Television). Its central method was direct observation, supplemented by interviews with most of the non-technical staff of the various programme teams in the Group. The author had full access to the production process at programme level, and the resulting data mainly reflected producers' perspectives (not those, say, of higher BBC executives or of politicians). The Current Affairs Group was responsible at the time for a varied range of campaign programmes, but this report is largely based on observations of the preparation of *Campaign Report*, thirteen editions of which were transmitted within the nightly current affairs vehicle, *24 Hours*.

The attitudes of producers have been grouped for consideration under four headings, each of which corresponds to a major focus of enquiry in the field of the sociology of communicators. They include the outlook of journalists and broadcasters on: the structure of rules and policies that is supposed to govern their activities; their sources (in this case leading politicians); the needs of their audiences; and the events they are supposed to cover.

PRODUCERS AND BROADCASTING POLICY

How should the relationship between policy in a communicating organization and its staff communicators be conceived? A common point of view
treats the latter as virtually passive recipients and executants of the
former. Such an interpretation need not be unsophisticated; it can take
account, for example, of instances of deviation from policy. Nevertheless,
there is a tendency to regard policy as something that moulds the work
of the communicators and not vice versa.

On the face of it, such a one-way model of this relationship should be
particularly applicable to an analysis of the election-time responsibilities
of British broadcasters. Britain is noted for its strong tradition of concern
for the political impartiality of the electronic media. Elections have always
been regarded as exceptionally sensitive occasions for radio and television. It is appreciated that during a campaign the broadcasters must
comment upon the personalities and policies of parties to which their
organization will ultimately be accountable after the votes have been
counted. Consequently, an elaborate structure of rules and policies has
been evolved to guide the election activities of television journalists.

First, there is the current state of the law, as it is authoritatively
interpreted by the legal advisers of the BBC, the ITA,[2] and the Postmaster
General.[3] This obliges the broadcasters (a) to refrain from the expression
of editorial opinions of their own on controversial matters, (b) to maintain
a balance between the airing of rival views on controversial matters, and
(c) to abstain from any activity which could be construed, under Section
63 of the Representation of the People Act, as an expenditure of money
to advance the cause of a political candidate. Second, there is a set
of understandings which are negotiated in advance of an election by
representatives of the three main parties, the BBC and the ITA, convened
in an informal committee. And third, certain policies emanate from the
broadcasting authorities themselves. A formative element in BBC policy,
for example, has always been a concept of 'fairness' – one expression of
which was the creation of safeguards to ensure that no party could exploit
radio and television in the final stages of a campaign to win a last-minute
advantage that its rivals could not counteract.

It was evident from the outset, however, that many producers did not
regard themselves merely as executants of these official policies. They
shared what may be described as a set of policy objectives of their
own. They wished to direct the contributions of television to an election
campaign into channels they regarded as fruitful. This concern, which was
most noticeable in the early and formative stages of the 1966 campaign,
was not necessarily opposed to the official policies the broadcasters were
expected to implement. It chiefly reflected the preoccupation of journalists
with the relationship between their own freedom and various inhibitions

and constraints that were associated with the political parties. It was in that context that a *24 Hours* producer forecast the strategy that would be followed in the preparation of its *Campaign Report*: 'We shall push at the boundaries wherever we can and try to get the rules relaxed by breaking some of the accepted conventions.'

The producers' strategy embraced at least four objectives. First, they aimed to encourage party spokesmen to confront each other in face-to-face discussions (and not to appear separately on election programmes without interchange with their opposite numbers). The willingness of politicians to engage in debate was in doubt at first, for the major parties had insisted on separate interviews with the three individuals who were due to take part in the immediate pre-campaign edition of *Panorama*.[4]

Second, the producers were keen to help to promote a top-level party-leader debate between the Prime Minister and his Conservative and Liberal counterparts. At a time when the parties were deadlocked over the conditions for putting on a televised confrontation, a member of the Current Affairs Group devised a complex formula which seemed to meet the stated requirements of each side. Although it eventually proved impossible to arrange such an encounter, the BBC did forward the reporter's proposal to the political parties, and its existence was publicly revealed in an interview on *Campaign Report* with Mr Heath.[5]

Third, the producers were determined to circumvent any attempts by one or another political party to veto the airing of an election issue by refusing to supply a speaker to discuss it on television. In fact, difficulties of obtaining party spokesmen were experienced on each of the first four days of *Campaign Report*'s appearance. But by persisting on behalf of chosen topics (though prepared to be tactically flexible), the producers managed to present items on most of the issues they wished to cover. On one occasion, *Campaign Report* countered the refusal of one of the parties to provide a speaker to discuss a provocative event by presenting filmed extracts from its press conference on the subject. And after screening a controversial discussion of the prospects for Britain's eventual entry into the Common Market, a member of the *24 Hours* staff concluded that:

> What we've achieved today is to smoke them out – to get them to participate in the programme on an issue they were unwilling to see dealt with. Having persisted in our determination to cover the Common Market, they finally saw they had to put up someone to discuss it.

Finally, the producers wished to ensure that television did not pay more attention to the Liberal Party than it deserved. This objective reflected their judgement that the third party was electorally less relevant to the political situation of 1966 than it had been in the close race of 1964. Although it was found in the end that the Liberal Party had received the full share of broadcasting time to which it was entitled by the 5:5:3

ratio,[6] out of five inter-party confrontations on *Campaign Report*, Liberals participated in only two.

How can the readiness and ability of producers to take these policy initiatives be explained? The answer lies partly in their reactions to a decade of evolution in the role of election television, a twofold result of which was, first, to break the parties' original monopoly of campaign broadcasting, and, second, to enlarge the scope of the election programmes produced by the television authorities themselves. The determination of the producers to contribute to policy may be traced specifically, then, to their more or less common conviction that the developments which had taken place up to 1966 were (a) desirable and (b) still incomplete. But a full analysis of the sources of their initiatives would have to take account of at least three more general influences as well.

1 *The internal role-definitions of their position to which television journalists subscribe*

These appeared to include two expressions of a sense of responsibility. One was to serve the audience adequately. Although opinions differed about some of its political needs, there was a common agreement that in order to present an election interestingly and illuminatingly to viewers, party politicians should be encouraged to debate with each other in a face-to-face context, the contributions of relatively irrelevant forces should be kept to a minimum, and party aspirations to veto the airing of certain issues should be resisted. Second, the television journalists seemed to be moved by a sense of responsibility to the standards of their profession. These demanded a readiness to exercise their own judgement upon the election issues that mattered instead of a tame acceptance of the parties' issue priorities.

2 *The character of the existing body of rules and policies*

Some producer initiatives were facilitated by a policy vacuum. When representatives of the parties and the broadcasting authorities met to finalize the arrangements for the use of television during the campaign, it seemed to the BBC participants that both the Conservatives and Labour had lost any interest in the staging of a top-level party-leader debate. They assumed that any attempt on their part to raise this subject might be construed as pressure to impose a controversial form of political television on the reluctant parties. But because this matter had not been settled one way or the other, the producers were able to take steps of their own to arrange a confrontation between the party leaders.

3 *The place of producers in the authority structure of the BBC*

Although information was not systematically collected under this heading, the effects of certain influences were noticed. One is the fact that in the normal course of their programme-making duties, producers of current affairs programmes like *24 Hours* and *Panorama* are accustomed to exercise a high degree of initiative and discretion. It is well known that the Corporation tends to operate a *post hoc* system of control by review rather than an anticipatory system of censorship in advance, and it would not be surprising if the initiatives taken by producers in the determination of programme content did not occasionally spill over into certain policy areas as well. Second, some producers may have perceived the policy-making authorities of the BBC as rather indifferent to the case for a more vigorous use of television in an election situation. They may have felt that the BBC's contribution to the pre-campaign negotiations with the parties had been unduly cautious and that the Corporation was somewhat compromised by its close contacts with party headquarters. Some producers may have concluded, then, that it was up to them to strike a blow for journalistic freedom.

PRODUCERS AND THEIR POLITICIAN SOURCES

It is common knowledge that by the end of the 1966 campaign much tension had been generated between BBC producers and certain Labour Party politicians. A point had been reached where a number of leading producers perceived themselves to be targets of a sustained campaign of pressure from the Labour Party. Some phenomena which were interpreted at the time as belonging to this campaign included: the Prime Minister's persistent refusal to be interviewed on *Campaign Report*; informal expressions of Labour's dissatisfaction with the BBC's attempt to promote a party-leader confrontation on television; and informal reactions of surprise and resentment about a number of the election issues that the makers of *Campaign Report* proposed to discuss on the programme.

The author's opportunities to observe the development of this situation were one-sided and incomplete. He could not see it through the politicians' eyes, and he arrived on the scene after much of the tension had already been built up. From his vantage point, then, the author was mainly able to observe the responses of the producers – in attitudes and in actions – to a situation of perceived political pressure.

Those responses did not include many visible signs of personal stress. Nevertheless, one attitudinal effect of the seeming exertion of party pressure on organs of news and publicity is to strengthen a tendency for staff communicators to ascribe to politicians *the role of would-be manipulators* – at the expense of other role orientations through which they could also be perceived (e.g. the roles of statesmen, experienced men of affairs, men of ideas, puppets of fortune, etc.). There were times during the 1966 campaign when virtually the whole occupational class was considered to be more or less tarred with this manipulative brush, although some politicians were regarded as far more tainted than others. As one producer pointed out, the circumstances in which producers and politicians often meet probably helped to generate this impression: 'We often see them at their most calculating, trying to project themselves as effectively as they can, but we rarely see them in situations where they are developing their own ideas genuinely.' But each seeming attempt to put pressure on broadcasters only reinforced this picture of politicians as would-be manipulators, not only of the electorate, but also of the mass media themselves.

The reverse side of this coin is a part of the television journalist's own self-image: a tendency to cast himself in *the role of public watchdog*, the essence of whose position is an ostensible, but to some degree vulnerable, form of independence. Some producers believed the bark of politicians was worse than their bite, while others found their efforts more menacing. They tended to agree, however, about the line of response that it was appropriate for journalists to follow on the plane of action.

In fact, it seemed that the typical reaction of producers to a situation of perceived pressure was not accommodation but resistance. Partly this was because something vital to journalists (their autonomy) was at stake. But it was also because repeated indications of a party's displeasure with the broadcasters' activities had helped to translate each bone of contention, however minor, into an issue of principle – when to yield to the party's wishes would have symbolized lack of pride, courage and self-respect. On one occasion, for example, a factor in a decision to present a certain election item was said to have been the fact that Labour had apparently responded to it 'in a snide way. We should not let them influence how we are going to cover the campaign – play it way down just because it suits their book to have a low-keyed campaign.'

Yet a stiffening of the broadcasters' will to resist was not an invariable consequence of the voicing of party complaints. After the Conservatives objected that Labour had enjoyed the advantage of a 'last word' on the immediate pre-campaign edition of *Panorama*, it was decided to offer them the chance of closing the next edition of the programme. A Liberal politician's informal complaint late in the campaign that *24 Hours* had paid scant attention to his party led to a decision to screen a longer interview than usual with Mr Grimond, its Leader. And a decision to arrange a mini-confrontation on housing was probably influenced by Labour's complaint that *Campaign Report* had previously drawn many of its topics from the Conservatives' election locker.

A common feature of these examples, however, was the appeal of a political party to a principle of fairness which the producers themselves regarded as legitimate. What provokes the resistance of producers, then, is not the application of pressure as such but its accompaniment by: accusations of bias (which they regard as unjust); steps that may be construed as threats (which they perceive as attacks on their professional autonomy); or a concerted series of incidents (which they interpret as evidence of a sustained manipulative intent).

TWO STYLES OF PRODUCER–AUDIENCE RELATIONS: A SACERDOTAL VS. A PRAGMATIC APPROACH TO ELECTION COVERAGE

The producers of the Current Affairs Group were not only at odds with their politician sources during the 1966 campaign; they were also divided among themselves about the amount and type of attention that television should pay to an election. This internal conflict was precipitated by the decision to present *Campaign Report* as part of *24 Hours* – a step which effected a temporary marriage of convenience between teams that had previously been responsible for the quite different (and by 1966 defunct) programmes of *Gallery* and *Tonight*.[7] It was mainly the *Gallery* tradition that shaped the original conception of the programme, but compelling reasons had arisen early in 1966 for incorporating it into the format of *24 Hours*, which by the autumn of 1965 had succeeded *Tonight* in a later time slot (10.15 p.m.) that *Campaign Report* was expected to fill once an election was held. The makers of *24 Hours* were proud of the growing audience they had been cultivating with signal success and were reluctant to go off the air for the period of the campaign. It was decided, there-fore, to broadcast *Campaign Report* as a part of *24 Hours*. The latter would remain in operation more or less as before the campaign, present-ing a mixture of election and non-political stories, but its regular staff would be augmented by producers and reporters with specialist experi-ence in the political field (including some from the old *Gallery* stable).

Thus, adherents of somewhat opposed philosophies of current affairs broadcasting were compelled to work together for a concentrated period. It should not be supposed that their approaches to television journalism differed at every conceivable point. They shared an allegiance to many of the same ethical norms of their profession – such as accuracy, impar-tiality and reportorial freedom. They respected each other's technical mastery of such skills of their craft as: an ability to write clear, simple and vivid passages of commentary; an eye for apt and compelling visual material; speed of response to the challenge of fast-moving events; and an ability to steer an interview into interesting channels. Nevertheless, one executive admitted, even before the campaign had officially begun, that some members of his assembled team would 'lean one way' while others would 'lean the other way'.

What exactly were the main points of difference between the two camps? There were disputes about the total amount of time that should be devoted to the election and about the relationship to be forged between its election and non-election items. But these were merely outcrops of a deeper conflict – one which a BBC official epitomized in the middle of the campaign as a clash between a sacerdotal and a pragmatic approach to election coverage.

On the one hand, the practitioners of the so-called sacerdotal style of campaign programming tended to think of themselves as providing a 'service' and of an election as an intrinsically important event which entitled it to substantial coverage as of right. From this followed their 'audience image' (see Gans, 1957). They expected implicitly to cater either for voters who were already interested in politics or for viewers who could be helped to grasp the political significance of campaign events. The task of television, then, was to meet the needs of such an audience with a coherent, thoughtful and illuminating body of programme content. These reporters were thus concerned largely with political values and rather less with production values. One of them considered that three kinds of material belonged in *Campaign Report*: a response to the leading campaign events of each day, 'logging' them for the record; an examination of the underlying issues of the election in some depth; and filmed illustrations of various facets of campaign activity. This individual tended to emphasize the information-supplying function of current affairs broadcasting. It was true, he said, that television could operate effectively on an emotional plane:

> Yet we must remember that viewers already have certain emotions about politics and elections. There is no need to stimulate and arouse them. The important thing is to try to provide information and inject an element of reason into the presentation of an election. This might be difficult at times, but you've got to continue to plug away at it – for that is what democracy is about.

The more pragmatically disposed producers, on the other hand, denied the intrinsic right of election material to programme prominence and repeatedly asserted that it must 'fight its way in' on its merits. They wished to avoid creating any impression that they felt *obliged* to cover the campaign. And instead of beaming the programme at an audience of mainly politically interested viewers, the pragmatists professed a strong dislike of merely: 'talking to the converted. That is just a bore. I would much prefer to aim our mixture of election and non-election items at the relatively uninterested viewer.' Above all else, it was important not to cultivate what one producer called 'a ghetto audience':

> We should not produce an election programme *per se*, nor should we create an election ghetto within the programme. I do not want to have a special chunk in the programme, for that is the way to reduce the *24 Hours* audience to a ghetto audience. We should try to break it up into five- to seven-minute lumps scattered throughout the programme.

But how were the conflicts between these philosophies resolved in the course of the campaign? As might have been expected, most editions of *24 Hours* bore the imprint of both styles. After the transmission of certain editions, one group of producers seemed rather more satisfied with the result than the other; on other occasions, the pattern of feeling was reversed. The collaboration between the two groups often proceeded fairly smoothly, although on at least three occasions sharp conflicts arose which had to be settled rather late in the day. Those disputes typically flared up in the afternoon after one of the political specialists had learned that little election content was booked for the evening's programme, had expressed his dismay, and had then offered a veritable shower of practical suggestions for repairing the omission.

Although both producer groups achieved and conceded some of their stated goals, the *24 Hours* team did not realize its objective of treating election material strictly according to its day-to-day merits, unaffected by any obligation to cover it. Several factors conspired to defeat it on this issue of principle. One was the weight of authority which the political specialists could wield in their own field. Another was a commitment to present a number of film reports which had been planned before the campaign, which could not have been discarded without considerable waste. Running calculations of the amounts of time that had been devoted thus far to each of the parties encouraged the screening of certain political items at certain lengths in order to help to get the final sums right. But perhaps the crucial factor emerged from the first of the three main clashes mentioned above – a conflict which had arisen because, on a seemingly dull campaign day, the *24 Hours* team had assumed that, 'Today of all days we should let the programme build itself naturally and compel election material to fight its way in'. An affronted political reporter's response to that proposition was that 'We can make things happen' by the interviews and discussions that are arranged in the programme. And he carried his point by the force of the argument that special resources had been allocated for election coverage, which should be used to serve their intended purpose.

PRODUCERS AND CAMPAIGN EVENTS

After completing a participant observation study of CBS coverage of the American party conventions of 1964, Herbert Waltzer (1966) outlined eight criteria for evaluating television presentations of any political event, of which one, put in the form of a question, was: 'did the networks arrogate the center stage at the convention for themselves?' Did television help voters to see and hear an important political occasion at first hand, he asked, or did the medium and its reporters become the main objects of attention instead?

If *24 Hours'* interest in the 'real campaign' of 1966 is measured by the extent of its use of actuality material from hustings speeches and press conferences, then in this respect Waltzer's criterion was not met. Although some material of this kind was presented in each edition of *Campaign Report* (comprising some 15 per cent overall), it was usually over-shadowed by other items, and it had often been selected to illustrate a particular issue around which it had been decided to build the night's programme. Full attention could be said to have been paid to campaign speeches in their own right in only about two of the thirteen editions of *Campaign Report.*

Why did *Campaign Report* provide such a sketchy coverage of the platform performances of party spokesmen? The combined influence of four factors helps to explain why such material played only a minor part in the programme's election output.

1 *The lack of a consistently positive orientation towards hard news among* 24 Hours *producers*
Although two members of the BBC News Division had been seconded to the programme staff, many *24 Hours* producers had been reared in the distinctive style of *Tonight*. And although some individuals interpreted (and welcomed) the changeover from *Tonight* to *24 Hours* as if it had converted a 'magazine' into a 'newspaper', few leading producers felt obliged at the time to build each edition of the programme around the major news stories of the day. Their main concern, they said, was to broadcast a programme that was 'worth watching' and that had something 'to add' to what other communications sources were saying about a topic. Merely logging campaign events would be 'tedious [if] . . . there was no attitude behind it'.

2 *A conviction that sufficient attention was being paid to the party campaign elsewhere*
In their own quotas of election broadcasting time, first of all, the parties had access to an important outlet through which to present their arguments to the public. But if a voter wished to find out what the politicians were saying on the hustings, he could turn for enlightenment to his newspaper. Even on television, it was alleged, the hustings campaign was being covered more than adequately in the main evening news bulletins – the duration of which had been extended from 15 to 20 minutes for the election period. Finally, there was some anxiety about overcrowding the air waves with the sound of party argument – from the main news to party broadcasts to *Campaign Report*.

3 *A perception of the nature of the 1966 campaign*
Many journalists (and not merely those who worked on *24 Hours*) apparently shared a common set of attitudes towards the 1966 election, which they suspected the electorate was finding tedious. Much comment in the

press and in the political weeklies developed an ironic contrast between the dull, placid and almost ritualistic character of the campaign, on the one hand, and the gravity of the real issues that still faced the country, on the other. In the context of this consensus, perhaps it is not surprising that the producers of *24 Hours* assumed that the parties' hustings manoeuvres deserved only scant attention – and that they aimed instead to promote discussion of those issues which they considered important.

4 *The constraints of programme design*

The design of the programme itself left little room for coverage of the 'real campaign'. It was natural that the arrangement of mini-confrontations should have assumed a high priority in the producers' strategy for extending the scope of election television. *Campaign Report* was staffed by several able interviewers whose talents deserved to be exercised. The intimate familiarity of one of the political commentators with opinion poll trends was exploited on several occasions. Even before the campaign had been officially launched, a group of producers had started to prepare film reports about campaign activities from various perspectives. Altogether, thirteen such reports were contemplated, and ten eventually reached the screen. In addition, the concern of the regular *24 Hours* producers to transmit non-election items from both domestic and foreign sources had to be satisfied. Under these circumstances it simply was not possible to 'log' the course of the 1966 election more fully than *Campaign Report* did.

A CONCLUDING NOTE ON THE DETERMINANTS OF CURRENT AFFAIRS PROGRAMMING

One major outcome of this study is an indication that the character of current affairs output is not rigidly governed by an unalterable set of fixed conditions. Much of the end product seems to be determined by a number of variable factors that are not usually perceptible to viewers or to other outsiders. The coverage by *24 Hours* of the 1966 election partly depended, of course, on the Corporation's organizational arrangements, on the financial, technical and human resources that were allocated to the production team, and on certain fundamental programme ideas that were laid down well in advance of the campaign. But we have seen that election programming was shaped, in addition, by the producers' own policy strategies, by the tenor of their daily relations with party representatives, and by rival styles of political coverage thought appropriate for the intended audience. This underlines the need for a further investigation of the sources of producers' internal definitions of their roles – from which many of the influences detected in this study had emanated.

Chapter 10

The construction of election news at the BBC (1979)[1]

This chapter presents some of the more outstanding impressions formed by the authors during an observation study of the production of television news at the BBC during the general election campaign of April and May 1979. This study was the latest of a string of enquiries, stretching back to the 1966 general election campaign, in which one or both of us explored the workings of the British political communication system from a variety of angles. Long-standing associations with news personnel at the BBC from these previous investigations had helped to develop relations of mutual trust and confidence that were essential for conduct of the 1979 study. Consequently, we were given permission to be present at any location of our choice in the various news production areas; to sit in on discussions of news executives and producers, both those concerned with forward planning and those involved in post-mortem analyses of recent output; and to discuss the implications of their work with the individuals engaged in campaign journalism.

BACKGROUND

The campaign role of British television news

Before the 1959 general election, British news bulletins studiously ignored all campaign events. Nowadays the regular coverage they provide is a quite central vehicle of the campaign. Their centrality initially stems from the news programmes' large audiences and credible reputation. That is why they are assiduously cultivated by party managers, who are anxious to plant their gems in the output, and hence become a prime electoral arena, in which the combatants daily parade themselves, make speeches, look authoritative, shake hands, and try to score points off their opponents. What viewers see of all this depends, however, on how the arena is constructed by the media professionals who are responsible for reporting and covering the campaign. In this respect television news is not merely a channel through which messages and images devised by the political actors are transmitted untrammelled to voters, like water flowing through a tap. How editors and reporters go about their journalistic job of presenting or 'staging' the contest is so formative that they become not just observers but an integral part of the campaign itself.

In 1979, the role of television news in the elections was determined by at least four features of note. First, the calling of an election induces a subtle shift of gear: enthusiasm mounts but controls tighten. As one editor put it, 'This is far and away the biggest kind of story that a TV news organization can be involved in covering.' However, many of the rules that guide the journalists' work more flexibly in out-of-election periods are more rigorously imposed during a campaign, including a more strict interpretation of what impartiality and balance demands, a more faithful echoing of the issue and event initiatives of party spokespersons, and more circumspection when venturing comment on the politicians' activities.

Second, election news is accorded a high status in British television, though its output has to be fitted into bulletins which must continue to cover each day's non-election news as well. One sign of its special standing is the fact that at the outset of a campaign many of the BBC's most experienced and trusted political personnel are assembled to work on the election news team. This may help to explain a major respect in which the thrust of British election coverage differs from its more 'game'- and less issue-oriented American counterpart (Patterson, 1980). Although British television news does not ignore the campaign game, much of its output concentrates on party leaders' substantive remarks about issues and policies. In addition, election news takes up a sizeable part of the available bulletin time, usually amounting to nearly half of the total.

Third, the fashioning of election news for television is a continual struggle to reconcile two potentially opposed policy goals. Campaign coverage must be both newsworthy and fair. On the one hand, news personnel are supposed to behave like professionals, applying traditional news-value instincts to each day's crop of campaign statements and incidents. On the other hand, each party is supposed to receive that share of attention which is merited by its strength in the country (defined by a mixed formula of votes cast at the previous election and seats contested at the current one). In practice, news personnel take as their guide the share of political broadcasts that have been allocated to each party during the campaign concerned – which prescribed a 5:5:3 ratio for the Conservative, Labour and Liberal Parties, respectively, in 1979.

Fourth, in advance of the 1979 campaign BBC policy-makers had resolved to strengthen the analytical contribution of the election news output. In part, this was a response to criticisms of the 1974 coverage as unduly encapsulated and passive (Harrison, 1975). In part, it reflected a modified role of the main evening news report itself that had been introduced in the intervening period, moving away from a mere bulletin of record towards provision of longer reports on major news events which aimed to set them in an explanatory context. One product of this approach was a decision to prepare a series of prefilmed items on the central issues of the election (such as prices, industrial relations, taxes, agriculture), summarizing in each case the positions taken by the main parties and how they compared with each other. Another and potentially more significant idea was to give responsibility to the BBC's Political Editor for presenting all of each evening's election news package. As the Deputy Editor of BBC Television News explained:

> Last time we placed the Political Editor's piece somewhere towards the end of the newsreader's contribution. The election news might have consisted of a succession of speech items, précised by the newsreader, a bit of film, then the Editor winding up on how the campaign was going. We all felt we should change this. What we badly need is not a two-line introduction or wind-up piece but something that will set things into their proper context. The idea is to get your senior political man also to be your anchorman, so that he is in a position to offer that. The Political Editor may well not only round off each day's substance of election coverage, summing up in his own way, but also insert interpretative comment inside the various items that are coming along as well.

The setting

The authors' observations were conducted on intermittent days in April 1979, spanning the four weeks of the election campaign. BBC coverage was based at its Television Centre in West London, where a special work area was set aside for this purpose. It was separate from the regular television newsroom, which continued to produce the non-election portion of the various news bulletins transmitted during the day. The special area, or 'the factory' as, significantly, it was called by the people working there, was manned by approximately fifty members of the BBC Television News staff, ranging from typists, copy editors, sub-editors and news organizers to the various reporters and analysts, including the then Political Editor.

The output of this 'factory' consisted of three 'packages' of campaign news, transmitted in the bulletins at 12.45 p.m., 5.40 p.m. and 9.10 p.m. The two daytime bulletins were 15 and 20 minutes in length, while the evening bulletin lasted 30 minutes, an extension of five minutes beyond its usual non-election length. Although the contents of the campaign packages varied from one day to the next, they most regularly drew on three forms of party-originated material: the press conferences held in London by all three main parties every morning of the campaign; feature material, such as shots of party leaders going on 'walkabout' in the city streets, shopping centres and housing estates, chatting up ordinary voters on the way; and passages from politicians' evening speeches delivered to party rallies in large cities throughout the country, chiefly intended for use in the main evening bulletin. In addition, the packages might include the latest opinion poll results; politicians' reactions to events of the day, which, strictly speaking, were not campaign news but could impinge on election issues, such as publication of official statistics on prices and the state of the economy, or developments on some industrial relations front; notice of minor party manifestos; and prefilmed items such as constituency reports or 'day-in-the-life' profiles of the top leaders' campaign activities.

CENTRE AND PERIPHERY: LOGISTICS OF COVERAGE

During our periods of observation our attention was particularly drawn to three prime determinants of election news output. One of these concerned the near-umbilical relationship that obtained between the campaign 'periphery', that is, the field where the political actors operated, and the production 'centre', where the news was compiled. At first this way of identifying the centre and the periphery may seem odd, even a reversal of the 'true' order, since in many ways the hub of campaign activity is where the politicians are performing. The most significant feature of the periphery is its highly concentrated character. That is, the places from which the news personnel secured raw campaign material were few in number and were repeatedly revisited on an almost totally predictable basis. They consisted almost entirely of the headquarters where the three main parties held press conferences every morning, the towns where party leaders chose to go on walkabout in the afternoon, and the halls in which they addressed party supporters at evening meetings. Even so, regarded from the perspective of the working journalist, the centre of the campaign almost seemed to be located, not 'out there' amidst the hurly-burly of speech-making and political posturing, but amongst the videotape machines and editorial discussions at the Television Centre.

The campaign day of the Television Centre began at 9 a.m. with a meeting of the executive producer and his senior editorial staff. This was devoted to a review of the previous day's production activity and news output, as well as a scanning of likely campaign developments in the forthcoming day. The meeting usually lasted about 45 minutes, after which most of the participants moved to the videotape area, where, joined by other colleagues, they observed the parties' morning press conferences. These were usually chaired by the top leader of the given party, who would be supported by up to half a dozen other figures, chosen according to the issues it hoped to develop on the day concerned. The conferences took place in party headquarters in central London and were transmitted directly to the Television Centre, where they were displayed on monitors and recorded for excerpting. Pen and notebook in hand, news personnel took notes of the proceedings, just as they might have done had they been physically present at the conferences. The Political Editor was usually present at one of the conferences, while another reporter would attend the other. Both would then return to the Television Centre soon after the press conferences came to an end. Similar procedures operated during the afternoon and evening. The afternoon walkabout material was piped back to the Television Centre, mainly in the form of a brief story written and fronted by the reporter on the scene. The likelihood of items from press conferences and walkabouts being used in the main evening bulletin depended, of course, on the availability and newsworthiness of other material. Decisions on these had to wait, therefore, until the next batch of statements by the party leaders arrived in the evening. Those which the parties hoped would be covered in the news were delivered at around 7 to 7.30 p.m. to take account of the deadlines involved.

Advance releases of key passages of politicians' evening speeches usually arrived at the 'factory' shortly before they were due to start. These were quickly skimmed to identify the main themes being stressed and to locate illustrative passages that could be pulled out for inclusion in the bulletin. Nevertheless, the speech as delivered was shown on monitors in the 'factory' area and listened to through headphones by several members of the production team, who would often exchange terse remarks about striking and usable quotes. Although a BBC reporter was always present at the meeting hall, the shortage of time, and the fact that the producers at the 'factory' were in possession of the raw material, meant that they could, and were obliged to, prepare items on the evening speeches with little if any help from reporters on the spot. Having everything in hand by 8 p.m. or so, they could then put the various stories of the day into that sequence which best reflected their relative importance, edit the extracts so as not to exceed the total amount of time allowed the election segment within the bulletin as a whole, and finalize the links that would move the viewer from one story to the next. We have described this daily routine in some detail to illustrate a crucial feature of the process, namely the extent to which the coverage of the campaign was conducted from the 'centre', as it were, rather than from the 'periphery' in the field.

Many consequences seemed to us to flow from a 'centre-dominated' coverage routine, which processes materials regularly received from only a few repeatedly visited stations at the periphery. First, the role of the reporter in the field was considerably reduced in importance, if not yet totally eliminated. What has been directly affected is the dependence of the editor in the newsroom on the judgements and impressions of reporters. Admittedly, the reporter assigned to a party leader's entourage was more actively engaged in fashioning stories later in the day. But these mainly dealt with the more gimmicky part of the campaign, devised by party publicity advisers to furnish broadcasters with attractive pictures. As the Deputy Editor pointed out in describing the reporters' role, 'They prepare the film reports, adding a certain amount of colour to the campaign coverage, but they are not expected to offer political comment.'

Second, the atmosphere at the Centre seemed subtly but powerfully to strengthen the influence of what in our field notes we termed 'TV news presentation requirements' at the expense of 'political significance judgements' when decisions were being made about which comments of campaigners to pass on to the audience. When summing up what those presentation requirements seemed to be, we noted them down at the time as follows: a need for crispness of expression; suitability of length (neither rambling nor unduly brief); a need for vivid and pithy phraseology; ready comprehensibility (not requiring an unduly extended exposition or elaboration); emanation from the activity of 'our own correspondent'; compatibility with a preconceived view of what the dominant election story or theme of the day might be; continuity with the previous day's theme or story; vigour of attack on the opposition; and the provision, when two or more such items were being taken from different party sources, of a complementary form of thrust and counterthrust or point and counter-point.

Moreover, we were impressed with the subordination to such criteria of certain actors who might otherwise have been expected to inject more solidly political criteria into the selection process. For example, the Political Editor, in discussing his part with us, continually played it down, treating himself as no more than one voice in a chorus, where others had at least as much right to consideration of their impressions as he himself. This is not to imply that political judgements counted for nothing. They noticeably affected many decisions, particularly when choices had to be made between excerpts from politicians' remarks that seemed more or less equally suitable on other grounds. But it was as if even a figure like the Political Editor had become socialized to the characteristic demands of television news and accepted their legitimacy and overriding necessity.

Third, in 'coverage from the centre', relations between broadcasters on the one side and politicians and their campaign managers on the other side become rather distanced. News personnel working at the Centre seemed to be relatively insulated from the hectic and heady atmosphere of the campaign trail, and to regard events with the more detached perspective that could be maintained in the sheltered environment of their 'factory'. This could explain why it was surprisingly difficult at times for some of them to become fully involved in what was taking place. Even though party differences were arguably sharper in 1979 than at any election since 1945, throughout the campaign individual reporters would tell us that 'It all seems very low-key today'; 'It is still unriveting'. Perhaps it should be noted in addition that the lack of direct contact with politicians could reduce the latter's opportunities to exert an influence on the broadcasters. Except for the occasional telephone call, the work environment we observed was relatively free from direct pressures or attempted intervention by the parties.

Nevertheless, fourth, the limited number of periphery sites that television regularly taps makes the broadcasters highly dependent on whatever materials the politicians happen to provide at those particular places. This enhances the campaigners' chances of getting the message they want to drive home into the news, not through overt pressure but indirectly by manipulating the situation where the journalists are working and by playing on their professional predilections and preferences. Several strategies are open to them for this purpose:

1 To relate the message to some issue that is being treated as dominant at the time in the ongoing news flow.
2 To couch it in terms that score high on a cumulation of 'TV presentation requirements'.
3 To put it in the mouth of someone thought likely to be highly attractive to the broadcasters as a personality at the time.
4 To keep all other material in the speech of a party leader likely to be followed by television as dull, quiet, or repetitious as possible.
5 To take some step that will signal the likely importance of the passage concerned in some extraordinary way.

It so happens that on one evening we observed a quite dramatic example of the effective use of one of these ploys. In the late afternoon it was announced in the 'factory' that a telephone call had just been received from one of the political parties' headquarters about its Leader's evening speech. No advance release would be available, but the message was conveyed that 'The bit you want is $3\frac{1}{2}$ minutes long and will commence some 4 minutes after the Leader has got up to speak'.

When we asked the Editor of the Day how the speech would be handled, he told us that he and several colleagues would listen to it in its entirety and then choose that clip from it which most deserved selection on news-value grounds. Nevertheless, as the time approached for the speech to start, and they began to put on their headphones to listen to it, a keen air of expectation built up in the 'factory'. At the start of the meeting the Leader was introduced by a local party dignitary and then began to speak in quiet terms about the area of the country he was visiting and the fine candidates who were fighting seats there. Then quite abruptly he plunged into what was obviously the passage to which the Television Centre had been alerted. It recalled a comment on industrial relations issues made by his rival at a press conference that morning, and vigorously attacked it as misguided, risking industrial peace and reneging on promises that had previously been made to many groups of workers – a blunder that, unless retracted, could cause 'untold damage to the country'. From that moment onwards, there was no doubt in anybody's mind that the originally pinpointed passage would be prominently highlighted in the evening news package. Indeed, as soon as it came to an end, all headphones in the 'factory' were laid down except those of the authors!

In sum, it is clear that election coverage by television news has become a heavily routinized operation. It consists in the main only of what has passed from a few favoured stations on the periphery to the centre for processing and transmission. Such a routinization must be highly convenient for the broadcasters, and it presumably eases the parties' tactical problems of publicity planning as well. Yet significant campaign material may be missed simply because it is out of reach of the umbilical cord. And the needs of voters for illumination and reasons to become involved may also be shortchanged as a result.

THE ELECTION BALANCING ACT: DISTRIBUTION OF NEWS ATTENTION

A Chief Assistant to the Director-General of the BBC once rounded off an account of the Corporation's election coverage policies by proclaiming that 'fairness is all!' (Hardiman-Scott, 1977). The reality, of course, is more complex: other principles also apply, and the commitment to fairness is not without a recognized and sometimes regretted cost. Even so, it highlights the second formative influence on campaign news construction that we noticed in 1979: the producers' determination to achieve an appropriate 'balance' when reporting the activities of the principal election contenders.

This was an ever-present source of concern to the news makers we observed, guiding their efforts in a host of selection, presentation and timing decisions. Their preoccupation with balance was only partly traceable to their legally defined responsibilities. The obligation to present controversial issues with 'due impartiality', which is inscribed in the Independent Broadcasting Act (governing advertising-financed Independent Television), and which after its passage was also accepted by the BBC, is couched in quite general language and spells out no specific duties. A more urgent incentive to be even-handed lies in the broadcasters' pragmatic awareness that when the chief parliamentary forces, to which they are ultimately accountable, are locked in a struggle for power, they must not be open to the charge of having influenced the outcome. Indeed, an alleged lack of balance is the most often-cited ground of complaint that is levelled against broadcasters in the political field, even forming the basis of an official accusation by the Labour Party in the aftermath of the October 1974 election. Moreover, many British broadcasters have internalized the fairness principle as well. In the words of a television news reporter we interviewed in an earlier study (Blumler, Gurevitch and Ives, 1978):

> When I see all that bias blatantly emerging from how the newspapers cover political affairs, then I am grateful that our broadcasting system does at least have that marvellous quality of striving to be unbiased. What is left, after all, if somewhere among the numerous approaches taken to political coverage, you don't find some form of neutrality?

But what does 'balance' mean, and how is it to be maintained? Hardiman-Scott (1977) provides a classic statement of BBC policy on this matter, including revealing hints of the dilemmas faced by the news personnel who have to apply it:

> In reporting an election campaign, there remain the problems of achieving a fair balance between the parties contesting the election. Should one rely solely on the editorial judgment of what is news? Or should you superimpose upon that judgment a requirement to give equal time to the parties? That, unfortunately, is not the end of the question. Should equal time apply also to minor parties, to extremist parties and to individual cranks? We do, after all, live in a Parliamentary democracy. The BBC has answered these questions with a compromise . . . . In reporting the election and the party campaign, the BBC applies its traditional journalistic news values. It reports, in other words, what seems to its professional editors to be of interest, of importance and of significance to its viewers . . . .
>
> So news values *are* the basis for reporting the election in television. But – and this is our compromise – if we are using recorded extracts of speeches by politicians in television news bulletins, then we say we must achieve a fair balance between the political parties. Thus, in the course of the campaign, we would expect about the same amount of television time to have been used in news bulletins for extracts from speeches by Labour and Conservative politicians, and rather less time for speeches from Liberal politicians. We use the share of the total vote obtained by the parties at the previous General Election as a guide to the share of time devoted to extracts from their speeches in our news bulletins.

This passage graphically summarizes the professional aspirations of BBC journalists, the constraints under which they work, and the presumed solution to their dilemma. News is governed by news values; the need for balance is introduced as an extra requirement that forces a compromise; and the solution is found in the adoption of a stopwatch approach to the allocation of timed coverage shares to the competing parties, based on 'objective' measures of their relative strengths in the country.

This quantitative interpretation of fairness, it should be stressed, is not legally prescribed. It results from formulae that have been devised by the broadcasters themselves, though the parties now expect them to be observed with complete fidelity as well. But of all possible operationalizations of the principle, it is the most measurable and therefore the least challengeable.

Admittedly, the policy did allow for one element of flexibility: quantitatively balanced news attention was to be achieved across the campaign period as a whole, not invariably within each individual bulletin. But there were at least three reasons for trying to be quantitatively balanced on a daily basis. First, it would look better; the day's product would be more defensible if attacked. Second, an imbalance favouring one party on a certain day would only create a corresponding (and possibly difficult to meet) need to overbalance in favour of its rivals on some subsequent day. And third, day-by-day balance was a way of avoiding involvement in an unfortunate last-minute scramble to get back into overall balance in the closing and arguably decisive days of the campaign.

'Balance by the stopwatch' is relatively easy to effect, even though news values sometimes have to be sacrificed to achieve it. But both broadcasters and politicians realized that there were other dimensions to the problem as well. One issue raised by the Labour Party in 1974 concerned the order of battle in which leading politicians appeared in election packages. Party managers are keen to win the initiative in campaign news coverage as often as possible and to appear to dominate the argument by pushing 'their' issues to the fore and by putting their rivals on the defensive. 'Leading off' in the news may seem one way of gaining such an advantage. For their part, the BBC producers aimed to concoct a running order that would flow smoothly and would reflect the political significance of what had been said on the particular day. But the need to 'ring the changes' over which party's message would front the news also weighed with them. When out of balance in this sense they soon looked for ways of redressing the situation.

Fairness of treatment also involved sensitivity to the kind of image of the party leaders that was being projected in the election packages, though of course this was more difficult to assess. To illustrate such a concern, during one discussion the executive producer told the Editor of the Day that he should:

> look at some of the shots of David Steel which have been used. The
> Liberals have complained that Steel looks ill-shaven. See if we can get

a more closely shaven one. They are also complaining that the extent of Steel's audiences wasn't shown . . . . We probably need a few more reaction shots of the audience.

Balance could also be sought by ensuring that the number of news appearances of each party leader was more or less equal.

How shall we weigh, in the 'balance sheet' as it were, the British broadcasters' scrupulously fair approach to campaign reporting? Though it shelters the political parties from blatantly slanted coverage and ensures attention to most of their pet themes, it also constrains the construction of election news in at least three major respects. First, the balance principle is in tension with the criterion of objectivity. Even if one side happens to be making far more of the running than the other, television will tend to do its best to ignore and conceal the fact. Second, it circumscribes the role of news values in the selection process – more so even than the official policy language of 'compromise' acknowledges. The journalists cannot afford to be predominantly guided by what would be most interesting and significant to viewers. Instead their point of departure must be the need to derive from the Labour, Conservative and Liberal activities of the day that particular even-handed mixture which can be most readily combined into an easily followed overall package. Third, balance inevitably moulds the form of election reports. Since election stories have to be built up from Labour, Conservative and Liberal messages, producers continually face the problem of deciding how to juxtapose the multi-party ingredients that they are regularly obliged to present: in other words, how to wrap them into a professionally satisfying package.

PUTTING IT TOGETHER: PACKAGING, AGENDA SETTING OR WHAT?

This last concern is closely related to a third major determinant of election coverage that repeatedly came to our attention: the 'factory' team's concern to fashion a set of items which, by virtue of excerpt complementarity, incorporation into some overall theme, and the provision of suitable connecting links, would seem to 'hang together'. It was as if the flow of raw campaign materials presented dangers to be shunned and professional goals to be achieved. The former stemmed from the multiplicity of comments and incidents which in principle could be used. Viewed in that light, the cardinal sins to be avoided were randomness and disconnectedness of presentation. Viewed more positively, however, the art of editing the campaign news was regarded as one of producing a coherent package. Indeed, much of the editors' time and effort was spent in pursuit of a unifying story line, on which the day's election events could be threaded. Thus, as each new campaign day dawned, the search was on for some overarching theme around which the packages of the several bulletins could be constructed, and to which clips of politicians' remarks could be related.

On the days of our observations, this preoccupation with thematic story-building took many forms. For example, it provided the centrepiece of a sustained interview with a leading journalist who, when asked at the outset to describe what election coverage should aim to do, replied that it should portray:

> the issues that are arising, the ones that rise of their own accord because of external events, those brought up by the parties because that is part of their strategy . . . and to follow this day by day and to try and discern and convey *some pattern in this* [our emphasis]. You rely very much on your own instincts, and lights of one colour come on when certain things are said. Sometimes no lights come on at all; they don't register on your scale. Sometimes lights of quite exceptional colour come on, and you realize that they fit exactly into patterns, or they are new, or they are better ways of saying something which you've been waiting to be said. You know that you are waiting for a Conservative response on a certain aspect of unemployment or a certain aspect of their attitude towards the National Health Service, and you remain within yourself dissatisfied while that response is not given. You've been listening to a speech about something else perhaps, and suddenly the thing you've been waiting for, which hasn't to do with one's own political preconceptions, but the answer comes. It's right, it's the right length, and this is perhaps the thing we should go into, and it fits neatly into your pattern. You seize it and you put it in. It's right; you've got no doubt about that.

This was not merely one person's way of rationalizing his own part in the production process. According to our observations, such packaging concerns surfaced at every stage of the campaign day. The post-mortems that were held after viewing the finished product, as broadcast on the 'factory' television set, often centred on packaging successes and failures as well. On one such occasion, for example, a producer complained that 'there was still no theme to the election package. It was presented well, but it was all bits and pieces.' The Political Editor also confessed, 'It was the bittiest edition I've taken part in so far.' The executive producer was not so bothered: 'We should not beat our breasts too much. We had no theme, and a lot of obligatory items to make room for, but tomorrow is another day.' But the Political Editor would not be consoled: 'There should be something there, even despite all that. One should be able to search for it and find that overarching theme.'

As many of these remarks show, 'good packaging' was defined by certain norms that were not always achieved in practice. But in aiming to edit the election news to such standards, what exactly were the television journalists trying to do to, or for, the campaign? This question is difficult to answer because their role is at once passive and creative. The bulk of the materials they process originate, not in their personal priorities, but from partisan sources. Yet they also strive to impose a structure on the materials flowing into the 'factory', which reflects their perception of how the most outstanding elements can be fitted into the day's election jigsaw.

Does this amount to a role of 'agenda setting' by the television news producers? They would deny it, presumably because in their eyes this term has an active interventionist meaning, as if they were being accused of promoting issues they personally deemed significant, despite or even in contradistinction to those the parties wished to press for. Yet the packaging functions they perform may have formative consequences, both for how the campaign is communicated to the public and for how the political parties devise their campaign strategies.

First, the editorial process of selecting, collating and juxtaposing statements, which may have been made independently of each other, often yields a severely 'boiled down' version of the campaign. At a time when the team may have witnessed numerous initiatives and monitored many arguments, it allows the news reader to open an election package with some terse statement like, 'Prices were a key issue in today's party press conferences.' Such a decision to lift 'prices' out of the numerous issues being voiced, and to underline it as the day's central theme, stems from the journalists' need for a viable 'hook', 'peg', or common denominator, not their own political values. But it undoubtedly shapes the campaign, if not via independent agenda setting, then in the twofold sense of (a) pruning it by cutting out material that cannot be fitted into a tight story, and (b) crystallizing it by bringing it to a convergent focus.

Second, one of the more important consequences of election news packaging is the amplification of the extracts chosen for transmission. A traditional view of the selection process in the mass media interprets it as a gate-keeping operation. In that view, selection merely involves decisions about which viewpoints ought to be allowed through the media gates and which are to be shut out. Yet this ignores the resulting amplification of a small portion of a speech into the total message. It is not just that the spotlight is focused on the broadcast extract, but that the extract comes to represent the essence and centrepiece of the originating party's message to the viewing audience for that day.

Third, in continually counterposing one party's stand on an issue with that of its rivals, the journalists appear to be promoting inter-party communication. It is as if the news personnel are trying to create a dialogue between the parties, where it otherwise might not have existed, and to trigger the politicians into comments and actions that might not have been forthcoming otherwise. Television journalists thus help to orchestrate the campaign, even if they did not write the original score.

Fourth, the campaign tends to be served to the audience in the form of an 'issue a day' – since today's most presentable materials are unlikely to be shaped by the theme that would have dominated the previous day's package. Elsewhere, we have ascribed this feature of the modern campaign to party publicists' efforts to capture the attention of the mass media with a new issue each day (Blumler, Gurevitch and Ives, 1978). From the foregoing analysis it may be concluded, however, that the issue-a-day approach to electioneering is a subtly composite outcome of the mutual adaptation of politicians and media personnel in the conduct and communication of the campaign to the public.

Fifth, it is evident from much of the above that the broadcasters regard coherent packaging as an expression of their responsibility to serve the campaign communication needs of their viewing audience. The production of thematically unified stories, unfolding a pattern in events, should help audience members to follow the campaign more easily and to find more meaning in it. As one journalist told us:

> You're always acting on behalf of your audience. At least it's much more intelligible if you pull out this fact, that fact and that fact and use them in a quite different order from the original one because they illustrate your representation of the argument. But if [he continued] you just reported everything as it happened, the audience would become terribly bored with it, and it wouldn't communicate. I mean we are in the business of communication.

The news professionals tend to see themselves, then, as knowledgeable and skilful packagers, sifting through the raw materials provided by the politicians, selecting those extracts which, in their view, are significant and lend themselves to being linked and juxtaposed with other remarks, preferably oppositional ones. Through these connections and juxtapositions they try to tell a story and construct a coherent package. Media academics sometimes come in at this point and label the results of the process as 'agenda setting'. Editors and reporters, however, find it difficult to view their work in such terms. Perhaps their hesitation is simply an example of the difficulty all social actors have in identifying the latent functions (or unintended consequences) of their behaviour. But if the broadcasters were designated 'co-orchestrators' of the campaign rather than 'agenda setters', perhaps they would be willing to acknowledge responsibility and accept the honour.

IN CONCLUSION: ASPIRATIONS AND CONSTRAINTS

In this chapter we have sought to identify certain salient features of the production of campaign news for television as we observed the process at the BBC during the British general election of April and May 1979. Such ethnographically derived insights served two purposes. One had to do with the relationship of journalists to their sources in the election news field. Much of our theoretical interest has focused on interaction between politicians and broadcasters, regarded as joint and mutually adaptive producers of political communications. In that context observation facilities helped us to note how election news-making both reflects and impinges on the interplay between television journalists and party campaigners. In addition, we were moved by a policy-based interest in the kind of campaign that is projected to viewers as a result of the routines that these two types of communicators jointly operate. Having committed ourselves a few years ago to the proposition that 'More weight must be given [in campaign programming] to what voters would find interesting, informative and geared to their needs' (Blumler, Gurevitch and Ives, 1978), observation offered first-hand impressions of the feasibility of such a goal – of the organizational constraints that may impede its pursuit and of the prospects for relieving them.

In fact, much of the story of the production of election news, as we witnessed it, could be told in terms of aspirations and constraints. During the observation period we frequently heard expressions of concern about taking certain steps which in the end remained largely in the realm of promise. For example, considerably fewer prefilmed items of issue analysis actually appeared in the news than were originally planned. Difficulties of length and scheduling frustrated this policy. To do justice to a designated issue more time was needed than a jam-packed bulletin could afford. And because editors preferred to screen such items on days when campaign events made them topical, they then created for themselves a professionally unwelcome duplication of themes and speakers between other election stories and the special issue analyses.

Similarly, the broadcasters resolved at one of their nightly post-mortems to cut down the number of party leader walkabout films they were showing, realizing that they had little inherent news value. Their intention was eroded, however, by the daily availability of such stories, manufactured by the politicians and their media consultants in forms that proved difficult to resist.

However, the central innovation that was intended to improve news coverage of the 1979 campaign was undoubtedly the proposal to embed the election packages in a more firmly defined surround of analysis and interpretation. Such a policy decision probably emerged from many influences, including the evolution of news philosophy in a more analytical direction since the previous election; BBC research into audience reactions to the coverage, which is carried out after every election; and the criticisms of those academics who had deplored the overly snippety approach of television news to campaign reporting (Blumler, Gurevitch and Ives, 1978; Harrison, 1975; Pateman, 1974). But the outcomes of lengthy postmortems, held by News and Current Affairs policy-makers in the aftermath of each campaign, would have played a part as well.

Consequently, the task of fronting and presenting the election news package was assigned to the Political Editor, the most senior journalist covering the political scene for the BBC, in the hope that he could inject a form of commentary that would be interpretative without being opinionated. Though we are in no position to pronounce this venture a success or failure, from observation we can state, first, that it was continually beset with difficulty, and second, that those involved rarely seemed satisfied with how it was working out in practice.

The problems of achieving a more reflective form of election coverage were probably rooted in certain working conditions and procedures of the news producers, including those determinants of their campaign output that have been examined in previous sections of this chapter. At a quite particular level, the difficulties of providing effective campaign analysis arose from severe time constraints in two senses. There was acute deadline pressure on the Political Editor, who an hour or less before the evening bulletin was due to go on the air could be seen still composing links between speech extracts and the other items in the election package. There was also a shortage of available time, in the ration negotiated for the election package inside the day's bulletin, for accommodating analytical remarks after the various stories and actuality clips had consumed whatever minutes and seconds they needed.

In addition, strict adherence to the norm of balance may have had an inhibiting effect on the supply of interpretation. Analysis often had to be reduced to what could be couched in a more or less impartial terminology, along such lines as: 'On the one hand, Labour is faring well in promoting its theme of . . . ; on the other hand, the Conservatives are fighting back by emphasizing . . .'. When forced into such an even-handed mould, campaign interpretation may lose some of its analytical punch.

Similarly constraining effects may have flowed from the team's preoccupation with packaging desiderata. These put a premium on the weaving of various campaign events, pledges and speech clips into a coherent story line, which emphasized in turn the need for suitable passages linking the day's several items. As we have seen, the Political Editor was keen to write these sequences himself. But when immersed in such tasks, it seemed to us that he lacked time to brood at leisure on the more reflective demands of his contribution.

It should not be concluded that the impulse to innovate in election programming is invariably bound to be thwarted. The record shows that it has made significant contributions to campaign broadcasting at each successive British election between 1959 and October 1974 (Blumler, 1975). Nevertheless, this case study does suggest that attempts to transform the election role of television news are likely to encounter at least four formidable sources of constraint, ones that are rooted respectively in: (a) the bulletin format; (b) the organization's prevalent working routines; (c) socialization to a corporate ethos, favouring straightforward approaches to the presentation of campaign events at the expense of more adventurous ones; and (d) the need to avoid anything that might upset the delicate balance of the broadcasters' relations with the political parties.

This account of the construction of election news has depicted the broadcasters' contribution to a subtle and largely undeclared division of labour between television journalists and party spokespersons in the political communication process during an election campaign. We have found that the role of the broadcasters, even when construed mainly as 'packaging' and deprived of much analytical thrust, still serves certain vital functions of identifying and crystallizing the themes of the campaign, as well as promoting an inter-party dialogue on the issues of the day. These are important functions in their own right, and they underscore the role of the mass media in general, and of television in particular, in nourishing the political debate in society and in focusing it more coherently than the political competitors could achieve if left to their own devices. Ironically, broadcasters often seemed reluctant to accept credit for this, preferring a more narrow definition of their contribution in terms of 'reflecting' and 'mirroring' the debate. To that extent they fall prey to a blinkered view of their societal role, emphasizing its more technical-professional aspects while obscuring its political consequences. Such a neutered view of television journalism needs to be unpacked and critically examined, not least for the broadcasters' sake, but also to continue the difficult quest, with their involvement, for ways of enhancing their political journalism.

Chapter 11

Setting the television news agenda (1983)[1]

Television news plays a critical but difficult part in the projection of a British election. Its importance is due partly to the exceptional brevity (three and a half weeks) of the packed campaign. This not only 'concentrates electoral activity and gives it an intensity lacking in the United States' (Rasmussen, 1983); it also divides the campaign into a sequence of discrete single-day units, each of which opens with the morning party press conferences and closes with the two main evening news bulletins. Naturally, the parties organize much of their publicity on a daily basis with the demands of television in mind, aiming 'to catch the midday news with the morning press conference; the early evening news with that day's carefully staged walkabout; and the main evening news with that day's first insert into the basic campaign speech' (Glencross, 1983). Consequently, much of the dynamic of the British campaign, the engine by which it is predominantly driven, stems from the demands and characteristics of daily television news.

Television news is also centrally implicated in the ritualization of the campaign process. Leading political communicators tend to go through similar motions to those of previous elections, because (whatever their disadvantages) they are at least familiar, they allow one to predict how others will behave, and they help to reduce uncertainty in the hectic circumstances of a short campaign. For journalists, however, the price of involvement in the election ritual is continual anxiety that the parade of statements and incidents they are expected to cover will not prove fully newsworthy. Observation during the 1979 and 1983 campaigns often found them *straining* to produce reports that would satisfy their professional standards, reflecting tension between an obligation to cover the campaign on a daily basis and a fear that election events on that day might not form a recognizably satisfactory story.

Three other news coverage difficulties may be mentioned. First, during an election the broadcasters' reputation for political fairness is at stake. Open alike to accusations of undue passivity (Harrison, 1975) and of intervention (Seymour-Ure, 1974), they are apt to be 'damned if they do and damned if they don't'. Second, they depend heavily for the election stories they fashion on the quality of what the principal campaigners put before them each day. In 1983 especially, the capacity of the three main contenders to supply suitable material was very uneven. One party (the Conservatives) appeared confident and well-organized; another (Labour) often appeared in disarray; and the third force, a novel Alliance (Liberals and Social Democrats), was fighting a general election for the first time. Third, there is some ambivalence inside the BBC over the ability of the News Division to report an election entirely on the strength of its own resources and routines. Consequently, these have been rearranged and supplemented at every election since 1970. Unfortunately, the new dispositions are often settled at the last minute; in 1983, people who had not previously worked together were required to do so with effectively no advance preparation.

Shortly after Parliament was dissolved in May 1983, the BBC granted the authors' request to observe the production of campaign reports for the lunch-time, early evening and *Nine O'Clock News* bulletins on BBC 1. As previously, we attached ourselves on intermittent days to the election news operation at the BBC Television Centre, where we were allowed to be present in any of the news production areas, to attend planning and editorial discussions, and to discuss the implications of their work with the campaign journalists.

The report that follows is part ethnographic, part analytical. At one level, it describes the production process as we saw it – which happened to be punctuated by periodic conflict between divergent schools of journalistic thought. At another level, however, we aim to generalize from the evidence about the agenda-setting roles and options of television newscasters in election campaign circumstances.

CONTINUITY AND CHANGE, 1979–83

The scene at the Television Centre in 1983 was both closely similar to and substantially different from that witnessed in 1979. 'Internal' policy decisions had introduced new roles and faces into the election news team, working relations within which had become rather less harmonious as a result. 'External' developments in the British party system also gave the campaign to be presented a different political complexion from its predecessor. But three sets of practices and attitudes, which had formatively shaped campaign reporting in 1979, still prevailed in 1983.

Enduring determinants of election news-making at the BBC

First, in both elections the organization of the coverage was highly centralized. Raw campaign materials, such as press conference exchanges and leaders' evening speeches, were relayed back to monitors at the Television Centre for selection, excerpting and processing – rather than being handled by journalists in the field.

Second, certain characteristically conscientious ways of striving for 'balance' between reports of the main election contenders were as noticeable in 1983 as in 1979. These included a strictly mathematical application of 'balance' by the stopwatch, requiring the news team to ensure that they had shown recorded extracts of politicians' remarks in proportions identical to their parties' election broadcasting shares (5:5:4 in 1983). But the balance norm was also influential in more qualitative ways. In 1983, for example, there was a concern to draw a suitable line between reporting Labour's divisions over nuclear defence and insistently referring to its predicament. Similarly, there was some concern not to exaggerate the political significance of fissures in Conservative ranks via the 'deviant' utterances of Francis Pym, James Prior and Edward du Cann. There was also a prompt readiness to respond to Alliance complaints of less prominent coverage of its campaign contributions than Labour and Conservative efforts were enjoying.

Third, certain 'packaging' arts and criteria often controlled the form and content of election items in both campaigns. Much of the production, particularly of lunch-time news reports, boiled down to the selection of excerpts that chimed in some confrontational or complementary way with each other; the sequencing of material to form a seemingly logical set of links from one extract, event or item to another; and the identification of some theme that would give a semblance of unity to the campaign day as a whole. Such a factor may heighten uncertainty among party publicity-makers, whose chances of planting their preferred messages in a bulletin will turn not only on their intrinsic news interest, but also on their relationship to other materials that will have caught the journalists' eyes on that day.

New organizational dispositions in 1983

The key coverage decisions for this campaign apparently reflected responses to two main sources of difficulty. One, essentially philosophical, pitted the Corporation's responsibility to the political system against wariness about the limited political appetite of the ordinary elector. On the one hand, the BBC, as a public service organization, felt that an election has an inherent claim to full and serious treatment. On the other hand, numerous complaints about excessive TV coverage from audience members, surveyed after each election since February 1974, had instilled a keen concern not to overstretch the tolerance for political talk of the average viewer. As one executive put it, 'We wanted to treat the election campaign as an important affair, but our problem was how to avoid over-exposure of viewers to it to such an extent that they would become bored with it.'

The other difficulty was more practical and concerned the nightly scheduling of campaign programming on BBC 1 and BBC 2. During the elections of October 1974 and May 1979, news coverage in the *Nine O'Clock News* bulletins had been supplemented by a late-night *Campaign Report* programme on BBC 1, in which election issues were taken further through a mix of round-table discussions, interviews, special reports and analysis.

In 1983, however, this pattern seemed less applicable. BBC 1 no longer had a regular late-night Current Affairs vehicle of its own. Instead, on BBC 2 *Newsnight* had evolved its own authoritative style of political analysis and comment. Apparently, the transfer of *Newsnight* to a BBC 1 slot for the campaign period was never seriously canvassed. Instead, it stayed on BBC 2 and was bidden to supply the forms of discussion and analysis provided at previous elections by *Campaign Report* on BBC 1. Nevertheless, some policy-makers felt uneasy about the lack of a more reflective element on the mass-audience channel. It was therefore decided to give the *Nine O'Clock News* a more substantial brief than in previous campaigns, including the services of a few politically knowledgeable specialists drawn from the Current Affairs Group. Specifically, it was extended – by 10 minutes in the first week of the campaign and by 15 minutes thereafter – on the understanding that about a half of the 40-minute total would normally be devoted to election material. Two of the Corporation's politically most experienced commentators, David Dimbleby and Fred Emery, were incorporated into the election news team, to front the campaign reports, to offer rounded assessments of election events and to inject specialist political judgements into editorial decisions. The Political Editor of the BBC, John Cole, was asked to supply a regular commentary on campaign developments. And a Current Affairs producer was assigned to the team with responsibility for preparing a series of special film reports on key election issues.

The 1983 formula was, however, a recipe for underlying conflict that periodically came to the surface during the campaign. Internal memoranda were circulated in the first week, provoking spirited discussions with policy executives. Sometimes the differences of approach erupted into overtly angry exchanges. Editorial team meetings occasionally took the form of struggles for ascendancy, reflecting the determination of one side or another to shape the output on that day, for a change. At times those involved even felt obliged to exert 'unremitting pressure' on behalf of their ideas.

Overarching the specific points of clash, broad differences of journalistic philosophy were evidently at stake. In essence, the two sides differed over the appropriate point of departure for election reporting. Many of the News Division, perceiving their role primarily as one of 'reflecting' daily events, assumed that the proper point of departure for election reporting was what leading politicians had said and done on the day concerned, whether deliberately or inadvertently. But those who came to the task from a Current Affairs background preferred what they sometimes termed 'a more issue-oriented approach', allowing viewers to compare one party with another for their stands on the questions involved, which could then be illustrated with speech excerpts.

The new dispositions of 1983 were not universally admired at the end of the campaign. Each side felt it had reason to be satisfied with the quality of many of its contributions, but few of the individuals we spoke to afterwards endorsed the overall conception. In the typical words of one critic, the exercise was an 'ill-thought-out attempt to combine News with a half-hearted Current Affairs operation'.

Altered political climate

Although similar to previous television campaigns in many ways, in one major respect the 1983 contest may have marked a turning point in the post-war history of election broadcasting in Britain. It was the occasion when the increasing instability of the British party system – evidenced in electoral volatility, partisan dealignment and greater support for challengers to the major parties – finally caught up with and impinged significantly on the election role of television.

Until 1983, arrangements for campaign broadcasting had emerged from a relatively ordered framework. Despite many developments and innovations since the 1950s, at its core the system of election broadcasting was stabilized by two things. One was the country's traditionally strong party system. The other was the forging of many close contacts and understandings, both formal and informal, between party and broadcasting élites. Together, these underpinned the role of the Committee on Party Political Broadcasting – which was able to decide on a consensual basis how BBC and Independent Television offers of campaign broadcasting time would be distributed across the competing parties. The same props also made possible a relatively controlled pattern of access to other election programmes for party representatives. Not only did politicians and broadcasters monopolize almost all forms of political expression during the campaign. Maverick and dissident party voices, often heard in out-of-election periods, were also virtually excluded once a campaign was launched.

In 1983, however, such traditions were disrupted by the aftermath of two post-1979 developments. One was the formation of the Social Democratic Party and its subsequent entry into an Alliance to fight the election in tandem with the Liberal Party. The other was the emergence in all parties of more vigorous, open and high-level dissent from official policies. Of course, the resultant splits were most virulent and uncontained in the Labour Party. But they also surfaced in more 'coded' forms in the public utterances of leading Conservatives; while a two-headed Alliance offered scope for a certain amount of jostling and invidious comparison between its component parts.

BROADCASTERS' RESPONSES TO 1983 CIRCUMSTANCES

Treatment of the SDP–Liberal Alliance

Unprecedentedly, the formation of the SDP (and its Alliance with the Liberals) posed problems that the Committee on Party Political Broadcasting could not solve on its usual consensual terms. In the absence of a previous election track record, the established formulae for distribution of party time were inapplicable. The two major parties naturally feared the enhanced notice and legitimation that a generous allocation might confer on the new force. Given the sizeable fluctuations of opinion-poll support for the SDP from its inception to the moment of the election announcement, nobody could be certain that it would be a lasting fixture on the party scene. In these circumstances, the BBC and the Independent Broadcasting Authority assumed responsibility for proposing a new set of guidelines on which all might agree. In March 1982, they jointly submitted a policy paper to the Committee on Party Political Broadcasting, suggesting revised ground rules both for the share-out of party broadcasts in a period of high electoral volatility and for incorporating newly formed parties, like the SDP, into 'the club' (its own revealing phrase). But its terms were not accepted and indeed were only cursorily considered. Meetings of the Committee became more acrimonious than in living memory. Its lubricating 'usual channels' machinery of prior consultation, which had often paved the way for agreement in the past, creaked and virtually broke down. For the 1983 campaign, therefore, the BBC and IBA representatives on the Committee had to decide, on their own responsibility, how much time to give the Alliance. Following the implications of their 1982 paper, they settled for a 5:5:4 distribution of party broadcasting (and consequently news-attention) time – which also happened to split the difference between the Alliance's claim for equal shares (5:5:5) and the Conservative and Labour wish to reaffirm the 1979 quota of 5:5:3.

In the light of political events since 1979, the BBC and IBA policy-makers did not see how 'in fairness' they could be less generous to the Alliance. However, things looked somewhat different on the BBC 'news factory' floor. It was not that anybody challenged the validity of the 5:5:4 allocation (although one or two journalists criticized the system of rationing news attention across the parties itself). In fact, when Alliance complaints of inadequate treatment reached the newsroom – a tendency to cover their leaders' remarks lower in the bulletin, failure to mention the Alliance in the news headlines, and lack of visuals showing warm crowd reactions to David Steel on walkabout – nobody seemed to resent the pressure or to regard it as unreasonable. Instead, adjustments were made in a spirit conveyed by the Editor of the Day, who said of the Alliance, 'They are getting twitchy about our tendency to take them on news values, and so are we.'

As that comment suggests, however, the news professionals sometimes regarded the journalistic worth of Alliance contributions as not quite on a par with the amount of attention that the norms of fairness (as enshrined in the party broadcasting quotas) would dictate. One root of this view may have been a journalistic predilection for clear-cut issues, capable of being presented in two-sided terms (Seymour-Ure, 1974). From this preference stemmed a tendency to project the election as a contest between two heavyweight boxers, into which a third fighter could not always be easily inserted.

Another barrier to its being taken seriously was a political perception of the Alliance's record. Journalists – who have been described by one of their number as 'experts in the credibility gap' (Kraft, 1983) – are keenly sensitive to discrepancies of political performance, when measured against prior claims, potentials and expectations. This told against the Alliance (especially its SDP component) in May 1983, when the journalists we observed sometimes commented on it as if it aimed to sport bigger political boots than it could really wear. For example, at a late point in a team meeting, after much time had been devoted to points made that day by Conservative and Labour spokesmen, the editor in charge finally moved the discussion on by ironically asking, 'And what about the four-fifths party?'. Another individual compared the Alliance with the position of Prince Philip: 'Equal but a little behind!' Some argued that the Alliance had not yet effected the transition 'from a party of protest to a party of government'. Certain broadcasters acknowledged that the communication system might ensnare the Alliance in a 'Catch 22' predicament: How could it improve its electoral standing if the major campaign media largely presented it as a sideline force? Nevertheless, some considered that the Alliance should have been able to attract more centrist electors at a political moment when a staunchly right-wing Tory government, with an uneven economic record, was opposed by a decidedly left-wing and divided Labour Party.

At best the Alliance was still on probation, then, not yet having proved itself. This points to the influence of a third discounting element among broadcasters' attitudes. In some cases, their 'cognitive map' of British politics was still geared to a two-party (or a two-and-a-half party) system. Typical was the producer who replied to questions on this that one would have to wait until the election returns were in to see whether Britain had a three-party system: 'The British political system is still very much a two-party system, with a third party which might or might not emerge as a viable party from this election.'

The significance of this cognitive factor was underlined by the spirit in which the journalists finally did take the Alliance more seriously in the last week of the campaign, as its opinion-poll ratings improved and those of Labour declined. As an editor explained, when asked why certain points about these developments had been drawn from Alliance and Labour press conferences for inclusion in the day's lunch-time bulletin, 'That's what the campaign has moved on to – whether the Alliance can come second instead of Labour.' It was as if, even at this more favourable moment for the Alliance, his cognitive map was unchanged: Britain still has a two-party system, but the interesting question now was whether the Alliance could replace Labour as the nation's second party.

FOUR APPROACHES TO ELECTION AGENDA-SETTING

Election campaign agenda setting by television is a complex and notoriously delicate subject. To some politicians and broadcasters, it implies an intervention by non-elected media personnel into a fight, the essential terms of which should be defined by the party combatants themselves. Past research reveals mixed broadcaster attitudes towards the concept. In the 1966 campaign, for example, certain BBC Current Affairs producers boldly staked out a claim to present items on issues the parties did not wish to be covered (see Chapter 9). In the 1970s, however, signs accumulated of an editorial and reportorial hesitancy to define their campaign contributions in agenda-setting terms (see Chapter 10).

When applied to media–*audience* relations, the notion of agenda setting is straightforward. At that level, it refers to the tendency, tolerably well-documented in research, for audience impressions of the relative importance of different political issues to correspond to the relative prominence given to those issues in media reporting (Weaver *et al.*, 1981). But when applied to media–source relations – or to the question of how the media campaign agenda itself is formed – the concept becomes quite complex. For one thing, the process may be joint and interactive, with each side making significant, albeit different, contributions to the agenda-setting outcome. For another, the media contribution can be made in different ways, yielding different messages and entailing different relations to the other interests at stake in campaign communication (those of politicians and voters).

Such diversity was a prominent feature of the responses of BBC news personnel to the 1983 campaign. Its distinctive political character had apparently triggered sometimes quite keenly felt differences among producers at the Television Centre over what their role in framing the campaign agenda should be. In fact we discerned – when editorial decisions were being taken, when the journalists were arguing with each other, and when they responded to questions we put to them – four different strands of thought on the issues at stake. They consisted of what may be termed (1) prudential, (2) reactive, (3) conventionally journalistic and (4) analytical positions on their own election roles. It should be noted that these categories represent our own way of sorting out the different approaches to election news-making available to, and advocated by, the professional journalists. They do not necessarily coincide with distinct camps in the team, although some influential individuals did more or less consistently favour certain approaches over others. Most news workers probably appreciated something about all four stances, differing chiefly in how they were hierarchically valued.

The *prudential* reaction seemed specially concerned to ensure that television journalism was, and would appear to be, politically beyond reproach – perhaps even politically innocuous. That is, it should not, actually or in appearance, intervene in the political course of the campaign. This attitude was expressed in such phrases as, 'making sure that we aren't leading with our chin', 'aren't stepping out of line', or 'conveying the impression that the make-up of the bulletin is politically determined'. For example, the producer responsible for a sequence of special reports to be prepared on the main campaign issues occasionally drew attention to the danger that they might focus on an issue which none of the parties was projecting, or on one that was being more heavily stressed by one party than another.

According to some observers, the *reactive* approach tended to dominate television news coverage of campaigns in the 1970s (Blumler, Gurevitch and Ives, 1978). This looked to party publicity initiatives (press conferences, walkabouts, evening speeches) which TV news had a duty to report, as the centrepiece of campaign stories. In 1983, it was espoused by some BBC journalists in such propositions as, 'The prime responsibility of election news is to provide a round-up of the main points made in politicians' speeches and activities of the day'; and, 'On television, the news of the campaign should be presented relatively straight, relaying points from politicians' speeches day by day'.

Exponents of this view tended to regard the campaign as an external event that took place somewhere 'out in the field', from which it was the task of television journalists to bring back the most interesting and encapsulatable highlights, often guided in this by what politicians themselves deemed significant, judging by their press releases and other evidence. This was by no means an uncreative process for it demanded much skill in juxtaposing and connecting the various available contributions and describing them in terms that audience members could be expected to understand. Thus, the totally passive image of a mirror does not adequately express the essence of this approach. Perhaps in this conception the role of the campaign reporter is best likened to that of a translator – converting what politicians are emphasizing into messages that viewers can understand. In 1983, it was most often followed in preparation of the lunch-time bulletin, perhaps because no Current Affairs person was assigned to its production. Its merits were most stoutly defended, however, by an executive who could not generate much personal interest in the campaign, who suspected that many voters were bored with it, and who was sincerely troubled by the tendency of politicians to tailor their actions and remarks to what they thought would come over best on television. In this last concern, he was being logical, since such a process of party adaptation blurred his distinction between television as an independent reporting agency and those happenings in the campaign field which it was supposed to observe.

At times the advocates of a more *conventionally journalistic* approach (so termed because they wished to filter election events through professional news-value criteria) had a 'field day' during the 1983 campaign – although they were often highly ambivalent about its developments as well. On the one hand, they were continually looking for what they sometimes called the 'bull point' of the day ('What's the bull point this morning?'), and, on the other hand, they were continually fearful that they would not find it! Often they were specially concerned with what should be the lead or top election story of the day, something that they wanted to be novel, not just a repetition or even a development of a theme that had been struck in the previous day's, or even in a previous bulletin's, output. And they wanted that lead story or bull point to be heavily laden with conventional news values, particularly those of conflict, drama, movement and anomaly. Consequently, their moods and reactions often fluctuated in response to the materials coming in to the Television Centre. Sometimes they soberly worked at what was to hand, sifting through the material in search of a major story that did not seem to be there, almost as if building bricks from straw. But sometimes they were intensely galvanized, particularly when a dramatic and unexpected incident or statement transformed their prospects – and the sequence of stories in the bulletin running order.

Adherents of this view were chiefly 'generalists', reporters who had been assigned to concentrated political duty for the duration of the campaign. Their outlook was typified by their occasional reactions to press conference proceedings, saying, for example, 'There's no news there; it was all about the party's manifesto'; or, 'It's all old hat, all about the economy'. At such times, however, 'no news' meant no dramatic news as defined by conventional news values. A BBC executive, who knew them well and admired them, characterized them neatly for us as 'typical journalists, who are like street-sweepers, continually hoping to find a diamond in the gutter'.

Such an approach seemed to put a premium on two qualities for campaigning politicians: an ability to avoid newsworthy gaffes and 'own goals'; and fast publicity footwork of a kind that would enable the alert and news-knowing politician to step in at the right moment to address (perhaps even to manipulate) this group's news values. In fact, on four of the six days of our attachment, the running order for the *Nine O'Clock News* was transformed more or less at the last minute by a syndrome that combined, on the one hand, a certain weariness on the team's part with what had promised to be the lead election story of the night, with, on the other hand, a sudden injection into the campaign of some startling or striking statement that caught the eye like, if not a diamond, then at least a piece of quartz, in the gutter.

A more *analytical* approach was mainly proposed by the heavyweight political commentators who had been brought into the election news team from other sectors of BBC Current Affairs television. In essence, they regarded the exercise by journalists of independent agenda-setting judgements as both inevitable and desirable. In their view, those of their colleagues who denied this were deluding themselves, since they were willy-nilly in the business of agenda setting. They were saying who the main campaign actors were, what the most significant utterances and claims of the day were, and in what context they should be followed and grasped by viewers. Failure to acknowledge this feature of election journalism was literally irresponsible.

The most concerned advocate of this position held that they had a positive 'Reithian duty', not only to capture attention, entertain and provide excerpts from politicians' speeches of the day, but also to 'tease out the central threads of the arguments and issues involved'. The aim was to attain coherence in reporting, although not 'the kind that comes from just looking for the most intense aggro and blazing rows between rival politicians'. Instead of screening just 'a slab of speeches and a slab of conference material and saying that's enough for campaign reporting', one should 'try to say what the events in the news might mean, in terms either of an exploration of the strategic objectives underlying a politician's statement, or in terms of some substantive clarification of the issues involved and policies proposed'. But, he went on, all this was 'predicated on the assumption that one gets it right'. And although it was naturally difficult for him to spell out what that last qualifier implied, it would presumably entail, he said, 'some correspondence between journalists' perceptions of what the issues to be aired in the campaign are and the priorities of society'. So if they 'got it right' in such terms, all was well and good; but if not, they could and should be open to criticism.

By the end of the campaign, it appeared to us that, of the four approaches, the analytical had proved most difficult to sustain effectively. Its proponents had their triumphs and moments of glory, but they had to work hard for them, and their efforts were often overshadowed by those of the conventional journalists, whose coverage mode seemed more dominant than in any previous British campaign. In part, this was because the 'own goals' and inter-party splits of the 1983 campaign were grist especially to the conventionally journalistic mill. But an institutional explanation carries weight as well. The Current Affairs analysts were not on their home turf, lacked space of their own to confer together, and had to work at a different pace with fewer resources than they usually commanded. They had been transplanted into a newsroom, where the News Division Editor of the Day was keeper of the running order and captain of the bulk of the team.

SOME IMPLICATIONS

One conclusion to be drawn from this analysis, obvious perhaps but often overlooked by polemicists, is that in a liberal-democratic society television journalism is a multi-faceted enterprise. In fact, the four different approaches to agenda setting underscore certain alternatives of choice and orientation, which have emerged in other forms from numerous studies of media occupational roles (McQuail, 1983, pp. 106–11). Thus, each seems to point to a different set of interests as ultimate points of guiding reference:

Agenda-setting orientation	Main point of reference
Prudential	The organization
Reactive	Politicians as sources
Conventionally journalistic	Occupational values
Analytical	The 'public interest'

But how journalists strive to project an election campaign is not just a matter for internal debate. Their choices and decisions have important consequences for all who depend on their coverage of major political events. First, the various approaches to journalistic agenda setting may trigger or constrain different electioneering tactics. Prudential attitudes may encourage parties to develop calculated strategies of sharply angled complaints. A reactive philosophy could favour close collaboration between party managers and campaign reporters and a signposting of the party's intended message of the day (or hour) to their mutual convenience. The conventionally journalistic approach seems to invite a propaganda of 'nuggets, nutshells and golden phrases' (Blumler, Gurevitch and Ives, 1978, p. 29), including the staging, where possible, of dramatic, combative and visually arresting incidents and accusations. The analytical approach, however, would presumably require politicians to elaborate their more substantive issue and policy positions.

Second, there are implications for how an election is perceived by broadcasters. Some BBC journalists viewed the 1983 contest as an ordinary news story writ large with customary news values to the fore: 'The campaign is just an exceptionally long and important news story not all that different from how you would have covered the Falklands expedition.' Others, however, thought that elections were *sui generis*. According to one 'analyst', for example, the very fact that the news bulletin had been extended, and Current Affairs resources been ploughed into the operation, 'signalled that an election campaign was supposed to receive other than normal news coverage'. In his eyes, an election campaign was not merely a parade of events but a process of critical choice for the nation.

Third, how journalists conceive their job may rub off on popular participation in politics and impressions of elections as meriting involvement or not. Predominantly prudential and reactive styles of coverage, for example, might transmit to the audience a sense of distance from a campaign, whose prime actors could be seen as routinely going through their ritualistic paces. For their part, many of the conventionally journalistic seekers after events with drama, conflict and novelty seem to take the view that the average audience member has a low threshold of interest, a cynicism about government and politicians, and no great ability to follow or sort out complex issues and arguments. 'What a lot of words,' was one reporter's exclamation after watching the morning's three press conferences on the Television Centre monitors. Thus, some felt a need to sweeten the pill of campaign stories with values to some extent extraneous to politics. By contrast, the analysts on the team appeared more confident that the choices underlying the rival political programmes offered at an election could be brought alive and made interesting for the viewer on their own terms.

Finally, the merits of the several positions may be evaluated for their central tendencies and thrust. The prudential emphasis seems to ignore the irreversible fact that television is itself now a participant in the political process. The reactive outlook is open to the charge of putting television news mainly at the disposal of the political parties, even though they have other slices of broadcasting time for advocacy. The conventionally journalistic approach may distort political priorities for the sake of more immediate excitement and gratification. If 'Men ... cannot govern society by episodes, incidents and interruptions' (Lippman, 1922, p. 228), then conventionally shaped news may 'not be a [fully adequate] guide to political choice' (Patterson, 1980, p. 174).

This line of argument appears to favour the analytical approach, on the ground that 'the peculiar type of event that an election campaign, by its very nature, is', may be 'better suited to presentation in news analysis than news bulletin terms' (Blumler, Gurevitch and Ives, 1978, p. 54).

An objection to such an analytical emphasis is that unduly heavy material will drive viewers away. As a thoughtful 'conventional journalist', reacting to a previous draft of this study, put it:

> Though analysis is fine in theory, many times fewer people would actually watch it with, presumably, a decreased impact on the electorate.... Lose their attention, and they'll switch over, and what happens to your informed electorate then? BBC 1 in particular is an entertainment medium and any programme editor who arrogantly forgets this is asking for trouble.

In the end, however, such an objection to a more analytical provision appears to answer itself. For if even election news has to be tailored to the needs of an 'entertainment medium', then viewers of it may be encouraged more often to laugh and scorn than to learn and weigh.

Chapter 12

The earnest versus the determined
Election news-making at the BBC (1987)[1]

Election communication for television is a subtly composite product that emerges from the mutually adaptive efforts of journalists and politicians in pursuit of overlapping yet distinct goals. In 1987 there were signs that their different purposes had crystallized into sharply opposed models of campaign message projection. From a BBC vantage point at least, earnest newscasters, applying a social responsibility view of their role, confronted partisan forces, each determined that, if they could not control the campaign agenda, nobody else would. To the former, communication was a tool of public enlightenment; to the latter, a weapon in a two-way power struggle – against rival parties and professional journalists.

We became aware of this conflict while observing, for the third election in a row, production of the *Nine O'Clock News* at the BBC on intermittent days during the 1987 campaign. As previously, access was essentially open and free, except to editorial conferences whose participants we could interview afterwards.

EMERGENCE OF THE MODELS, 1983–7

The broadcasters

'The BBC treated the event with due seriousness.' This was how a senior executive interpreted the Corporation's decision to inject massive resources from the Current Affairs Group into the *Nine O'Clock* coverage of the 1987 campaign. That step was remarkable, even heroic, given the disasters that had attended a similar attempt to strengthen the analytical component of election news in 1983 (see Chapter 11). Universally condemned as a failure, the 1983 attempt had no unified objective or line of command. The leading presenter from Current Affairs had felt like Prince Charles over the water, under-supported on alien turf. Opposed camps (News versus Current Affairs) had formed and struggled continually for ascendancy, differing over philosophy, running order priorities, the nature of the campaign and their appropriate roles in it. Not surprisingly, like the team, the programme had rarely knitted together. It had been a 'searing experience', from which the participants emerged 'battle-scarred' (as 1987 informants recalled).

Why, then, did the BBC venture an even bolder combined operation to present the 1987 campaign? Essentially it was because momentum for the closer integration of News and Current Affairs had accelerated irreversibly over the intervening four years. By 1987 both the Editor of Television News, Ron Neil, and the Head of the Current Affairs Group, Peter Pagnamenta, were true believers. BBC 2's *Newsnight* was widely regarded as a shining model of such a fusion. Another praised example, the *Six O'Clock News*, designed specifically to blend news and analysis, was scheduled on BBC 1 from 1985. Moreover, the furtherance of this trend was guaranteed when, shortly before the election was called, John Birt, a noted critic of conventional television journalism for its 'bias against understanding', was appointed Deputy Director-General of the BBC.

The parties

Nevertheless, BBC relations with the parties had gone through a bad patch, including several vociferous complaints of bias. Contending that its 1983 electoral support justified more extensive news coverage than it was getting, the Liberal–SDP Alliance applied for a judicial review in July 1986 (dropped after previously confidential BBC records on party appearances in programmes were released). There were also heavily publicized Conservative accusations of bias in BBC reporting of the American bombing of Libya from bases in Britain. Although no equally prominent complaint emanated from Labour, the Corporation presumed it could expect similar vigilance from a party for which retention of official Opposition status was a sheer survival matter. In the background, there was also anxiety over the BBC's institutional future. New communication technologies and a free market ideology had given the government opportunity and incentive to restructure British broadcasting in ways that might eventually imperil BBC funding and status. It could therefore be worrying if anything happened during the campaign to exacerbate anti-BBC sentiments among national politicians.

Moreover, BBC officials sensed that for all parties the name of the modern election game had become deliberate agenda setting: 'Everybody is making a determined attempt at agenda setting now; at a general election every party hopes to conduct debate on the issues advantageous to itself.' Apparently, it had been 'suggested quite heavily that the broadcasters would have to follow the issues laid down by the parties'. One party had 'said that they will only make their spokespersons available to speak on issues which they have decided are the proper ones'. Of course, campaign conflict with the parties over priority issues is not new, and nobody expected such demands to be taken to their literal extremes. Nevertheless, many in the BBC felt that attempts to set the television news agenda had become a more central, considered and concerted element in the strategies of all three parties than at any previous election.

THE PROGRAMME CONCEPT

Instead of pulling in its horns, the BBC resolved to pursue the 1983 path towards its more ambitious conclusion. The *Nine O'Clock News* would be doubled in length from 25 to 50 minutes. Of this, up to 35 minutes might normally be devoted to campaign materials, including news of the parties' activities; analytical commentary; regular reporting of opinion-poll developments; up to six three-party debates (each preceded by a filmed 'set-up' giving background on the issue to be discussed); interviews with leading politicians; and up to eight film reports on key issues and how the campaign was being received by voters in the country. For these purposes, a generous near-£2 million budget was set aside, and an unprecedented migration from Current Affairs was arranged. Compared with the transfer in 1983 of only two presenters and two producers, in 1987, in addition to David Dimbleby (presenter), John Cole (Political Editor) and Peter Snow (poll reporter), the *Nine O'Clock* newsroom would be filled with 'doctoral fire-power' – a veritable army of Current Affairs producers stripped from other programmes. Five reporter-producer and camera teams would also be brought over to make longer films under its own assignment editor. The Institute for Fiscal Studies was commissioned to prepare a factual guide to economic and financial issues that might feature in the campaign, and an Institute expert would be regularly on hand for back-up information and advice. A similar briefing on how to interpret opinion polls, their methods, uses and limitations, was also distributed to the team.

According to pre-campaign interviews with the planners, four considerations shaped this far-reaching approach. First, focusing analysis on prime news points and giving news an explanatory surround was the way that journalism was moving in the BBC anyhow: 'It is true that this is a one-off exercise for this election; but it is also bound to be seen as a pilot to determine how these systems might interrelate with each other in the future.'

Second, a News and Current Affairs merger did not have to be like a shot-gun wedding; with proper planning and ample resources it could work well. Third, executives aimed to redress the imbalance in pre-planning priorities, whereby at previous elections great attention had been given to the results programme but 'very little proportionately to how the campaign coverage, which could help determine the ultimate outcome on Polling Day, would be presented'. Fourth, there was a strongly asserted public service principle, holding that at election time more of what *Newsnight* usually offered a minority audience on BBC 2 should be made available to the mass audience on BBC 1.

But would that audience stay the solid course plotted for it? We were struck by the planners' unanimous refusal to be deflected by fears of 'election overkill':

> When people complain that there is too much of something, they are perhaps best interpreted as saying that what they are getting is not on the right lines for them. The privilege of democracy obtains in only thirty-nine countries, of which we are one. We are bloody lucky to have carried into our living rooms a large amount of material showing what politicians are saying and prioritizing when competing for votes.

How, then, would the 1987 operation overcome the weaknesses of its 1983 predecessor?

First, there would be more lead time to plan in the light of anticipated problems. Thus, the programme's Editor and Deputy Editor were designated as early as autumn 1986, charged to think through questions of staffing, equipment and editorial policy. Second, steps to ensure smooth teamwork would be taken. 'Ecumenical figures' were appointed as Editor (Tony Hall) and Deputy Editor (Paul Norris), each having previously worked in both the News and Current Affairs Departments. They brought relatively youthful producers and reporters into the team, less likely to be wedded to separatist philosophies of News or Current Affairs. A clearly defined editorial structure was established, giving the editor responsibility for all *Nine O'Clock News* output. A more unified programming style without an election 'ghetto' was envisaged. Third, the entire team was dedicated to exclusive *Nine O'Clock News* use, in contrast to 1983 when many individuals also worked for the lunch-time and early evening bulletins.

EXECUTION

How did these intentions fare in the heat of the actual campaign?

Plan and performance

On the whole, the team accomplished what it set out to do, deviating little from the original plan. The aim of giving a high and guaranteed priority to election coverage was adhered to throughout the three and a half weeks. Typically, the programme opened with election news (only rarely leading on some other national or international story), and 35 minutes were spent on campaign material. Even when it was learned that the audience had fallen sharply in the first week, the team stood its ground.

It is true that there was some learning on the job, but most of the resulting adjustments were minor. First, the notion of the programme as a 'seamless web' had to be abandoned in the first week as unacceptably top heavy. Yielding 35 minutes of unrelieved election coverage, it was decided to break this up into a tripartite pattern, signposting for viewers what kind of material was coming up next. Thereafter, part I was largely devoted to the 'essential election news of the day', part II to main non-election news and part III (about 22 minutes nightly) to items of campaign news 'development, discussion, reflection and analysis', including debates and interviews, longer films, and opinion-poll reports. Second, a way of treating part I election news more analytically evolved during the campaign. This fell to John Cole, who occasionally delivered a short essay, weaving together party press conference or hustings material to identify a key contrast between the parties. Third, in the event, two of the eight pre-commissioned films on which much thought and production effort had been expended – on 'Inner Cities' and 'Divided Britain' – were not screened.

Team working

The determination to run a smooth election-coverage ship was fully realized. Most team members showed enthusiasm for the new approach, and no 1983-like storms erupted. Factors favouring harmony may have included recruitment (bringing in likely sympathizers); more time for pre-campaign planning and trial; the Editor's firm but unabrasive leadership style; and a more congenial working space than the cramped 'bunker' of 1983, including (a 1987 innovation) personal recourse for every team member to a battery of word processors, strung along six bench-like desks in the main election newsroom.

ELECTION ROLES OF TELEVISION JOURNALISTS

From our 1983 observation and interviews, four different notions emerged of the roles that television journalists should play when covering a campaign: prudential; reactive; conventionally journalistic; and analytical (see Chapter 11 for their definition and elaboration). We also reported in 1983 that, of these perspectives, the analytical role had proved 'most difficult to sustain effectively', while the 'coverage mode' of the conventional journalists 'seemed more dominant than in any previous British campaign'.

Considered in these terms, the 1987 approach was very different – predominantly *Reactive plus Analytical*, pursued more or less back to back. Thus, we were struck by the much reduced influence of the 'conven-tionally journalistic' mentality on the making of the programme. Com-pared with 1983, there was much less headline chasing, less seeking after the sensational, less dismissal of overly sober political material, less drive to fasten onto what was 'new' and what might be the 'bull point' for the top story of the day.

We were also impressed with the strenuous efforts made to ensure that the debates and interviews of part III secured constructive contributions from the participating politicians. Typically, David Dimbleby spent 4–5 hours daily just preparing this segment of the programme. He was plied with a great deal of background information on the issue to be discussed, including details of party stands. Formulations of probing questions were offered, hashed over and revised. Even dummy runs, with producers role-playing the politicians, were conducted. In addition, a filmed 'set-up' was carefully prepared to precede most exchanges. As explained, its aim:

> was to dispense in the preamble with the factual ground of an issue, so as to enable the discussion to concentrate on the real questions that belonged to it. So much time can be wasted when all the politicians do is trade their pet versions of appropriate figures, slanted to their own sides of an issue . . . . So the main purpose is to clear the ground before getting down to the nitty-gritty of the issue at stake in an area of debate.

The debates themselves were often organized more as a series of three separate one-on-one interviews (Dimbleby to the Conservative, to the Labour spokesperson, to the Alliance representative) than as a discussion, because in a more free exchange (it was feared), somebody might try to hog the available time or one or more participants might wander off the point.

In 1987 we also became aware of yet another view of the television journalist's campaign role, one we had not previously noticed, although it is quite widely held by American political correspondents. On this view, now that the bulk of election news is carefully pre-packaged for the cameras, those who relay such events are under an obligation to open viewers' eyes to the manipulation of the underlying message. In a BBC reporter's words:

> Thinking of the campaign as it is organized by the political parties, all we can do is point out that things do not happen by accident. It is not a mere whim for Kinnock to have chosen a red rose as the party's symbol, to have selected a certain passage of Brahms for repetition . . . . What we should do in this context is to point out the degree to which deliberate campaign management goes on and what the principal managers hope that viewers will see and will not see.

And when we asked why television journalists should try to expose such practices, he replied:

> Television is such a passive medium that people might often just sit before it and let the way in which the election is presented just wash over them . . . . But we can see behind that and are in a position to show how that has got where it is. It is important to show that the campaign is being fought in a way that campaign managers want it to be fought, which may not be in the interest of viewers and voters.

Thus, the tendency of American reporters to 'disdain' the very news they are presenting could be increasing in this country as well. In both systems, the practice seems to rest on: (1) the assumption of viewer gullibility in the face of party propaganda in television news; (2) a belief that workers in television are well placed to see how campaign management is conducted and have a responsibility to convey that understanding to the viewing public; and (3) a fear that if they do not expose such campaign machinations, they will become merely passive purveyors of party propaganda instead of independent journalists. The recent growth of such attitudes here presumably reflects an impression that the British state of the art of professional electioneering for television is now approximating its more pervasive and thoroughgoing entrenchment in the United States.

One consequence of the predominantly Reactive-Analytical formula of 1987 was that access to the audience was almost monopolized by politicians and journalists, particularly since so much of part III was devoted to debates and interviews. Although such concentration is natural, it can shut out the concerns of other interests, unless they happen to be voiced by either of the more 'authorized' election communicators. Apparently this problem was raised in a News and Current Affairs meeting early in the campaign, when it was suggested that programmes from departments other than Current Affairs – an arts programme, a science programme or a religious programme – might occasionally step into the gap, looking at the election from the standpoint of other interests at stake. The objections were revealing. One was the difficulty of achieving a proper balance of contributors (say, between left-wing and right-wing doctors). The other concerned the BBC's control machinery for ensuring that politically sensitive programmes are made by people used to assessing the judgements involved, which would not apply to producers in other departments, who might veer dangerously off course. According to the participant, the conclusion was that, 'In an election period it should only be the politicians who regularly get on the air'.

THE 'AWKWARD PARTIES'

So what were the producers' relations with their predominant campaign sources like? How did this affect their work on the expanded election news?

External relations

In one respect, BBC–politician relations were not so troubled as expected. The more threatening climate of the mid-1980s was *not* a prelude to a campaign of attempted intimidation and blazing rows. Nevertheless, the producers we observed often seemed as if surrounded by 'awkward parties', whose sensitivities and reactions made their jobs more difficult and less pleasant than they might have been. Party forces were rather like a set of heavy clouds, hovering in unrelieved grey over the Television Centre, that rarely erupted into actual storms. Producers understood the reasons for this:

> For the parties it's a matter of life and death; hence the constant horse trading over who will appear and on what terms . . . . They are also more aware of the tricks of our trade now – for example, over how interviews are edited – and that how they are exercised could put them at a disadvantage.

Broadcaster perspectives on campaigning politicians seemed to be shaped by three dominant perceptions. First, they regarded the parties as determined would-be agenda-setters. As a newsreader put it, 'The really extraordinary and different thing about this campaign is how persistent the efforts of the parties have been to set the news agenda in their own terms.' At one point we listed the strategies of attempted party agenda control that had been drawn to our attention as follows:

> Co-ordinating a leader's activities to reiterate a chosen theme or issue throughout the day – centring the morning press conference on it, symbolizing it in an afternoon walkabout and addressing a party rally in the evening about it.
> Putting only one or two leading speakers on the hustings on a given night to limit the cameras' ability to go to somebody who would not be voicing the chosen message of the day.
> Declining interviews on subjects off the party's preferred agenda or making them particularly difficult to arrange.
> Holding more than one press conference on the same theme on a given day, addressing it from different angles or through different spokespersons.
> Attempting to put a rival party on the defensive by raising a series of questions about an issue unfavourable to it for journalists to press on it.

Systematic complaining along the lines of: Why are you proposing to deal with so-and-so when such-and-such is so much more important? Why have you been leading with our opponents' favoured issues more often than ours?

Second, the parties were regarded as ever-vigilant monitors of broadcasters' news choices and angles. When we asked a reporter assigned to a party entourage what was most noteworthy about his role, for example, to our surprise he replied:

The public scrutiny of what we do. As journalists we make certain judgements, but the pressures on us can be enormous. This is especially the case now after two or three years of ever-growing party scrutiny of BBC affairs. Everything you say and do you know is quite intently being monitored by the Labour and Conservative parties. This does not distract me from doing what I think I should do, but we are very conscious of it.

Third, the parties were perceived as moaners, continually commenting negatively on broadcasters' intentions and output:

Questioning of our political judgements by the political parties is par for the course. When visiting —— Party headquarters the other day, I was told that we had been leading on the —— Party's position and issues more often than theirs. Clearly this was designed to keep me on my toes – and I suspect with deliberate intent. I start conversations with them on the assumption that everything I say may later be held against me.

Internal restraints

Campaign coverage is also circumscribed by various internally accepted limits. For one thing, the broadcasters were ambivalent over their own agenda-setting role. If to some degree inevitable, it should be secondary to party agendas, transcending them only in clearly justifiable circumstances. For another, pains were taken to ensure something of a party balance in top-of-news story choices. Again the outlook was ambivalent:

We would want to be driven by journalistic imperatives – so that if an issue developed a strong element of charge and counter-charge or had elements of ambiguity or lack of frankness – then we would want to follow that. On the other hand, you have got this constraint of being seen to be fair, and that has to do not only with the amount of time that is allotted to presentations by speakers from all the parties but also with what they want to get onto centre stage.

Yet another example concerned use of the term, 'tactical voting'. Realizing that TV '87 was a 'get-the-Tories-out' campaign, programme editors were instructed not to introduce the notion of 'tactical voting' unless it emerged from the players themselves.

A focus of particularly close attention concerned presentation of opinion-poll findings. Well in advance of the election this was noted by policy-makers as a 'booby-trapped' area. Because the 1983 experience showed that the parties could seek to generate campaign momentum from interpretations of opinion-poll findings, it was decided that care should be taken to ensure that nothing the BBC did could be unduly exploited for such a purpose. Consequently an elaborate policy was evolved, including the following elements:

> Full and regular reporting of published opinion-poll results, avoiding sporadic coverage that might inadvertently favour one or another party. Attempts to inform the audience throughout the campaign about polling methods, such as sample sizes, fieldwork dates, error margins, etc. No BBC commissioning of national voting intention polls. Given the large number of polls already available, 'If our result told the same story it would be redundant; but if it told a different story, it could be a worry to us'.
>
> BBC polls to be commissioned only to gain specific journalistically interesting information not otherwise available – as in a poll of young voters or by inserting questions into a Gallup survey to elicit electoral responses to certain issues and personalities. And after some hesitation, a *Newsnight* proposal to conduct a panel survey of sixty selected marginal seats was accepted on the understanding that, while tracking trends in such constituencies, it could not be extrapolated to the national scene.

This last decision, however, was responsible for the most difficult internal controversy of the election, including much argument and revision of scripts. The problem arose because in the third week of the campaign the *Newsnight* panel produced a result that seemed to foreshadow a 'hung parliament' if generalized to the country at large. Whereas those responsible for presenting the result in the *Nine O'Clock News* and *Newsnight* wished to underline this prospect, senior management insisted on adherence to the original understanding that the poll could not serve as a national projection. In the end, the latter prevailed, and the former had to resort to tortuous verbal circumlocutions when presenting the story.

Philosophically intriguing was the case of those two non-screened film reports on 'Inner Cities' and 'Divided Britain'. Because they had not made it into the early coverage, they could not, we were told, have been shown later in the campaign:

This would appear to be bringing to the top of the agenda an issue that would not have been justified by the events of the day. It would have been easier to justify such a film – showing the BBC standing back and setting an issue in a context that had only been touched on by politicians – early in the campaign. Sensitivity increases the later you get into the campaign. It could have been interpreted as an Opposition issue had it been screened in the last week.

The explanation illustrates how the meaning of what reporters do or say changes, not because of the actions or words themselves, but due to the context, the timing and the surrounding political atmosphere. What could be seen as political analysis at one moment or in one situation is seen as a political statement at another.

The consequences

It should not be concluded from the above that the programme makers merely handed the television campaign over to the politicians to shape to their own images. There were a number of ways in which the *Nine O'Clock News* sought to be more than a party platform:

The forum function regularly performed by part III, particularly the care taken in preparing for the interviews and debates that featured so centrally in it, including the preceding 'set-ups'.
The scope given to John Cole to fashion think-piece essays, drawing on material from party events, not to reproduce them so much as to use them to underscore some fundamental contrast of party approach. A decision to limit party walkabout material largely to the prefatory parts of correspondents' packages, which instead would focus chiefly on evening rallies and speeches.
The overall aim of situating party statements and events within thematic and explanatory contexts.

But there was also a risk that such a pile-up of external scrutiny and internal inhibition would make the campaign coverage task seem:

More worrying	I would always refer upwards to protect my back.
	Many people are worried and looking over their shoulders.
Less fun	Now more things seem to be governed by rules, and producers have mainly to think about how to organize things so that what they have done fits some notion of the rules that are supposed to apply . . . . All this makes the process less interesting, both for us and probably for viewers as well.
More delicate	It means that everything has to be watertight.
Less meaningful	There is this tendency where we react to the parties and feed off them, and they react to us or feed off us. It is rather like my son's hamster in a cage. With advanced

> technology ... it is as if the hamster's wheel can now spin
> faster ... and is in a transparent ball ... through which he
> can see the world. Yet the hamster's horizons are still con-
> fined to the same limited diameters as before.

WAS IT WORTH IT?

Television and democracy

For a quarter of a century television has exerted a formative influence on British public debate. Keen to reach its mass audience, politicians and pressure groups have adapted their message-making ways to the medium's cameras, interviewers and brisk rhetorical conventions. Although the pending era of multi-channel broadcasting, break-up of the BBC–ITV duopoly and audience fragmentation may eventually reduce its role, in 1987 this was still pivotal. It accordingly remains appropriate to consider the criteria by which the campaign contributions of television to democracy may be evaluated.

First, since 'Election campaigns, for all their faults, may be the major learning experience of democratic polities' (Katz, 1974), television coverage should be designed to inform and enlighten those following it. By this standard, the makers of the 1987 *Nine O'Clock News* passed with flying colours. They succumbed neither to cynicism about viewers' interest levels nor to perceptions of television as essentially an entertainment medium. Compared with the American networks' days at the election horse races (Patterson, 1980), their unflagging commitment to the provision of a substantive diet was impressive.

Second, election television should serve as a forum for a national dialogue about the future of society and be designed to constrain politicians to address the public in as illuminating terms as possible. Here too the *Nine O'Clock News* earns high marks for the numerous debates and interviews screened in part III. Although politicians often complain that the mass media tend to ignore their more serious contributions to public debate, in this case the news team took the initiative to seek them out.

Third, journalists should aim to perform an accountability function, framing and putting the questions for which politicians should be answerable to voters in the light of their records, promises and campaign statements. Our observation suggests that the thorough back-up and preparation behind the part III debates and interviews were designed with precisely this end in mind, seeking suitable questions for David Dimbleby to ask and strategies to oblige the politicians to answer them.

Judged by such democratic criteria, then, it is difficult to fault the programme, which treated the 1987 campaign not as a parade of events or an elaborate game but as a 'process of critical choice for the nation' (see Chapter 11).

The audience verdict

Although most of those associated with the venture, or in sympathy with its original objectives, were proud of its achievements, a few News Division members criticized the programme as boring: 'They haven't taken the trouble to make it interesting; and if they fail in that, they will lose viewers hand over fist.'

Did that happen? The answer is, 'Yes, to a not insignificant degree'.[2] Whereas in the four weeks before the campaign, the average *Nine O'Clock News* audience was 7.6 million nightly, for the four weeks of the campaign, it fell by a quarter to an average of 5.7 million. Details for separate time segments suggest that much of the loss reflected the fact that fewer viewers than before the campaign watched the news from the outset; that there was a certain amount of switching off or over in the first half-hour of the programme; and that a further slight decline took place in the last 20 minutes. Moreover, although the *Newsnight* audience fell to a similar degree, ratings for the BBC's daytime news programmes all held steady.

Caution is necessary in ascribing responsibility for these results specifically to the *Nine O'Clock News* model. As summer approaches, people tend to watch less television; ITV scheduled highly competitive programming from 9 to 10 p.m. during the campaign; and on many evenings the *Nine O'Clock News* followed a party election broadcast. Of these factors, the last could have been most significant, but its influence is impossible to calculate exactly, and the most plausible interpretation is that an appreciable number of usual *Nine O'Clock News* viewers decided not to watch it. That conclusion is somewhat mitigated by the fact that ITV's *News at Ten*, which was extended by only 5 minutes during the campaign, also suffered audience erosion though not to the same degree. From a four-week pre-campaign average of 6.2 million, it fell by 11 per cent to a 5.6 million campaign-period average.

In assessing this record of audience response, four considerations should be borne in mind.

First, the success or failure of an ambitious effort of this kind should not be evaluated by audience ratings alone. The net contribution to public enlightenment of a more popular programme with different content might have been appreciably less than the *Nine O'Clock News* achieved in 1987.

Second, even when judged in audience exposure terms, the daily ratings should not be the only criterion, since many viewers were probably exposed from time to time to the programme's more analytical style. Despite lower average ratings, its cumulative reach over the full campaign period could have been quite substantial. Moreover, those who stayed with it were apparently not just Current Affairs buffs. A breakdown of the programme's audience for pre-campaign and campaign weeks shows no significant change in age, sex or social class terms.

Third, the fall in the *News at Ten* audience suggests that some viewers at least were not rejecting the BBC format specifically but whatever they found unsatisfactory and unpalatable about the campaign on television at large.

After all these considerations have been allowed for, however, it must be asked, fourth, whether the audience decline could have been checked and more done to sustain viewers' interest. A BBC executive told us as early as January 1987 that the programme makers should 'think back from the viewer and not go about things simply from the standpoint of organizational dispositions', but while with the team ourselves, we were exposed to few signs of people saying to themselves or others, 'How can we make this relevant and meaningful to the average viewer?'

This has nothing to do with élitism. Rather, the viewer as a point of reference for producers becomes remote because during a hectic campaign so many other pressing and immediate preoccupations block him or her from sight. Although much of this is inevitable, in 1987 the resulting distractions may have been compounded by the political climate of the time, including all the external pressures on the producers to watch their steps and the internal concerns to avoid booby-traps. Although such an influence cannot be measured, it cannot have been beneficial in the sense of encouraging and helping broadcasters to 'think back from the viewer'. After all, it still holds true that, 'whether viewers feel that an election has been interesting and informative to follow will depend in great part on the enterprise and imagination that producers have been able to give to its coverage' (Blumler, Gurevitch and Ives, 1978).

Chapter 13

Struggles for meaningful election communication (1992)[1]

In many competitive democracies, election campaign communication is increasingly tension-laden. Three sectors of heightened conflict may be identified.

First, inter-communicator struggle – politicians vs. journalists – for control over news agendas has intensified. Before and during the British general election of 1992, the increased professionalization (some termed it 'Americanization') of the major parties' approaches to campaign publicity had put a special spin on this tussle.

Second, intra-journalistic dilemmas have been sharpened. During the 1992 campaign, these took on a distinctive flavour at Britain's 'cornerstone' public broadcaster, the BBC – between being serious (focusing on the issues, informing electors, performing a democratic civic role) or responding to conventionally journalistic impulses (pursuit of the horse race, campaigners' gaffes and anything humanly dramatic); between recognizing campaigners' rights to set the terms of electoral choice and asserting journalists' autonomy to contribute to the debate; and between core journalistic norms of objectivity and impartiality and helping viewers to make sense of the issues and conflicting party claims. Moreover, the onset of structural changes in British broadcasting, shattering the BBC–ITV duopoly and raising questions about the future of the BBC after Charter renewal, had brought to the fore: a competitive dilemma, between providing more substantial coverage than Independent Television News (ITN) but risking falling behind it in audience appeal; as well as an identity dilemma, between serving a principled purpose and looking pragmatically to organizational survival.

Third, a chorus of doubts over the relationship between media-dominated election campaigning and democratic values has been approaching a crescendo in many ostensibly democratic societies (see Bennett, 1992; Buchanan, 1991; Entman, 1989; Jamieson, 1992; Patterson, 1993; Sabato, 1991; and Swanson, 1992). As Graber (1992, p. 25) concludes:

Although the canons of news reporting have remained unchanged for many decades, the news product has deteriorated when judged as a resource for public opinion formation. The information needs of citizens have skyrocketed in the age of the global society and the guardian state intrudes ever more deeply into personal and collective behaviors. The news media have not kept pace. That is why the paths of democracy and news have been diverging.

Much food for thought on all these tensions stemmed from our observation attachment on eight days during the 1992 campaign to BBC Television News, focused mainly on the Corporation's flagship bulletin, the *Nine O'Clock News*. We approached this occasion with two primary questions in mind: First, how have changes since 1987 in the British communication system (especially developments in political party publicity methods and the commercialization of ITN within ITV) affected the production of election news at the BBC? Second, what implications for public service coverage of election campaigns flow from the philosophy of John Birt (then the Corporation's Deputy Director-General and Director-General designate), whose influence was known to run strongly throughout BBC News and Current Affairs? Access for our research was exceptionally open and generous, including not only attendance at policy and editorial meetings, newsroom observation, and interviews with executives, editors, correspondents and producers, but also, for the first time, presence at a post-mortem meeting, where a dozen principals candidly reviewed their campaign performance a week after Polling Day.

In fact, when invited to voice our own assessment at the conclusion of that meeting, one of us summed up as follows: 'You did the best job of election coverage possible within the limits in which you had to operate.' Both the compliment and the qualification on it were sincere.

On the one hand, the public service spirit was vigorously alive in BBC News and Current Affairs and drove many impressively conceived endeavours to provide meaningful campaign coverage. Advance planning and personnel dispositions were set in train from spring 1991. For the daily output, a division of roles between News and *Newsnight*, more clear and satisfactory to all concerned than in 1987, was agreed: News, much fortified and deepened in its editorial resources and experience since the last election, was considered able to cover the campaign without the heavy Current Affairs imports thought necessary in 1983 and 1987; while *Newsnight* was expected to provide an arena of debate and more free-wheeling commentary than would be appropriate for News. Overall, a strong and purposive team had been assembled, working on closely collegial terms, even when discussing contested options – in marked contrast to the fierce splits that disrupted their 1983 counterparts (see Chapter 11).

On the other hand, the limits circumscribing such an effort, some externally imposed, some internally generated, were also formidable. In certain respects they appeared more constraining than at any previous election reporting operation we have observed.

THE PUBLIC SERVICE APPROACH

Changes afoot in British broadcasting may have had a unifying influence on BBC journalists. They shared a public service perspective on their election mission and presumed that they primarily bore its attendant obligations. Three propositions reflect BBC applications of this idea to the 1992 election:

1 *Public service implies giving extensive, prominent and well-resourced coverage to the campaign.* Consequently, the *Nine O'Clock News*, normally 30 minutes long, was extended to 45–50 minutes and given a three-part structure: part I to report the day's campaign news; part II to report the day's non-election news; and part III to present a range of more reflective approaches to the campaign, including pre-prepared films, often a report on the latest opinion-poll results, and a two-way exchange on the overall politics of the current situation between the newsreader and the BBC's authoritative Political Editor (John Cole).

2 *Public service implies that the coverage should be predominantly serious and substantial.* The more conventionally journalistic assumption, that politics is essentially boring and therefore must be spiced with jolting news-value angles, was conspicuously absent. As a producer put it, 'The old newsroom attitude of knowing in your gut that something demands a certain kind of attention no longer prevails.' One producer even confessed that they were prepared to test 'viewers' boredom thresholds' to do justice to the campaign.

There was one major exception to all this in the devotion of a regular slot in part III to a jazzy, unashamedly horse-racist, graphics-animated coverage of opinion poll findings. The most costly element in the programme (for the graphics and the back-up research), it was justified on the grounds that (a) 'In part this election *is* a horse race, and I'm sure that's how many viewers regard it' and (b) 'It's something that leading politicians themselves now give tremendous weight to', a significant campaign factor, then, on which viewers should be kept informed.

Nevertheless, even this feature was surrounded by reservations, laid out in a printed set of guidelines, that were unique to the BBC. The BBC was not to sponsor any voting intention polls of its own.[2] Undue weight should never be given to single poll results, however spectacular, since they might not reflect a trend. And poll coverage should be confined to part III.

3 *Public service implies that the coverage should be rationalistic – based, that is, on much prior thought and considered planning.* This proposition particularly reflected the influence on BBC journalism of John Birt.

What did this involve? A Current Affairs executive described it in terms of a paramount 'mission to explain'. This should apply not only to weekly public affairs programmes but also to daily journalism for the mass audience so that its need for information would not be shortchanged by the mere packaging of daily events and party statements. This required prior consideration at editorial level of the implications of the most significant current developments to which the audience should be alerted, drawing on strong resources of 'in-house expertise'. Another feature of this philosophy was its stress on *responsible* journalism. As one informant put it, people should have 'opportunities to check the suitability of what they are providing' and guidelines for gauging what might count as 'suitable' in problematic situations.

The Birtian approach, then, values philosophic clarity, managerial leadership and creation of a team aware of shared purposes and standards. In line with this, since 1987, a merger of the BBC's formerly separate News and Current Affairs Divisions had been completed; many individuals with Current Affairs backgrounds were appointed to leading positions in News programmes; journalists unable to work to the prevailing outlook were weeded or eased out; four large and well-funded specialist units – for Westminster politics, foreign affairs, business and economic affairs, and social policy, respectively – were set up to serve all factual programmes; and steps were taken (e.g. the occasional convening of seminars to review programming and the handling of critical situations as well as to anticipate forthcoming ones) to fashion and induce acceptance of what some termed a 'new journalistic culture' at the BBC. As a senior executive told us, 'I think you'll find we've got an exceptionally confident team here, particularly sure of their values.' Consequently (in the words of an executive from another department), 'The election is being covered by people who have now worked together for such a long time that they practically approach their tasks and problems as if of one mind'.

Given this 'upmarket' drift and certain contrary developments at Independent Television News (Semetko, Scammell and Nossiter, 1994), it was perhaps natural that how ITN was covering the election often seemed on BBC journalists' minds. Transcripts of *News at Ten* were available to Editors for perusal the next morning. A newsreader, noting that *News at Ten* had not been extended for the campaign, commented that:

> The gap between the BBC with its public service orientation and ITN with its commercial one is undeniably widening. We are entering a situation where we will be the sole repository of public service values in News and Current Affairs.

ITN's performance was accordingly a frequent source of comment. Thus, it was variously said, ITN:

'Have an ability to go for the jugular.'
'Are sometimes more intelligible when dealing with economic affairs.'
'Lack our more analytical approach and seem to do more channelling
of party propaganda on to the audience.'
'Seem to have a more relaxed attitude to internal balance.'
'Has gone tabloid; I sense their heart's not in it.'

Findings from the Broadcasting Research Department, showing that the
Nine O'Clock News audience had not fallen disastrously and that the BBC
was rated more highly than ITN on a number of campaign coverage
attributes (for fairness, accuracy, informativeness, trustworthiness, etc.)
were therefore welcome to all.

THE CONSTRAINTS

In 1992 campaign practice, however, the BBC's public service approach
seemed to be circumscribed by five major sources of limitation.

Party publicity management

The most pivotal of these limitations was the thoroughgoing professionalization of the parties' strategic approaches to their media campaigns. In
a brief encounter with John Birt in the newsroom one day, the first author
defined this as the intensification of publicity competition, concerted
efforts to dominate the news agenda, increased reliance on specialist
political consultants and campaign managers, and a ceaseless determination to cover all publicity-relevant bases, leaving nothing to chance.
BBC executives and journalists were certainly keenly aware of being
surrounded by highly professionalized party teams, immersed daily in the
message environment they were creating largely for television news. In
the words of one:

> There has never before been the same degree of self-consciousness
> about this complex of phenomena. Everyone is now walking into this,
> knowing to an agonizing, navel-scrutinizing extent how the two pieces
> of the process are relating to each other.

Much was said in this connection about the parties' morning press
conferences, which for the first time started daily as early as 7.30 a.m.
An Editor perceived these conferences as closely controlled affairs
through 'rules preventing anything happening because no supplementaries
are allowed, an exercise in damage limitation all round'. An executive
saw them as theme-setters, controlling politicians' other comments on the
day concerned:

> It seemed the debate during the day had been set off more by press

conference statements than by interviews. It was as if the party strategists had laid down what would be said in interviews by virtue of their preceding [press conference] presentations.

Moreover, as the campaign progressed, the newspeople found the parties concentrating on a limited set of issues, only those that each calculated would best advance their cause with voters. There were also signs of Conservative adoption of a 'hardball' campaign ethic, based on the assumption, accepted by many US campaign consultants, that the quickest and most effective way to act on the balance of public opinion is to mount a strongly negative attack on one's opponent.

Such single-minded party professionalization posed three main problems for the broadcasters. Probably the most vexing and subtle was: *how to make a significantly independent contribution of their own to the campaign, without intruding improperly into what should be a choice for voters between whatever the political parties were offering in their own terms.* Key figures in News and Current Affairs keenly resented the fact that a rash of analyses had appeared in the serious press, mounting what one executive termed 'a fashionable attack' on TV journalists as little more than the parties' tame poodles, passively relaying to viewers whatever soundbites politicians chose to craft and whatever photo-opportunities party managers chose to stage. In fact, BBC journalists had engaged since 1987 in a 'great debate' (a participant's term) over how much coverage photo-opportunities and reports from correspondents with party leaders on the campaign trail should receive. Some playing down of such materials without rejecting them altogether seemed to be the 1992 compromise over this.

The BBC's core response to this problem was a two-sided formula: its campaign role should be *'reactive but with value added'*. It was to be reactive in the sense of being obliged to report the parties' main campaign initiatives day by day. This duty derived from the BBC's long-standing sense of itself as a creature and servant of British parliamentary democracy, which is organized as a confrontation between Government and Opposition in the House of Commons. The BBC's role was also to be 'value-added', however, by putting party statements in a context helpful to viewers. As the Editor of Television News expressed it, 'The parties are entitled to campaign in their way, and we are not entitled to ignore it. But we are entitled to put it in perspective.' The coverage's 'bread and butter', he went on, was what the parties were saying and doing on a given day. 'It would be a negation of our role to refuse politicians that kind of direct access [, but] we are not to be used simply as the politicians' newsagents' windows without their claims and arguments being tested in some way.'

But what more specifically did the value-added element amount to?

For the News team it included two main kinds of contributions: one unmasking, the other informing. The first was to open viewers' eyes to what the parties were up to tactically – to expose their publicity intentions and why they were saying and doing what was coming across on the screen. In the words of a Current Affairs executive, 'One thing the News people have done more of in this campaign is not only to report what the parties are doing, but also to give an assessment of their reasons for doing it.' Of course, such a response to candidate electioneering has long been prominent in American campaign coverage (Blumler and Gurevitch, 1991). BBC producers, however, considered they should indulge in such a vein of comment only in moderation, stopping somewhere short of a full-throated 'disdaining' of party-fashioned election news. 'One shouldn't be so sceptical and derisive of the process [one said] that you undermine it – for you're part of the process itself.'

The other value-added contribution was to call as often as possible on the BBC's large cadre of specialist correspondents 'to provide [as one explained] information on the basis of which one can come back to the hustings argument with some perspective for judging it'. Whenever possible, then, the specialist voice would either be interwoven with what the parties were saying on some issue or would be incorporated into an informative follow-up package after a report on what the parties had said. In addition, the notion of a so-called 'Election Briefing' item was conceived 'to create' (as one put it) 'enough space so that, depending on the agenda of campaign news that day, we can take a half-step back, saying they have been going on about such-and-such and then asking what is the most important information which this fits'. Another producer elaborated:

> If we are supposed to have a role in an informed democracy, that means trying to present the arguments as politicians would choose to do (and giving them the right to do that) but to pull things together in a context laced by the information you have to share with the audience.

A second problem arising from party professionalization was the limited agenda of issues on which the 1992 campaign pivoted, comprising mainly (a) economic management issues, especially the recession and how it might be overcome, (b) the parties' taxation and spending policies, (c) the future of two social policy areas, health and education, and (in the last week) (d) constitutional reform. As a producer summed up, 'The parties rarely stepped out of the circle of the economy and social affairs.'

Although the parties were concentrating thereby on central issues vital to electors, many others of some significance (one Editor seemed to have a checklist in his mind) were almost entirely ignored – for example, the environment, relations with Europe, defence and security, the rising crime rate and local government finance. Admittedly, some of the dozen films prepared for presentation in part III were designed to deal with such less emphasized issues. But when asked whether any of these contributions had entered into the public debate, the responsible executive producer unhesitatingly replied: 'No. If you want to do that, you get famous people to say provocative things. The decision not to have politicians in these items ensured they were low-key.'

Although the third problem for BBC newscasters of advanced party professionalization is more difficult to define than the others, something characteristic of the 1992 campaign could be missed if one failed to identify it. A highly organized and controlled campaign can seem to lack some of the essential ingredients of attractive and meaningful communication: spontaneity, a bit of unpredictability, a sense of adventure that could lead to discovery, a sense of wrestling with reality instead of always trading smoothly in appearances and perceptions. As an Editor told us, 'The parties are so effectively buttoned up, there ain't no surprises.' As an executive concurred, 'With so much planning on their part and ours, there was almost no room for the unexpected. It sometimes threatened to denude the campaign, taking the juice out of it.'

Institutionalization of complaining

A second potentially limiting influence in the newscasters' environment was the frequency with which party representatives telephoned programme editors directly, commenting on or complaining about how a bulletin had presented the election news. Already almost a built-in systemic feature of British campaign communication in 1987 (see Chapter 12), by 1992 this had developed yet further.

A reason why this can happen in the British system is that senior BBC executives regard it as legitimate. As one told us, 'We don't want to convey the impression that if people complain, it's pressure and shouldn't happen.'

Some new wrinkles introduced into the process in 1992 included: making a complaint after the 6 p.m. news in the hope of inducing some change in the 9 p.m. bulletin; drawing attention to some weakness in something just advanced by another party and offering to provide a high-level speaker for an item on it; and sending a round-robin letter to all programme editors, warning them to be careful about being taken in by some tactic that a rival party was expected to try out. Some of the party comments we were told about were so detailed that the phrase 'backstop editing' occurred to us to characterize the role being assumed, as if politicians were casting themselves as makers of superior news judgements.

It is impossible to determine whether such tactics had any influence, particularly since, in contrast to the aggrieved and depressed response of the 1987 team to party complaining, the typical reaction in 1992 seemed more one of resigned acceptance of it as a now entrenched part of the systemic game. As a recent recruit to BBC journalism explained:

> You go through a process of brutalization in arguments with the Conservatives and with Labour. At first you lost sleep over it. But when it happened again, and again, and again, you realized that this is politics and not the end of the world.

Taking objectivity to an extreme?

At times we were inclined to apply this label to the third type of limitation we noticed, internally imposed of course. This is the principle that nothing the BBC does should be construable as having tended to influence a significant partisan outcome. For example:

> A specialist correspondent said that if she unearthed a 'shock-horror scandal' in a public service, she would hold the story until it had appeared somewhere else.
> An executive criticized a news bulletin for having presented a heated press conference exchange as like 'a disaster for the government', adding 'We have got to take a low-spin approach for preference to an event like that'.
> An executive cautioned that, when controversy erupts over economic statistics, editors should 'check with the Business Unit, think three times and don't go unattributed', but instead say, 'One party is using the figures this way and the other that way'.
> Care was sometimes counselled over the language of stories so they did not appear to support one side's perception of a controversy.

But two sets of dramatic opinion poll results – earlier in the campaign and again in the penultimate week – suggesting that Labour was opening up a sizeable voting intention lead, provoked exceptional tumult on this objectivity front. Whereas many members of the team wished to give them full attention in part I of the programme, this would have flouted the Corporation's guidelines (which were known to the parties), and there was much querying (some of it flippant) over when a clutch of results could be regarded as forming a trend. After references up a long chain of executive command, it was eventually decided that the poll news should not be mentioned in the bulletin's opening headlines, could be mentioned briefly in the newsreader's follow-up introduction to part I but would otherwise be relegated as a formed story to part III. A justification for drawing such a fine line was that a headlined mention 'would put the whole weight of the BBC behind it'.

Fairness run wild?

This is a possible label for the fourth source of limitation on BBC election news-makers. In addition to its statutory obligations, the BBC has always prided itself on its voluntary fidelity to the principle of fairness when covering party affairs, particularly during election campaigns. By 1992, however, the scope of this principle had seemingly been extended to a remarkably broad number of respects in which news treatment accorded the opposing parties might be compared:

The amount of time given in bulletins to recorded extracts of politicians' campaign statements (though not necessarily so closely stopwatched as in previous elections).
Place in the running order, especially frequency of leading the bulletin.
Balancing occasions when much more time is given to one Leader than another.
Week-by week scheduling of Leader interviews in programmes.
Reporting of second-string politician speeches.
Live reporting from press conferences.
'Equivalence of tone' in Leader trail reports.
Similarity of placement of favourable opinion poll results in the bulletin (i.e. reporting a restored Conservative lead in the same headlines, introduction, Part III pattern as previously for Labour, on the ground that 'We must be sensitive to a legitimate charge that we're not giving the same prominence to some possible Tory fightback as we did to Labour's lead last night').
Coverage of particularly newsworthy constituency candidates.
Complementarity in the framing by specialist correspondents of concluding assessments on some contested issue.

As one reporter put this last point: 'The need for balance in the specialist packages . . . is very different at election time and sometimes very frustrating. You always have to end up your piece with an anodyne thought.' All this explains why one of us remarked to a senior executive during the campaign that BBC election coverage seemed to have become ever more rule-related in recent years -- to which he agreed, only quibbling over 'rule-related', preferring 'guideline-related' instead.

Taking account of the combined impact of the last three limiting factors – non-stop party complaining, objectivity to an extreme, and fairness run wild – it seemed to us that BBC news producers were continually being encouraged to err on the side of caution. 'It's important not to put a foot wrong,' an executive advised Editors on the morning of a particularly virulent cross-party row. Many team members seemed to agree both that prudence was a 1992 watchword in the Corporation and that this was an advisable policy: 'I suppose we're a bit too safe, but it's as well to play it that way.' 'If this policy leads to accusations of being not daring and adventurous enough, so be it.' As a senior executive summed up: 'The thing I say to all our people is that: You are the most powerful source of information for most people, and you must expect this sort of thing. *But don't make mistakes that could give the critics ammunition.*'

Role of the audience

A final limitation on the 1992 coverage concerns the shadowy role that the audience seemed to play in it. Normatively, it was supposedly paramount, the ultimate source and beneficiary of public service, several of our informants said, 'It all comes down to what we do for the viewer and listener,' John Birt himself told one of us: 'If that is not our object and approach, it all loses point.' But audience needs and likely reactions tended to be assumed and taken for granted, reflecting perhaps the ease with which a rather Platonic (i.e. idealized) notion of the audience member can be incorporated into the ethos of public service provision. In other words, the audience was more of a concept than a real force. For one thing, it rarely entered into the editorial discussions we observed and overheard. Admittedly, it sometimes entered for reassurance – as on the occasions when tolerably favourable viewing figures and broad-gauge comparative assessments with ITV coverage were received and circulated throughout the team. But comprehension, received meanings and potentials for involvement were relatively neglected criteria of audience reception of the coverage.

In mitigation, it may be said that bringing the audience in as a real force is inherently difficult, because of its multiplicity of needs and diverse ways of tuning into political affairs. In 1992, however, the problem at the BBC may have been exacerbated by two more specific features of the campaign coverage situation, noticed by some informants themselves. One was a technological factor mentioned by a more critically minded producer – the isolating and insulating influence of editors' and journalists' dependence on newsroom computers:

We're all linked nowadays to computers, and we can tell the story without moving out of the room – just by logging on. If something doesn't exist in our computers, it hasn't happened. The outside world has to come to us through the computer. . . . The issues we decide are important from day to day may well be isolated [therefore] from the issues that are important 'out there'. . . . There is so much on the computer that you can't keep track of it all, so you try to fit it into your agenda.

Another factor, rooted in the inter-institutional web of mutual dependencies among politicians and journalists, was mentioned by a producer after the election, when discussing the failure to detect a late-campaign opinion shift to the Conservatives. Relating this to 'the lack of an authentic ears-to-the-ground dimension to our coverage', he added:

> We were in no position with our dispositions to understand what was moving voters. We were almost entirely focused on the press conferences, the Leaders on the trail, reporting how the campaign was going, as if it were primarily a media–party-based affair.'

THE PRODUCERS TAKE STOCK

We were impressed with the post-mortem review meeting we attended, which showed the team in a somewhat different light from how they had appeared during the campaign. Although pride in certain achievements occasionally came to the fore, a note of professional self-satisfaction rarely surfaced. Instead a range of important coverage issues was aired in terms that demonstrated how much the participants had thought and cared about them; and speakers did not hesitate to propose different ways of conceiving and implementing their roles 'next time' from those assumed in 1992. Debate was lively, and divergent views were expressed, though without heat, as if reflecting individual differences of emphasis rather than factional positions. If there was a hint of underlying structure to the differences, it may have been between *utopians* and *realists* – with the former presuming that coverage another time could be significantly different in certain respects from 1992, especially for the assertion of a more independent broadcaster contribution, and the latter occasionally drawing attention to reasons why certain features were likely to abide.

To convey something of the character of the occasion, we set out below the main issues addressed under five headings, illustrated with a few things that were said about each of them:

1 *Commitments to campaign trail assignments and reports*
   'Correspondents assigned to the leaders are not really in a position to question searchingly what is happening there. Do we need our "big hitters" to be there all the time?'
   'We are still too soft with photo-opportunities, which can mislead viewers.'
   'We should get away from a coverage pattern of a fifteenth shot of John Major saying nothing and a fifteenth shot of Neil Kinnock saying nothing.'
2 *Lack of attention to popular reactions (relative to coverage of other voices)*
   'That's the number one question: How can we plan next time so as to stand a better chance to gauge the popular verdict?'
   'Absent from the coverage was a feeling for what was happening in

the field. We must get away from programming based entirely on politicians.'

'There was too much shown of us at press conferences – almost interviewing each other.'

'Getting closer to the ground is the key for news.'

3 *Agenda setting*

'We should swing more solidly behind the issues and do more of our own agenda setting.'

'We should interpose ourselves more rather than less.'

'We have a strength to set the parties' agenda. If we say we are going to focus on health, they will follow suit.'

4 *Range of coverage*

'We hardly covered anything other than the two issues each that Labour and the Conservatives believed were theirs. We strayed out of this a bit with the Election Briefings but not enough.'

'On the range of issues, by the end of the campaign we had got there in the sense of having dealt with most of the important ones. Nevertheless, something on Europe at the tail end of the campaign is not enough, and one package on the environment is not enough for a four-week campaign.'

'Many Liberal-Democratic policies escaped our scrutiny.'

5 *Other matters*

'Perhaps we should aim for a marginally shorter coverage next time.'

'Though the 9 was terrific, it was sometimes very predictable. I missed the occasional showing of an incisive single interview, something that would take an issue or an event and mount a killer interview with somebody crucially involved in it.'

'The 5:5:4 balance was particularly difficult this time. I had to drop two or three good sequences due to that. The weight of obligations on us are a bar to adventure and to doing more interesting things.'

Various explanations for the searching spirit of this occasion (not necessarily mutually exclusive) may be suggested:

1 Since the daily pressures and constraints of the campaign period no longer applied, members of the team could think more freely about their election roles.

2 The journalists' professional ideology, often suppressed during the election, had reasserted itself – as if 'disdaining' their own campaign-period behaviour.

3 It was an organizationally useful safety-valve occasion.

4 The exercise was a genuine attempt to consider and find ways of providing a more significantly independent and worthwhile pattern of coverage at the next General Election in circumstances that would, as always, be full of difficulties and dilemmas.

However applicable the first three interpretations, the last function of the meeting should not be cynically dismissed. Even from the United States there are signs that media organizations, reacting to external and internal criticisms of their reporting in the 1988 presidential election, have become 'self-conscious about [their] past performance' and determined to 'do something about it' (Freedom Forum Media Studies Center, 1992). In Britain too, thoughtful journalists, committed to public service, aware of threats to the integrity of civic communication, and dissatisfied with disparities between their professional identities and their election roles, could become significant elements in the 'constituency for the reform of democratic political communication that seems to be [gradually] emerging' (see Chapter 8).

THE OBSERVERS TAKE STOCK

Electoral competition waged by highly professionalized political parties can have a deadening effect on the process of campaign communication – coming close to delegitimating it if American experience of the 1980s is any guide. If so, only journalistic enterprise stands some chance of retrieving or improving the situation, from which standpoint the more buttoned-up and prudential side of the BBC's approach to the last election is troubling.

In 1992 its journalists managed to be serious, dedicated, conscientious, responsible *and* cautious. There is much to admire in this model – and to build on (in the spirit of the post-mortem review described above). The election contest is not just reduced to a horse race or an elaborate game. Whatever the imperfections, it resists cynicism about the democratic ideal of an informed electorate served by responsible political communication. Public service traditions and the determination of the BBC to be a serious public service broadcaster may have helped to ensure that the 1992 campaign was still a relatively substantive one. But in the long run such a combination of qualities may not be sustainable: without a stronger pulse of satisfying vigour and freedom in support, dedication may eventually wither. In any case, if public service broadcasting is to flourish in the more taxing and competitive period that is imminent, it must above all be enterprising and sufficiently confident of its own place in the civic order to *be* enterprising.

The legitimacy of enterprising journalism, like the legitimacy of public service broadcasting, must ultimately depend, however, on its relationship to the audience, the shadowy character of which in the 1992 campaign is another worrying sign for the future. An interviewed executive seemed to sense this when concluding from the spate of party complaints directed at the BBC, 'That is why we need to measure the audience's response to our coverage throughout, for otherwise almost all the response we get is partisan.' But in the new phase that public service broadcasting is entering, such 'measurement' needs to move much closer to what viewers and listeners are striving to get out of programming, how they receive its informing efforts, and especially what it does and does not add to their understanding, than has yet been ventured by any major television service in the world. Followers of the 'Birtian model' in particular need to check how far the 'value added' to election stories has been successfully communicated to news audiences.

Most serious for the future civic role of public service broadcasting, however, is our impression that applications of the norms of fairness and objectivity were unduly restrictive. That judgement was challenged by leading members of the BBC team in exchanges over a previous draft of this report. They maintained that their independence had not been subjugated (said one, 'Through thick and thin, BBC journalists ... set out neither to appease nor to provoke, but to do their very best to broadcast what was journalistically right'). They claimed that their stance reflected considered principles of election journalism. The curbs on opinion poll reporting had been vindicated by the final election result, they pointed out, and in a 'many-headed monster like the BBC', central control was justifiable (according to one informant) because 'It was essential ... that the BBC spoke with one voice.'

Although much of this response is understandable (except perhaps for the rejection of pluralism implicit in the last comment), it fails to address our central concern. It was not cravenness that troubled us so much as the one-sided inculcation of a culture of responsible carefulness, little leavened by corresponding support for boldness. Of course a commitment to impartiality is critical for television and must remain so in a society with a partisan national press that often blatantly violates it. But in 1992 at the BBC it was impossible to escape the impression of valid standards being pursued in an unbalanced way at the expense of other valid norms, notably freedom of expression itself. When broadcasters feel so closely bound to the terms of party debate, their scope to advance it will inevitably be severely limited. That conflicts with viewers' concerns, often elicited in research, for a fair but vigorous televised source of political news that will stand up for their interests without pulling punches (Morrison, 1992). Even broadcasters' credibility may be at risk, if their coverage can be plausibly depicted as predominantly collusive.

Chapter 14

Longitudinal analysis of an election communication system

Newsroom observation at the BBC, 1966–92[1]

INTRODUCTION

Comparative research on political communication systems has become 'something of a growth stock' in recent years (Swanson, 1992a, p. 19). Creative conceptualization has flourished; specimens of cross-societal empirical enquiry have burgeoned (see Chapter 6). Nevertheless, a significant blind spot still detracts from this otherwise impressive record: how political communication systems develop *over time* has received little analytical attention, reflecting a more general tendency for macrosocial communication researchers to equate comparative work almost 'exclusively with spatial distinctions' (Blumler, McLeod and Rosengren, 1992, p. 8) to the neglect of temporal trends.

Changes in political communication systems seem to come either in major (sometimes cataclysmic) bursts, immediately visible for all to see, or they move, less perceptibly, at a glacial pace. Perhaps three types of change can be distinguished. The transformation of the political communication systems in the Eastern European countries over the last few years constitutes a classic example of the first, 'major burst' of change, coming, as it did, in the wake of the wrenching revolutionary reordering of those societies' political and economic systems. Other relatively large-scale changes may arise, second, when far-reaching media legislation is passed, or a major reorganization of media institutions is undertaken, often to accommodate existing structures to the impact of changing conditions, such as the introduction of new technologies. The implications for political communication processes of the current commercialization of West European broadcasting systems may exemplify this mode of change. Third, in more stable circumstances, i.e. when the institutional structures of the prime communication sources remain more or less intact, important changes in political communication arrangements may be more incremental in character and escape notice. Only with hindsight, by adopting a historico-comparative perspective, and by focusing on the more specific details of organizational culture and professional practice, can such glacially paced changes be identified.

This essay concentrates on the last form of change. Its source material is our unique series of attachments for observation research to the BBC's News and Current Affairs Departments in the British general elections of 1966, 1979, 1983, 1987 and 1992, spending between seven and twenty days out of three to four campaign weeks with them (see Chapters 9–13 above). Although not designed as such, these observations constitute the most sustained longitudinal examination of election communication practices from inside the newsroom of a major journalistic organization of which we are aware. We have therefore set out to review the full sequence of studies, aiming to chart the nature and degree of any significant changes that may have taken place and to reflect on the forces that brought them about and gave them shape.

A BACKCLOTH OF CONTINUITY

No reader of the first and last case studies in the series can fail to be struck by the magnitude of change between 1966 and 1992 at the BBC. Nevertheless, incremental change in communication systems (however cumulatively extensive) tends to take place within a framework of certain more or less enduring characteristics. Before presenting the main dimensions of change in the BBC's election coverage along which our observations may be grouped, we therefore outline the most systemically relevant elements that tended to persist throughout the period.

Elections as special events

On every occasion the election concerned was treated by the BBC as a transforming event (not merely a long-running news story writ large), requiring extraordinary measures to rise to the challenge. These included rearrangement of schedules, pouring in extra resources, redeployment of political staff, introduction of special programmes, segments and filmed reports, and substantial extensions for the main evening news bulletins in 1983, 1987 and 1992, with about half the air time devoted to election materials.

Substantive emphasis

On every occasion it was taken for granted that the main thrust of BBC election coverage should be substantive. In considering prospective materials for campaign reports each day, news personnel predominantly looked for the issues and party policies on them that most merited attention at the time.

Analytical approach

On every occasion an attempt was made to inject an analytical component into the election coverage of mass audience news bulletins. The BBC persisted with such efforts even though they were often 'beset with difficulty' (see especially Chapters 10 and 12). Thus, in 1966, heavyweight political analysts were assigned to *24 Hours* to help what had been a news magazine built around lighter features to provide a sufficiently serious nightly *Campaign Report*. In 1979, the BBC's Chief Political Editor served as anchorman for all campaign stories to confer due analytical weight on their presentation and content. In 1987, much of the latter part of an extended *Nine O'Clock News* was devoted to inter-party debates and sustained political interviews. In 1992, the BBC's specialist correspondents were mobilized to provide a 'value-added' back-up to campaign news events, lacing them with much background information and comment.

Commitment to fairness

The coverage was invariably stamped by extraordinarily conscientious applications of the norm of fairness in relative treatment of the messages of the competing parties, transcending any legal obligation to show 'due impartiality'. This typically entailed not only an extremely close matching of the amounts of news time given to party events and statements with the parties' allocated quotas of free broadcasting time, but also even-handedness in many other respects – for example, over the relative position in bulletin running orders of packages on the competing parties, as well as 'equivalence of tone' in commentaries from reporters assigned to Leaders on the campaign trail.

Privileged access for politicians and journalists

At every election, campaign communication was treated as the near-exclusive province of politicians and journalists – shutting out or marginalizing other voices, such as party dissidents and representatives of cause and interest groups (see especially Chapter 12, p. 159). It was commonly understood that the appropriate point of departure for campaign coverage was competing party stands on election issues, within which BBC reporters and commentators had to try to carve out some meaningfully independent role for themselves to perform.

Allegiance to public service principles

Of course much of this reflected the dominant public service definition of the BBC throughout the period. Indeed, an impressive feature of the BBC is that, despite all the social, cultural, political and economic changes through which it had to steer over the past two decades, the Corporation persistently and religiously adhered to a considered notion of its public service role, not merely paying lip service to it but actually being guided by it in fulfilment of its campaign tasks. That said, its sense of what public service entailed was strongly tilted towards support for the parliamentary parties and their designated spokespersons.

PROCESSES OF CHANGE

Examined as a longitudinal sequence, however, the election observation studies do register successive developments in two far-reaching processes of change. Compared with 1966, in 1992 the campaign communication scene looked quite different in both *external* and *internal* respects. Both inter-communicator relationships between parties and broadcasters (looking outward) and intra-organizational coverage practices in the newsroom (looking inward) had been transformed. The first may be defined as a shift *from relative distinctness in the functions of the two sets of communicators towards their increasing mutual adaptation and involvement*. The second is reminiscent of Weber's (1925) notion of the routinization of charisma and manifested itself as a movement *from impulses of inspirational enterprise among the working journalists towards a more comprehensively rationalized control of their efforts*.

Developments in party–broadcaster relations

Four phases in the development of relations between the two sets of campaign communicators can be discerned from our successive observation posts:

1 Distinctness of campaign communicators' (politicians and broadcasters) functions.
2 Party adaptation to television.
3 Party professionalization for news agenda control.
4 Consummated mutual adaptation.

Before the 1960s

The first phase emerged in the early 1960s, however, from a preceding period of what may be termed, with little exaggeration, *broadcaster suppression*, when election communication was treated as if belonging almost solely to the political parties. In the 1950s, for example, the Representation of the People Act had been interpreted as disallowing any broadcast reporting of election campaigns; and the BBC adopted a 14-day rule, forbidding coverage or discussion of any issue likely to be debated in Parliament within the following two weeks. Thus, in the 1955 election, television newscasts studiously ignored the campaign, while in 1959, election events were covered only cursorily in late-night bulletins.

Such abnegation was increasingly regarded as arbitrary, however, as an ever more confident corps of political broadcasters explored the potential of television to inform and enlighten large numbers of viewers and felt entitled to make their own contributions to electoral awareness. As Even (1986, p. 20) explains, 'By the 1960s,' the former 'passivity had given way to a more aggressive style of interviewing and more interpretive reporting.' According to Blumler and McQuail (1968, pp. 39–41), three developments in the 1964 campaign 'marked a watershed in election broadcasting in Britain'. First, news bulletin coverage was fuller and more adventurous than at any previous election. Second, the regular Current Affairs programmes of political comment and discussion, which had been taken off the air during the 1959 campaign, were allowed to 'stay in business' in 1964, devoting successive editions to in-depth analysis of significant campaign issues. Third, the BBC introduced an entirely new kind of programme, *Election Forum*, in which a panel of interviewers put questions, sent in by viewers, to the leaders of the Liberal, Labour and Conservative Parties, followed by searching supplementaries of their own. As Blumler and McQuail summarized, whereas previously television had mainly 'provided a platform from which the politicians addressed their prepared messages to the public', now television 'had also become a window, through which the elector could observe the activities of the politicians and the independent reactions of informed individuals to the policies and claims of party spokesmen'.

With this as background, we now turn to our observation reports to trace how party–broadcaster relations evolved over the next quarter century, starting with the 1966 election, when hopes of sustaining and extending the more assertive journalistic thrust of previous years were still prevalent.

Phase of distinctness of campaign communicators' functions

In 1966, BBC News and Current Affairs personnel seemed to suppose that a segregated division of labour should prevail between political and journalistic contributions to campaign communication, each to be driven by their own goals and neither to be modified or compromised by adjustment to the other. Politicians proposed and journalists reported and probed.

The 1966 case study (Chapter 9) reflects this outlook in several ways. It mentions the 'more or less common conviction' among members of the BBC team that the developments which had taken place in the role of election television up to 1966 'were (a) desirable and (b) still incomplete'. They consequently 'wished to direct the contribution of television to an election campaign into channels they regarded as fruitful', sharing 'a set of policy objectives *of their own*', which 'chiefly reflected the preoccupation of journalists with the relationship between *their own freedom* and various inhibitions and restraints that were associated with the political parties' (emphases added). These included attempts to encourage party spokespersons to confront each other in face-to-face discussions; attempts to promote a top-level party leader debate between the Prime Minister and his Conservative and Liberal opposite numbers; and a determination to focus their *Campaign Report* programme on issues of their own choosing (including, on occasion, tactics to overcome party efforts to block such discussion).

The broadcasters' belief in the importance of their distinct contribution also underpinned their reactions to complaints from party sources, including what they perceived as 'a sustained campaign of pressure from the Labour Party' and its then Prime Minister. As the 1966 report puts it, 'the typical reaction of [the] producers to a situation of perceived pressure was not accommodation but resistance', partly because 'something vital to journalists (*their autonomy*) was at stake' and partly because 'to yield to the party's wishes would have symbolized lack of pride, courage and self-respect' (emphasis added). It was natural, therefore, for the television journalist to cast himself 'in *the role of public watchdog*, the essence of whose position is an ostensible, but to some degree vulnerable, form of independence'.

Phase of party adaptation

Broadcasters subsequently realized that the campaigning parties were increasingly adjusting the timing, length and substance of their messages to the perceived requirements of the lunch-time, early evening and main evening news bulletins. This phase began in 1970 and persisted through the two elections of 1974 on to those of 1979 and 1983 and was marked not only in our 1979 and 1983 observation reports but also in *The Challenge of Election Broadcasting* (Blumler, Gurevitch and Ives, 1978), in which we reviewed coverage practices in the earlier campaigns of the 1970s. Its emergence was prompted, on the one hand, by the increasing centrality of television news as the predominant site on which election battles in Britain are waged, and, on the other, by the increasing instability of the British political system, evidenced by rising tides of electoral volatility, declining sentiments of party loyalty, and mounting scepticism about political institutions generally and the credibility of party propaganda specifically. All this made campaign communication more important, with so many votes now available to be won or lost, yet more difficult, in the face of electoral wariness about party claims.

The 1979 report (Chapter 10) accordingly depicts party managers as 'anxious to plant their gems in the output [of television news bulletins] . . . in which the combatants daily parade themselves, make speeches, look authoritative, shake hands, and try to score points off their opponents'. The parties' campaign events were therefore synchronized to bulletin schedules, aiming to catch the mid-day news with material from morning press conferences, staging Leader walkabouts in visually appealing settings for early evening news coverage, and inserting passages into Leader speeches at party rallies in the evening for inclusion in the main nightly news (1983 report, Chapter 11). Much of the accent of this period was on making the party message conform to what television was perceived to prefer.

Despite the flattery of being courted so assiduously, such adaptation provoked unease among some of the targeted journalists. It raised the question of whether they had been co-opted to party propaganda service. Although still going through the motions of selecting materials for campaign stories on news-value grounds, their actual options could be severely narrowed by party adroitness in catering to their professional predilections (see Chapter 10, p. 128).

Phase of party professionalization

In this period our informants perceived the parties as having shifted from the predominantly reactive process of adapting to television towards a more proactive determination to control the broadcast news agenda and hence to beat professional journalists at their own game. Characteristic of the 1987 election, three main signs of this development were prominently highlighted in our report of that year's observations (Chapter 12).

First, we found a pervasive awareness throughout the BBC that attempts to set the television news agenda had become 'a more central, considered and concerted element in the strategies of all three parties than at any previous election'. Second, the producers felt as if surrounded by 'awkward parties', who frequently and systematically bombarded them with complaints about their intentions and output, hoping thereby to influence the coverage. Third, we noticed for the first time in 1987 the growth of a disposition among BBC journalists to attach 'health warnings' to the very stories of party events they had to transmit. 'On this view [we explained], now that the bulk of election news is carefully pre-packaged for the cameras, those who relay such events are under an obligation to open viewers' eyes to the manipulation underlying the message.' We concluded that the emergence of this attitude probably reflected 'an impression that the British state of the art of professionalized electioneering for television is now approximating its more pervasive and thoroughgoing entrenchment in the United States'.

Phase of consummated mutual adaptation

The end of this road (so far) was reached in 1992, when the broadcasters perceived the parties as mounting a comprehensive orchestration of their approaches to television. In this phase, despite isolated break-outs from the pattern, both sides were prepared for each other's strategies and tactics, à la professional tango dancers, closely attuned to each other, able to adjust each step to that of the other, and unlikely to surprise the other (Chapter 13).

Pivotal to the 1992 situation was (in our report's words) 'the thoroughgoing professionalization of the parties' strategic approaches to their media campaigns'. This included 'concerted efforts to dominate the news agenda, increased reliance on specialist political consultants and campaign managers, and a ceaseless determination to cover all publicity-relevant bases, leaving nothing to chance'. Accordingly, one producer said, 'Everyone is now walking into this, knowing to an agonizing, navel-scrutinizing extent how the two pieces of the process are relating to each other.'

Although this phase may not appear qualitatively different from its predecessor, singling it out for separate consideration is justified by the numerous further developments, indicative of a more comprehensively sought control, that came to our notice in 1992:

1 Earlier party press conference timings (kicking off at 7.30 a.m.), because (as one newsman said) 'Each party is determined to try to dominate the day's agenda from the morning through the rest of the day', starting with breakfast news.
2 Tighter control over press conference proceedings.
3 Co-ordination of all campaign-day activities by the theme chosen for launch at the morning press conference.
4 Close concentration of party messages on only a small number of issues. This was in marked contrast to the tendency for most past campaigns to have been 'served to the audience in the form of an "issue a day" ' (1979 report, Chapter 10).
5 Deliberate recourse to negative campaigning tactics, particularly by the Conservative Party.
6 Institutionalization of complaining, with (a) the parties almost routinely objecting to features of their treatment in the news and (b) the broadcasters showing a 'resigned acceptance of [party complaining] as a now entrenched part of the systemic game'.

7 An increased tendency for the broadcasters to regard the 'unmasking' of party electioneering ploys as central to their campaign role, aiming to 'open viewers' eyes to what the parties were up to tactically – to expose their publicity intentions and why they were saying and doing what was coming across on the screen'.

Routinization of charisma in the newsroom

Four dimensions of change in the organization and spirit of BBC News approaches to election campaigns can be discerned over the last quarter century:

1 A move from enterprise to caution.
2 A move from partial to complete hierarchical control.
3 A move from dissensus to consensus in the newsroom.
4 Some marginalization of concern with the audience.

Of course these dimensions are interrelated, comprising different facets of the same overarching process towards a routinization (in the Weberian sense) of newsroom practices of election coverage. They are also very likely related to the developments charted above in broadcasters' relations to party politicians. With the increasing centrality of television in British elections, and the increasing dependence of the parties on how their campaigns are projected in broadcast news, it was as if the role of television in elections had become too important to be left to unfettered journalistic enterprise.

From enterprise to caution

Perhaps the most striking change we observed in the newsroom was an increasing tendency to caution among the journalists and executives responsible for campaign coverage.

Leading members of the team assembled to cover the 1966 campaign seemed to combine qualities of the test-pilot, the nonconformist and the adventurer. Of course, their radicalism should not be overstated: neither rebellious nor anarchic, many had earned reputations for having 'safe political hands'. But confident of their independent professionalism, they were prepared to 'strike ... blow[s] for journalistic freedom' in their various coverage initiatives. Their 'overriding aim was to use television to achieve a more revealing campaign than the political parties were likely to provide through their own unaided efforts'. Their strategy – of pushing at the boundaries wherever they could and trying to get the rules relaxed – was expansionist. They did not draw back therefore from independent agenda setting, managing to present items on most of the issues they wished to cover even in the face of political party resistance.

They also resented complaints-based party pressures and were determined to resist any they thought unjustified.

At subsequent elections, however, this entrepreneurial spirit gradually dimmed, and assertions of their entitlement to set the campaign agenda were muted. This is not to say that the search for ways of making a significantly independent contribution to the campaign was entirely abandoned. But our 1979 report depicted most BBC news producers as eschewing an agenda-setting role for themselves, 'because in their eyes this term has an active interventionist meaning, as if they were being accused of promoting issues they personally deemed significant, despite or even in contradistinction to those the parties wished to press for'. It is true that in 1983 a small coterie of current affairs commentators and producers, who had temporarily joined the election news team, stoutly maintained that the exercise by journalists of independent agenda-setting judgements was both inevitable and desirable. They fully realized, however, that few of their colleagues shared this view.

Meanwhile, the influence of what we termed a 'prudential orientation' was noticeably growing. Just one strand among several other less cautionary attitudes in 1983, in 1987 several glaring examples of prudential policy came to our attention: instructions not to introduce the notion of 'tactical voting' in programmes, since in implying Labour–Liberal/SDP Alliance collusion, this could be construed as anti-Tory; refusal to commission voting intention polls, which might appear to lend BBC support to the leading party; and decisions not to show two film reports late in the campaign, the subjects of which 'could have been interpreted as . . . Opposition issue[s] had [they] been screened in the last week'. By 1992, 'the limits' appeared to us 'more constraining than at any previous election reporting operation we [had] observed', while many producers 'seemed to agree both that prudence was a 1992 watchword in the Corporation and that this was an advisable policy'.

To what might this line of change be attributed? We can think of four, to some extent interrelated, sources of influence which might account for it.

Change in the organizational culture of the BBC

Of course this is not the place to offer even a pint-sized overview of the organizational evolution of the BBC from the mid-1960s to the early 1990s. Nevertheless, many observers of the Corporation appear to concur that over this period its reigning ethos has been less supportive of enterprise. The change may be illustrated by comparing the personalities and public images of the Director-Generals who headed the BBC from Hugh Greene to John Birt. Since the foundation of the BBC under the supreme leadership of John Reith, it has been assumed that the philosophies and personalities of holders of the top position in the Corporation could have formative influence on the culture of the organization. Historical accounts suggest that in the mid-1960s, under the forceful leadership of Hugh Greene, described by one of his political lieutenants as an 'adventurous, determined ... shrewd and experienced journalist' (Goldie, 1977, p. 307), broadcasters in the various programme departments of the BBC were given their heads and encouraged to express their creative talents to the full. This was followed by periods of some retrenchment under the directorships of Sir Charles Curran and Ian Trethowan, culminating (after the brief tenure of Alisdair Milne) in the elevation of Michael Checkland from the Accountancy Department, who was succeeded in turn by John Birt's characteristic 'stress on *responsible* journalism' (see Chapter 13).

Cultural change in the 'spirit of the times'

The creativity said to have been characteristic of the BBC during Hugh Greene's reign was not, of course, an isolated phenomenon, unique to the BBC. The 1960s tend to be retrospectively regarded as a particularly vigorous period of post-war British culture, promoted by generational changes of spending power and status, liberation from the burden of the imperialist legacy and freshly surging impulses of indigenous popular culture. The rise of the Beatles, the ascendancy of British fashion designers, the thriving counter-culture of Carnaby Street, the flowering of British theatre and cinema – all exemplified a vibrancy and excitement in which television also participated, in drama and arts programming as well as journalism.

Political changes

There is little doubt that fluctuations of political mood can have profound effects on all aspects of BBC performance, perhaps first and foremost on its journalistic functions. Notwithstanding its professed autonomy as a public service broadcaster, the BBC has always exhibited a high degree of sensitivity to expectations of the powers that be. The political spirit of the mid-1960s, which elected Labour Governments for the first time since the post-war Attlee administrations, was probably more propitious for ground-breaking broadcasting than the Thatcher and Major regimes of the 1980s and 1990s. In the earlier period, it was widely considered that Britain's traditional institutions had fallen into decrepitude and needed to be questioned, shaken up and revitalized. In all parties, 'modernization' was a favoured objective. In television that ethos was reflected, not only in the approach to election coverage observed in 1966, but also in a mushrooming of satire programmes projecting an iconoclastic view of politics and politicians. The most bold and striking of these, *That Was the*

Week That Was, stemmed from the same *Tonight* empire that had also spawned *24 Hours*, which formed in turn the programme base for the 1966 *Campaign Report*. This stands in contrast to the inability of the electorate over four elections from 1979 to 1992 to shake off fears of a Labour government and the inertia of Conservative rule.

The politics of broadcasting

The mid-1960s was a time when the power relations of broadcasters and politicians seemed closely balanced. As the former increasingly exercised their own programmatic muscles, the latter became more conscious of their dependence on television to reach large numbers of voters. As Jones (1993, p. 67) points out, 'instead of broadcasters seeking access to politicians for news stories and comment' (as had been the 1950s norm), 'it was now the politicians who sought access to the air waves to influence a mass audience'. Many politicians were uneasy over this situation, however, which appeared to threaten both their authority and their interests. To some extent they reacted by learning how to bend media workways to their advantage. But they did not hesitate to wield a heavier hand as well, particularly in the 1970s and 1980s, described by Jones (ibid., p. 72) as 'decades when the politicians turned up the pressure [on] broadcasters', showing hostility, provoking rows and intimating that licence fee settlements and other politically determined entitlements could be at stake. When faced with such antagonism in the 1960s, a more independent spirit of broadcaster resistance could be buttressed by the prospect of eventual release via the electoral pendulum, turning out a resentful government and installing a different party in power. In the 1980s, however, the pendulum had stalled. Another factor in later campaigns was the prompt alertness of all parties to alleged errors and loss of even-handedness and their readiness to complain vociferously about them. Under such a barrage, it is not surprising for a politically accountable public broadcaster's independent resolve to shrivel. Such tendencies to caution were probably reinforced by the onset from the mid-1980s of a period of broadcasting system change, leaving the BBC to face a review of the terms of its Charter in the 1990s. Much of this converged on the Corporation with a vengeance in 1992, when the Home Secretary said shortly before the campaign of that year opened that the future of the BBC could depend on how properly it behaved during it.

From partial to complete hierarchical control

Creativity in organizations stands in inverse relationship to control. Tightly regulated organizations leave little room for employees' independent creativity. Conversely, the more workers are given their heads, the more creative they can be. This basic rule of corporate life is particularly significant for organizations engaged in cultural production. Hence the importance of professional autonomy in media enterprises.

Our sequence of observation studies points to a shift in BBC News and Current Affairs from a more flexible form of organizational control to a more hierarchical, rule-regulated one. The environment described in the 1966 case study was one in which certain rules of what was regarded as fair and proper coverage of an election campaign obviously obtained, but the control by senior management was relatively loose and incomplete. The members of the production team were not only *under* policy guidance; on some important matters, they were also able to *make* policy, on the wing as it were, for themselves. The extent of their ground-floor freedom was epitomized by Blumler's conversation with the then Chief Political Assistant to the Director-General, who, after having read the 1966 case study report, expressed particular interest in it, since it had told him a lot about what went on in Current Affairs production, *of which he had not been aware.*

The organizational environment depicted in the 1992 report could not have been more different. The structure and workings of News and Current Affairs personnel had been transformed under the influence and determined leadership of John Birt. Priority was given to 'philosophic clarity, managerial leadership and creation of a team aware of shared purposes and standards'; journalists unable to work to the prevailing outlook were 'weeded or eased out'; and various steps were taken 'to fashion and induce acceptance of what some termed a "new journalistic culture" at the BBC'.

Many of the previously identified influences productive of a more cautious political journalism help to account for the shift to a more complete hierarchical regime as well. An organization that comes under severe external pressure will tend to tighten control to avoid offering up unwanted hostages to fortune. Specially influential here may have been the politics of television of the 1990s, in which the Thatcher Government communicated to all concerned its demand that the BBC be run like a tight ship, rigorously making economies, eliminating sources of inefficiency and re-gearing itself for operation in a more competitive broadcasting environment. Only strong leadership from the top, carrying its way through all branches of the organization, would stand a chance of satisfying such expectations.

From dissensus to consensus in the newsroom

Yet another manifestation of this sweep of intra-organizational change appears in a reduced range of election coverage roles that producers espoused over the period and a corresponding moderation of conflict among their holders.

An intriguing feature of our earlier case studies is the depth of disagreement (even severe conflict at times) reported between holders of divergent views. Members of the 1966 team, for example, waged a running battle for much of the campaign over such issues as 'the total amount of time that should be devoted to the election, . . . the relationship to be forged within the programme between the election and non-election elements', the kind of audience to be addressed, as well as the tone of voice (civic seriousness vs. a lighter touch) suited to it. In 1983, we noticed a multiplicity of perspectives on broadcasters' campaign roles, embracing 'prudential', 'reactive', 'conventionally journalistic' and 'analytical' stances, respectively. These divergent positions on political journalism had laid the basis 'for underlying conflict that periodically came to the surface during the campaign', with 'differences of approach' often erupting 'into overtly angry exchanges' and editorial team meetings occasionally taking 'the form of struggles for ascendancy'.

In 1987, however, a more harmonious operation was achieved, a determined effort having been made to create a team whose members could work together, while in 1992, an even more collegial atmosphere prevailed. Most participants seemed prepared to work to a common approach, differences centring chiefly on more readily resolvable specifics of judgement. Debates on different approaches to the day's news prospects rarely ensued. As an executive from another department revealingly put it, 'The election is being covered by people who have now worked together for such a long time that they practically approach their tasks and problems as if of one mind.'

Again, this move from formed factionalism to wide-ranging consensus reflects many of the influences described in preceding sections. However, two other more specific factors may have also favoured diffusion of a common outlook. One was a merger of the formerly separate News and Current Affairs Divisions, initiated before the 1987 election and completed before the 1992 contest, removing a structural basis for philosophic differences. Another was the strong impulse, personal to John Birt, to reform BBC journalism quite fundamentally, endowing it with a 'mission to explain' and purging it of anything that might smack of triviality, sensationalism or irresponsibility. One previously entrenched view stood no chance of prospering in this climate: 'The more conventionally journalistic assumption, that politics is essentially boring and therefore must be spiced with jolting news-value angles, was conspicuously absent' from the 1992 newsroom.

Marginalization of concern with the audience

Preoccupation with rules, guidelines and a more hierarchically controlled work environment could have another consequence for broadcast journalists: it might direct their attention internally, towards the organization; upward, towards their superiors; and outward, towards their most powerful sources – thereby distancing themselves from the audience. Some suggestions of such a drift do appear in the observation studies, albeit with less definiteness than the other changes that have been analysed in this section.

Whereas during the earlier campaigns we overheard producers at work referring at least occasionally to presumed audience requirements, 'the receding audience' was an overt theme of our later reports. In 1966, for example, a basic point of clash between the opposed groups of producers was said to be 'the different relationships that [they] wished to establish between their programme materials and members of the audience'. In 1979, the journalists' heavy emphasis on producing thematically unified and easy-to-follow election stories was described 'as an expression of their responsibility to serve the campaign communication needs of their viewing audience'.

But we made a point of declaring in our 1987 report that, 'while with the team . . . , we were exposed to few signs of people saying to themselves or others, how can we make this relevant and meaningful to the average viewer?'. And in 1992, we commented on 'the shadowy role that the audience seemed to play' in coverage decisions, with 'audience needs and likely reactions' tending 'to be assumed and taken for granted' and rarely entering 'into . . . editorial discussions'.

Why might audience concerns have been marginalized over the period reviewed? Three possible explanations can be suggested:

Increased professionalization

To the extent that professionalization enhances the status of 'specialists' at the expense of 'generalists', this may have been a factor. Such a development has certainly been central to the 'Birtian revolution' in BBC journalism. An analogy with the medical profession may illustrate how the audience could recede into the background. General medical practitioners are assumed to deal with their patients as whole persons, since they are expected to diagnose and treat a diverse range of their problems. Specialist doctors, on the other hand, are more likely to view their patients as sites of specific symptoms. By extension, the 'generalist' journalist may be more attuned to the needs and wishes of his/her audience, whereas the 'specialist' will be more concerned with the complexity of the issues he or she is supposed to handle and with their many contributory sources.

Increasing interdependency of politicians and broadcasters

This may have also pushed audience concerns into the background. Since the 1960s, the parties have learned the ropes of news production, and political journalism has become a part of the political process, involving journalists as virtual co-producers of the campaign. In these circumstances, it is not surprising that broadcasters have become increasingly oriented towards their political communication partners and decreasingly mindful of the audience.

Commercialization of British television

The increasingly pressured and competitive situation of the BBC in the British broadcasting system may have played some part as well. Although this should increase the importance of attracting and gratifying an audience, it also puts a premium on validating such success through ratings, statistics of viewing patterns, and, in the case of the 1992 news team, broad-gauge assessments of how BBC election coverage was evaluated by samples of viewers in comparison with that of Independent Television News (its commercial rival). But in such circumstances, 'comprehension, received meanings and potentials for involvement were relatively neglected criteria of audience reception of the coverage'.

SUMMING UP

The case study material suggests that changes in BBC newsroom attitudes and practices took place in the context of and may have been shaped by at least three broader processes of change:

1 Politico-cultural changes in British society
2 Changes in the conduct of election campaigns
3 Internal changes in the BBC

Politico-cultural changes

The range of dimensions for possible consideration here is, of course, very extensive. For our purpose we would single out two profoundly formative features of recent British history which we deem to be especially relevant: (a) the gradual but continuous decline of Britain's economy; and (b) the long reign of the Conservative Party under Margaret Thatcher and her successor. The combination of these forces undermined exploratory optimism in politics and culture and favoured retrenchment and a tendency to conservatism in many aspects of British life, including its broadcasting organizations.

The conduct of election campaigns

Many consequences have flowed from the emergence of television, in a period of high electoral volatility, as the main site on which campaigns are staged. Electoral competition became more intense, and politicians could not afford to wage it casually. They fashioned events, images and messages specifically for television, turning broadcast journalists more into co-producers of the campaign than external reporters of it. The specialist help they hired – publicists, consultants, advertisers – put campaign conduct in the hands of a new profession. At the same time, they exerted relentless pressure on broadcasters, who were doubly vulnerable to it due to their political dependency and their commitment to meticulous fairness. The transformation of television journalists from observers of to participants in the campaign may have had a profound influence on their sense of responsibility for its shape, favouring care and caution rather than enterprise. Altogether, the changes probably contributed to the tightening up of hierarchical control and the creation of a more rule-regulated environment.

Intra-organizational change

We noted earlier that an abiding feature of the BBC has been a certain public service definition of its role in British politics. This regarded civic communication as predominantly a province of the parliamentary parties, whose spokespersons accordingly deserved generous access, serious attention and sensitivity to their expectations. Not excluded from and sometimes a point of tension within this notion was a responsibility to help the audience make sense of the debate. Increasingly, however, fulfilment of that obligation had to be sought within the primary givens of political party offerings.

The past quarter century has witnessed major changes in television broadcasting, some of which may have reinforced these leanings to the political establishment. Three in particular come to mind.

First, there has been an immense infusion of new technology, both hardware and software, into television. Absorption of the technology opened up previously unimagined possibilities for the presentation of News and Current Affairs programming, ranging from the satellite transmission of live events to the use of computers for generating and injecting highly sophisticated graphics into stories. One product of this development has been the incorporation of technological mastery into the notion of broadcast professionalism, inducing preoccupation with the presentational and technical features of news production (flow, graphics, linkages, etc.). Although no straight-line implications for campaign reporting should be assumed, a possible consequence is some weakening of independent informing zeal and some readiness to accept the political messages offered so long as they can be packaged attractively.

Second, the personnel of BBC News and Current Affairs have also changed over the period. The youngsters who were pushing back the frontiers of political television in the 1960s have been replaced by a new cohort of Editors, producers and executives who are now responsible for campaign operations. Many among this generation of news professionals have been socialized into the present-day technologically oriented, rule-regulated, hierarchically ordered and politically cautious work culture. They also appear more at ease with bureaucratic conditions than their predecessors.

Third, there was the need to transform the organization and culture of BBC television journalism, which John Birt tackled with conviction. However, this did not stem only from his personal philosophy of responsible reporting. It originated in a confluence of pressures to which the Corporation would have had to respond one way or another: for greater economy in the use of resources; for distinctiveness of journalistic approach in a more competitive broadcasting system; and for safety in a more threatening political climate.

A FINAL EVALUATIVE WORD

The trend to institutional caution traced above should finally be considered in relation to assumptions in Western political thought about the contributions of the press to the health and vitality of democracy. Although the BBC is still regarded as a role model of political independence for public service broadcasters, its shift to a predominantly informative and explanatory role has entailed withdrawal from anything that might smack of significant intervention in the campaign process, including independent agenda setting and performance of a 'watchdog' function. The 'watchdog' notion foregrounds the explicitly political character of media work. Television journalists may not always find its adoption comfortable. Yet at a time when media considerations have entered so deeply into the calculations of all leading political actors, broadcast journalists cannot avoid or shun it. An insulated media professionalism is not enough.

Another democratic obligation of the media is that of giving access to the otherwise voiceless. In a period dominated by big government and big media, entrance into the public sphere by groups and interests not aligned to those institutions is increasingly difficult. If, for the sake of 'objectivity' and moved by instincts of prudence, the 'big media' suppress the voices of those who seek to be heard as well as their own voice, the diversity of the public sphere will be diminished. Here too is a cautionary tale.

Conclusion

Chapter 15

The crisis of communication for citizenship

In and out of the ashes?

When the foregoing body of writings, reflecting our career-long preoccupation with political communications, is reviewed as a whole, two general points clearly emerge.

One is firmly embedded in all our essays. We have never wavered from our conviction that system-based features of political communication give characteristic shape to a society's public sphere, favouring certain sources and styles of political discourse over others and enabling or impeding a democratic engagement of leaders with citizens.

The other thought arises from retrospective reflection on the dynamics of change in the two countries whose political communications we have studied most closely, Britain and the US. In that period the political communication process has been getting into ever deeper trouble. An impoverishing way of addressing citizens about political issues has been gaining an institutionally rooted hold that seems inherently difficult to resist or shake off.

This is not to allege that occasions when people, politicians and the press have engaged in 'open, critical public debates about the uses of power' (Bennett, 1993) have been entirely lacking. Our democracies do have their better moments and their better days. Nevertheless, the political communication process now tends to strain against, rather than with the grain of citizenship. While politicians often behave as if planting ever more clever messages in the media could be a miracle cure for their power predicaments, journalists often deploy disdain, scorn and shock-horror exposure as ripostes to their threatened autonomy. Meanwhile, the voter is left gasping for 'civic-ly nourishing air' – not expecting to be given it and surprised when it is offered. Our civic arteries are hardening.

What has gone wrong? In our view, the two observations stated above are connected. Although political communication arrangements are systemically structured, they are not frozen in time but continually evolve. At any given moment political communication systems exist in a complex condition of volatile and precarious equilibrium. Our more analytical essays, however, rarely addressed their propensity to change. In what follows we aim to supply that missing element by explicitly considering the motors of political communication development. This is not merely for the sake of conceptual completeness but has a more important diagnostic function. We intend to show that the main changes which have modified key relationships within our political communication systems over recent years are directly responsible for the present crisis of communication for citizenship.

THE FLUIDITY OF POLITICAL COMMUNICATION SYSTEMS

Structurally, a political communication system comprises (as stated in Chapter 2):

> two sets of institutions, political and media organizations, which are involved in the course of message preparation in much 'horizontal' interaction with each other, while on a 'vertical' axis, they are separately and jointly engaged in disseminating and processing information and ideas to and from the mass citizenry.

At least four sources of instability are built into the organization of such systems, however, two external to the actors concerned and two more internal to their mutual relations.

One exogenous source of unsettlement is change in the communication technologies by which political messages are produced and disseminated. Depending on how they are adopted, regulated and used, technological innovations can offer politicians new opportunities for projecting their messages; pose 'demands' they must satisfy; and reconfigure relations among key communicators and receivers. The most obvious and dramatic instance, with consequences that were being registered at the time of our earliest analyses, was the increasing prominence of television as a medium of political communication. This restructured the audience, enabling sectors of the public previously little exposed to political materials to be reached more regularly by them. It reduced selectivity in voters' exposure to party propaganda. It subordinated or transformed previous modes of party communication with voters (e.g. large rallies). It emphasized norms of fairness, impartiality and neutrality in contrast to the partisanship of many established newspapers. It introduced a visual dimension and many new programme formats to which politicians had to adapt. Latterly, changes in political communication have been initiated by the diffusion of cable, satellite and computing technologies, which have multiplied message outlets, fragmented the audience, spawned yet more novel formats and potentially facilitated communication interactivity.

Second, political communication patterns may be responsive to relevant changes in the structure and culture of the surrounding social and political system. Chapter 14 affords a specific case in point, ascribing the BBC's increasingly more cautious election coverage to (among other things) political and cultural retrenchment and greater conservatism in British society. Other external influences on political communication arrangements might include changes in media regulation (e.g. the break-up of public service broadcasting monopolies in Western Europe); in the top-most concerns on a society's political agenda (which may be more or less easy for politicians to tackle – and to talk convincingly about); and in norms of political culture (e.g. supporting more or less public involvement in what is termed 'politics as such' in Chapters 5 and 7).

A third source of change may be traced to the drives of politicians and journalists to understand each other's strategies and continually to adjust their mutual relations in response to the other side's next steps and ploys. Again, the three-decade account of the trajectory of such relationships among television journalists and party politicians in Britain amply illustrates the scope for such fluidity (Chapter 14). Structurally, such changes are rooted in the ongoing struggle by both sides for greater autonomy and control over the political communication process as a response to their dependency on each other and to the constraints such dependency imposes. Politicians are continually on the look-out for more effective ways of ensuring the delivery to voters of as full and unchallenged versions of their messages as possible. Journalists are ever on guard against their feared conversion into mere propaganda mouthpieces and are concerned wherever possible visibly to stamp their own judgements and trademarks on political reporting.

Fourth, several factors induce instability in political communicators' relations to would-be audience members. These include ebbs and flows in people's interest in politics and their ambivalence towards political communication itself. Thus, as audience interest in political messages declines, politicians and journalists come under pressure to adapt their output accordingly – perhaps by shortening the message or trying to make it more arresting, compelling or relevant. Changes in people's support for political institutions – as in the weakening of voters' identifications with political parties in many competitive democracies and of their trust in politicians' statements – also prompt adaptive manoeuvres. Changes in the structure of the competition for electoral support (say, in the number and relative strengths of rival parties) or for audience patronage (say, in the number and type of television channels) may also impinge on the length, focus and style of political statements and stories.

Thus, changes in political communication systems can be accounted for by the disposition of the three main sets of actors – politicians, journalists and audience members – to respond adaptively to the continually evolving perceptions and behaviours of each other within a continually changing environment, the dynamics of which are technological, sociological and political.

THE MAIN SYSTEMIC TRENDS

Global processes of change seem to be affecting the organization and conduct of political communication in many democracies, albeit unevenly (Swanson and Mancini, 1995). All appear to be on the same path, although they are situated at different points on it due to differences of political and media systems and of socio-political cultures. In most of these societies, a number of external developments have been recasting modern political communication systems.

One has been the weakening allegiance of voters to the main political parties since the 1960s, including many individualizing, consumerist, mobility-promoting social trends that have shattered or diluted such loyalties. This has accelerated electoral volatility and correspondingly increased the importance of mass media communication and news appearances through which a larger number of votes may be won or lost. Consequently, politicians and others seeking to influence public opinion have felt impelled continually to cultivate and sharpen up their publicity efforts via the mass media.

Second, such electoral volatility and the increasing centrality of the media have coincided with the onset of relatively intractable political problems – e.g. those of economic management, safeguarding the environment, escalating demands and costs of social provision, rising rates of crime, drug-taking and other indicators of social breakdown – added to which there has been the eruption of a host of global trouble spots. Yet with societal consensus fragmenting, there are more disparate constituencies for politicians to try to satisfy. An ever-ready ability to handle the media and the rapidly changing flow of front-page news has thus become indispensable for politicians of all stripes.

Third, changes in communication technology have been responsible, initially for the growth of television as the main source of people's information and entertainment – enabling less politically committed viewers to be reached by crisp messages and obliging politicians to acquire new tricks of the rhetorical trade; and latterly for a proliferation of channels both nationally and locally, multiplying the outlets and demands for political news and appearances. The resulting intensified competition across all media has put still further pressure on politicians to provide arresting material for headline coverage.

Fourth, an inexorable process of modernization has encouraged the deliberate rationalization of most forms of organized activity, involving sustained planning, reliance on tested techniques, greater influence for experts and specialists and the systematic collection of information (preferably quantitative in form) to guide problem solving. The subjection of politics to this approach is captured by Butler and Ranney's (1992) observation that 'Elections, once oddly amateur and intuitive, have become increasingly technical and self-conscious operations'.

THE RE-CASTING OF POLITICAL COMMUNICATION

Arising from all this, four major trends in the organization of public communication can be identified.

1 A thoroughgoing professionalization of political advocacy

Arguably the most formative development in the political communication process of present-day democracies, the professionalization of political communication is the near-universal response of political parties (as well as many other would-be shapers of public opinion) to the dissolution of previously more firm anchorages of political attitudes, the increasing centrality of television and the proliferating demands of multiple news outlets for instant comment and appearances. American politicians have led the way in the professionalization of publicity and still embrace it with fewer reservations than their counterparts elsewhere (Blumler, Kavanagh and Nossiter, 1995). But the essays in Part II above map in detail the steady advance of this process through the British polity from the mid-1960s to the early 1990s. In an early essay (see Chapter 2, pp. 17–19), we treated the mass media but *not* political parties as examples of professionalized organizations. It is as if, since that time, politicians have been impelled to absorb, match, and ape mass media professionalism.

But what exactly has such professionalization involved? Its contributions to political communication may be summed up in terms of the following impulses.

First, professionalization is the antithesis of amateurism. Waging publicity competition through the media, massaging journalists' news values, putting the best spin possible on significant stories, fashioning political advertising, designing opinion polls and interpreting their results – all these require the skills of experts, who are single-mindedly dedicated to the goal of victory in such competition, and for whom all other goals, including policy and politically educative ones, are subordinate if not irrelevant.

Thus, a new role, that of the specialist political consultant, has been injected into modern democratic politics, and its incumbents enjoy much influence and high status. A survey (Hagstrom, 1992) has documented how advanced and ubiquitous this specialist component of professionalization is in the United States today. This showed that every serious candidate standing in a recent presidential, senatorial, or gubernatorial race had hired a pollster and a media consultant and that the trend was spreading fast to campaigns for lower offices. When a candidate decides to run for office, his or her first act after initial fund-raising is usually to hire a media consultant. Most surveyed candidates also said that choosing a media consultant was the most crucial decision they made during a campaign.

One index of the importance of consultants is the proportion of overall campaign expenditure that goes to their fees and expenses: in the US election of 1990, this was 45 per cent of the total money that congressional candidates spent (Fritz and Morris, 1991). Another indicator is their influence on the campaign agenda: in a survey of consultants, 44 per cent agreed, 'When it comes to setting issue priorities, candidates are neither very involved nor very influential' (Levine, 1994). Consultants are often more adept at discovering weaknesses in opponents' characters and records than at designing positive campaigns: 'The result is a heavy emphasis on negative campaigning' (ibid.).

As another contribution, possibly reflecting the relationship of political consultants to the world of marketing and advertising, professionalization has revamped the concept of electioneering, assimilating it to a process of political marketing. This treats the voter more as a consumer to be wooed than as a citizen to be enlightened or engaged in debate. It equates the party or candidate with a product suited to meet consumer needs and allay people's worries and fears. It encourages data-driven campaigning, based on an increasing use of public opinion polling, survey research, and focus group exercises to discover voters' perceptions, moods, needs and desires and their ratings of rival parties, leaders and candidates. Such data are then used, on the one hand, by the news media to report which parties and leaders are ahead or behind in the polls, and, on the other hand, by parties and candidates to shape, fine-tune, and monitor their campaign efforts. The marketing approach tends to militate against broad-based discussion of public concerns during elections and drives a deeper wedge between policy-oriented statesmanship and electorally oriented appeasement of voters.

One consequence of this has been the adaptation of political appearances, rhetoric, and leaders' images to presumed media requirements. Much of this is now taken for granted as commonplace – e.g. argument through crisp, punchy, and arresting soundbites and the staging of political events with high visual or symbolic appeal. But the process of media adaptation has also fuelled recourse to negative campaigning, which meshes compatibly with the dominant values of a news-driven polity: journalists' predilections for bad news; their penchant to define events in conflict terms; and a need for brevity, making it easier in 30 seconds to pick holes in one's opponent's credentials than to outline a case for one's own candidature.

Calculated cultivation of the media has an even more disturbing potential: the transformation of politics into a sort of virtual reality. Crucial here is the distinction between substance – the objectives, tasks and policies that politicians actually pursue – and appearance – the perceptions of their aims and activities that politicians strive to project. Many combatants of media-based competition are tempted to assume that in the publicity sphere only mass perceptions of politics matter. The crux is not necessarily what happens in the political world but how political happenings are *perceived*, putting a premium, then, on getting the *appearance* of things right. As Kelly (1993) characterized this outlook in a *New York Times* profile of David Gergen, a guru of American political consultancy:

> it has come to be held that what sort of person a politician actually is and what he actually does are not really important. What is important is the perceived image of what he is and what he does. Politics is not about objective reality, but virtual reality. What happens in the political world is divorced from the real world. It exists for only the fleeting historical moment in a magical movie of sorts, a never-ending and infinitely revisable docudrama. Strangely, the faithful understand that the movie is not true – yet also maintain that it is the only truth that really matters.

This captures many of the factors that contribute to the crisis of civic communication: cynicism; lack of substantive nourishment; and lack of respect for the presumably gullible voter.[1]

Finally, however, adaptive reactivity to media is not quite sufficient for the consummate professional. As Gergen himself advised President Reagan early in his first term, 'To govern successfully the government has to set the agenda; it cannot allow the press to set the agenda for it' (Hertzgaard, 1988). Proactive strategies of media control are therefore needed, including such devices as: limiting journalists' access to candidates only to favourable moments and situations; carefully staging and controlling the visuals of political coverage and relying on them to counter any critical facts or reporter comments; taking part in solipsistic interviews – answering not the reporter's questions but one's own; and especially concentrating all one's publicity on a preferred message, offering journalists no choice of any other theme to go to media town with.

In Chapters 12 and 13 we describe the various tactics the British parties adopted to dominate media agendas in the 1987 and 1992 elections. Jamieson (1992) has documented a recent American 'advance' in this struggle for communication control – the fashioning of political commercials with qualities that lend themselves to take-up in the news. In her view, the successful permeation of much network and local news by such 'adnews' during the 1988 presidential election was due to 'reporters' fascination with pseudo-events and focus on strategy'. As a former CBS executive, quoted by Jamieson, observed, 'The Roger Aileses of this world are now able to create ads in order to have them air in television news.'

2 The journalistic fight-back

Journalists have not taken the professionalized bombardment lying down, however, for they do not relish having their news choices severely narrowed by those whose activities they are supposed to cover. Although they may often report what has been served up to them on a plate, fashioned to satisfy their news values, they recognize, and resent the fact that they are being 'used' to pass on what the news massagers have dreamed up. Thus, in campaigns dominated by media-savvy politicians and consultants, journalists feel in danger of losing their independence (see especially Chapter 13 for strongly felt expressions of this among BBC news personnel).

Certain characteristic features of political coverage may therefore be regarded as attempts by journalists to re-establish control over their own product. One is a fixation on process rather than substance, treating politics more as a game with effective and failed strategies, dramatic ups and downs, personalities large and small, heroic and villainous, victories and losses, than as a sphere of policy choices. Related to this is the frequent commissioning and reporting of opinion polls. Yet another reaction is inordinately heavy coverage of any blunders that the professionalized politicians may happen to commit, indulging in what has been called 'feeding frenzies' (Sabato, 1991).[2]

Most telling, however, may be journalists' practices of 'disdaining' political and especially campaign news, covering events in a manner designed to demonstrate the reporters' distance from their propagandistic purposes, indicating that the event has been contrived, describing how it has been crafted and presenting it as a public relations effort to be taken with a grain of salt (Levy, 1981).

American and British political journalists often justify this approach as a service to potentially gullible voters, aiming to 'open their eyes to what the parties are up to tactically – to expose their publicity intentions and why they are saying and doing what is coming across on the screen' (see Chapter 13). But such a rationale may be quite misconceived, since in cuing voter scepticism, they are often pushing at an open door. As long as three decades ago, a survey of British voters' attitudes to campaign television had already tapped a broad vein of wariness among viewers about the 'dangers of being taken in by a spurious image' (Blumler and McQuail, 1968, p. 288). As the authors summed up:

A graphic picture has emerged from this survey of the conflicting feelings about political persuasion which buffet many electors. The qualities they look for in politicians highlight the existence of a tension between their desire to be ruled by men of integrity and their fear that such individuals are rather rare birds in the political zoo.

Journalistic disdain serves only to reinforce the latter.

3 Normative uncertainty about the ethical rules of the new publicity game

This has arisen from shifting roles, increased conflict and intensified competition – among politicians for electoral support and among media outlets for audience patronage. When does the journalist cross the line between healthy scepticism and corrosive cynicism? What is fair or unfair game in the exposure of leaders' lapses from political or personal grace? How hard should 'hard-ball' negative campaigning be waged? What distinguishes acceptable attempts by politicians to puff up a favourable publicity wind from manipulation that is beyond the pale? How much of 'the truth' should politicians tell, and how far should journalists be moved by the assumption that politicians are congenital liars? What should the more 'serious' news media do about the gossip, rumours and scandalous stories that emanate from the tabloid end of the press?

On the political side, such doubts and dilemmas reflect uncertainties over the ethics of 'hard-ball' campaigning: Is it permissible to try to win by all possible means? On the media side, the soul-searching stems from journalists' self-image as professionals who are supposedly bound by ethical commitments. But for both sides the present situation seems far removed from that notion of an 'emergent shared culture', with ground rules specifying how politicians and journalists 'should behave toward each other', to which we devoted a substantial section of our 1981 essay on role relationships among politicians and the press (Chapter 3, pp. 36–9). On this matter times really have changed!

What underlying trends explain the recent sharpening of such dilemmas? One may have been the erosion of trust in government and political leaders. In the United States experience of the Vietnam War and Watergate encouraged media decisions not to treat leading politicians as a protected species and to activate the watchdog role more often. Another factor may have been increased media competition for audiences, tempting journalists of even more serious organs to go down the tabloid road, while still wanting to observe a solid boundary between their own and tabloid standards. A third reason why the 'emergent shared culture' has come under strain has been the intensified conflict between media élites and political élites, arising from the greater perceived importance of media agendas to politicians and the resistance of journalists to news-control efforts by politicians.

Consequently, many journalists seem to be torn between two opposed prescriptions nowadays:

1 Politicians should be held accountable only for those acts that have a demonstrable public significance.
2 Politicians are fair game for almost anything you can throw at them.[3]

But whereas conformity to the former rule enhances democracy by keeping the media focus on matters of public importance, a full-throated adherence to the latter may undermine the civic culture by increasing public cynicism. The problem is that in the more competitive climate of both media and politics, the balance is tilted more often to the latter.

4 Widespread projection of an image of the 'turned-off' citizen

Media commentary on politics is increasingly suffused with references to the public's disenchantment with their leaders and institutions. In both the United States and Britain, mentions in the press and television of voters' 'contempt for politicians', a 'public sentiment that the current crop of politicians cannot make government work' and 'a pervasive sense of cynicism about how little governments can accomplish' are now commonplace and are rarely balanced with positive references to civic involvement. Sometimes such disenchantment is ascribed to politicians' failings,[4] sometimes to the worsening communication system itself.[5] The news media are thus continually projecting the *systemically influential* perception that the respect of many voters for their political leaders and institutions has been plummeting. Indeed, the media could be said to be constructing for audience members how they are, and therefore *should be*, regarding their politicians and institutions.

Whatever its validity, to the extent that such a perception prevails, it sanctions negative campaigning. As an interviewed British consultant put it (Kavanagh, forthcoming):

Knocking adverts work. People are so disillusioned with politicians that you cannot convince them of your good points. But they are prepared to believe that the other lot are worse .... People are so fed up with politics that you are now pushing at an open door. If they have doubts about the other side, you have to make them hold them even more strongly.

That perception also diminishes media readiness to provide sustained and serious coverage of politics, weakens confidence in the audience appeal of extended discussion and appears to justify the stereotyping in factual and fictional materials of politicians as cynical manipulators.

CRISIS CONSEQUENCES

The trends outlined above contain the seeds of the crisis of communication for citizenship. Such a proposition implies no over-romanticization of former times. Of course, the make-up of 'political communication man' has always included elements of partisan deviousness, journalistic sensationalism and electoral indifference. In the past, however, it could be assumed that the role of publicity in politics was not only to reflect but also to counteract such shortcomings. Today, it is as if the shortcomings are built into the very structure of the publicity process; faith in the corrigible potential of media disclosure has been undermined if not abandoned; and the ties of communication to citizenship are severely frayed if not severed.

But what is meant by a crisis of communication for citizenship? What are its components?

First, the very move of the media to the centre of the political process entails a degree of *de*politicization. This is because in Western democracies the press (and especially television) base their claims to legitimacy and credibility with the public on their *non-political* status and on their disavowals of explicitly political, particularly partisan, motives. Such a stance underlies in turn their preoccupations with personalities and the flow of events rather than with policies. That shift in the portrayal of the political process is then transmitted to audience members as an appropriate perspective on politics.[6]

Paradoxically perhaps, the 'political vacuum' at the heart of the media, particularly in the United States, has been invaded by media personalities, who, under the protective umbrella of the First Amendment, have assumed positions of inordinate political visibility and influence. While the prime example is Rush Limbaugh, the ultra-conservative 'talkmeister' on radio and television, many other talk show hosts have assumed similar powers. They represent a new breed of politically influential 'non-politicians' who enjoy power without political responsibility.

Second, the present system disseminates an over-supply of oxygen for cynicism – through the fractured integrity of political language, the visibility of manipulative publicity efforts and the increased flow of negative messages. A related product is a highly pejorative, oversimplified, and, in many cases, probably an unfair stereotype of the standard politician as someone who only cares for power and personal advancement, is not bothered about the problems that matter to ordinary people and is constitutionally incapable of talking straight. Audience disillusionment with political leaders and their utterances is a natural outcome of such a bombardment. Two to three decades ago it was supposed that only a small anti-political minority of the electorate suffered from the condition of 'political alienation', defined by Levin (1962) as 'the feeling of an individual that he is not a part of the political process'. Today such alienation threatens to become the norm rather than the exception.

Third, less and less of the political communication diet serves the citizen role – due to the predominant presentation of politics as a game; the irrelevance of campaign agendas to the post-election tasks of government; and the diminished space and time devoted to policy substance, resulting from provision of ever shorter soundbites. This is not to claim that a brief message is always shallow or unenlightening[7] but that, other things being equal, it often oversimplifies the issues and blocks meaningful argumentation. In any case, the soundbite providers and controllers are rarely moved by a concern to offer illuminating ideas in captivating capsules. Much of the snappiness of modern political communication arises from the influence of advertising on political persuasion, from that part of the journalistic culture which regards political talk as inherently boring and from the assumption that people have incredibly short attention spans.

Fourth, because voters' needs to understand and make sense of civic problems are increasingly confounded and frustrated, they are virtually excluded from having any say or significant stake in public communication. The increasing preoccupation of politicians and journalists with their own complex and fraught patterns of collusive conflict results in what Rosen (1992) aptly terms a 'public sphere commandeered by insiders'. Its emergence is illustrated in Chapter 13 by a BBC producer's acknowledgement that in the British election campaign of 1992:

> We were in no position with our dispositions to understand what was moving voters. We were almost entirely focused on the press conferences, the Leaders on the trail, reporting how a campaign was going as if it were primarily a media–party-based affair.

Fifth, developments in the relationship of the media system to the political system have catapulted the press into a position of surrogate opposition. And since it is the duty of an opposition to oppose, reporting is yet more imbued with the qualities of challenge, vigilance, criticism and exposure at the expense of giving credit where it may be due, fairly recognizing the difficulties involved in shouldering political responsibility and a rounded political coverage overall. As media framing of politics has become increasingly negative (Patterson, 1993), leaders, bereft of strong parties, have lacked a sounding board to counter the press' discordant orchestration. All this has injected an extra element of conflict and mutual recrimination into the relationship of media personnel with politicians.

Indeed, we are tempted to suggest that this relationship is entering a new phase. Chapter 14 showed that it was possible to periodize, without undue schematization, certain critical developments in the British political communication system since the advent of television. Thus, before the early 1960s, broadcasters were relatively subservient to political authorities. The 1960s was a time of more assertive broadcaster intervention into British politics, aiming to cover political activity and utterance on more journalistic terms. The 1970s witnessed an increasing adaptation of the parties to newsmedia demands; while in the 1980s they tried more proactively to manipulate the journalists. And from the 1987 election onward, the journalists increasingly responded by 'unmasking' the politicians' propaganda efforts.

But was that the end of the systemic road or are we observing the emergence of yet another systemic phase? If so, it could be termed *a chronic state of partial war*. Since those relationships have always been and still are part adversarial, part collaborative (recall the analysis of Chapter 3), the state of war is not total. Nevertheless, in contrast to the periodic eruption of one-off rows between politicians and reporters in the past, the adversarial climate today seems both more fierce and more abiding – justifying the 'chronic state of war' tag.

A number of systemic developments have probably combined to produce this condition:

1 The gradual disengagement of formerly politically affiliated media organs from past party ties.
2 For reporters and editors, the problem (and resulting frustration) that professionalized politicking creates of getting some genuinely independent news out of the processes of conventionally collaborative political journalism.
3 For politicians with career ambitions, the fact that the stories and pejorative forms of more aggressive, critical and investigative political journalism are evidently capable of breaking them.[8]
4 Increased competition within both camps – for the attention of readers and viewers among journalists and for their votes among politicians.
5 The greater intrusion of tabloid organs into politics, not only spilling over into quality coverage but also shifting the boundaries of what counts as proper coverage.
6 The attempts of both political and journalistic figures to persuade the audience that the other side is to blame for the seeming squalor of public life and its media coverage.

Finally, an irony of the present situation is that, although democracies face many urgent problems requiring a considered canvassing of difficult choices, and although frequent attention to such problems in our expanded communication system ensures broad public awareness of them, formats of constructive discourse about them are in rare supply in the established news media. With the possible exception of top-level candidate debates (in the US but not the UK), conventional civic communication today seems to be dominated by point-scoring, tallies of rivals' advances and slipbacks in the game of political snakes and ladders, childish soundbites, interview gamesmanship and a plethora of scarcely believable attempts to establish plausibility.

Not a pretty picture – nor an involving one!

OUT OF THE ASHES?

But is some systemic relief at hand perhaps? Could our charred communication process emerge from its ashes, phoenix-like, 'with renewed youth to live through another cycle of years'?

According to the conclusion to Chapter 8 (pp. 107–8), the prospects for improving civic communication depend in the first instance on the emergence of a constituency prepared to advocate and initiate reform. Paradoxically, the worst trends and excesses of our present system do have at least a potential for building such a constituency.

Some *political leaders*, for example, are not only deeply unhappy about being driven by media forces but also perceive electoral scepticism as a formidable obstacle to projects of constructive government. As a British politician has urged (Mandelson, 1994): 'The need for new ideas – and higher standards in public life – to cope with ... voter cynicism is not restricted to America. It is probably one of the most pressing problems in every advanced democracy, Britain included.'

Present conditions may offer *journalists* more fun, but Chapters 12 and 13 spotlight the frustrations which they may also suffer when trying to perform a more constructive role than incessant 'braying and nay-saying' involves. A striking reaction on this front has been the so-called public journalism movement in the United States, which is said to have been 'born out of frustration over the 1988 presidential campaign coverage' (Shepard, 1994). A growing number of local American newspapers are exploring ways of reconnecting themselves with citizens and the political process, assuming something like the role of community organizer. Their activities have included refocusing political coverage on the concerns of ordinary people, sponsoring round-tables, forums and town meetings to air community problems, pressing politicians to address those that emerge, and generally helping the proponents of change. Although the motives behind this effort are not entirely altruistic (e.g. to counter flagging circulation or to improve the paper's public image), it is, in essence, a media-based initiative to revitalize civic communication.

Finally, a growing body of evidence, including careful research, suggests that much political communication fails to do justice to the informational needs and interests of *voters*. An example is the contrast between the questions, about their campaign strategies and personal shortcomings, which American journalists tended to put to the presidential candidates in the first debate of the 1992 election series, and those predominantly about policies, which were posed by ordinary citizens in the second debate. Drawing on her extensive research into the ways in which people process political information, Graber (1994) considers that mismatches, between journalists' approaches to election news topics and how average people approach those topics, largely explain voters' 'expressed disgust with poorly conducted and poorly reported ... campaigns'. This supports our own conclusion to Chapter 8 that more suitable forms of 'political discourse and coverage could strike neglected chords and would find an audience ready and willing to attend to them'.

It is therefore interesting to note that the most significant break-throughs in civic communication are being launched from this 'popular' end of the process at present. In both the United States and Britain (more modestly in the latter), the status of the public voice is being upgraded. Instead of being positioned only to attend to and overhear the views and arguments of others (politicians, journalists, pressure group spokespersons, experts), the opinions, experiences, problems and priorities of ordinary people are being elicited more often, and they are being encouraged to discuss social and political problems in a number of new communication vehicles. These include call-in programmes, electronic town meetings, computer bulletin boards, extended interviews with call-in segments and, especially, televised talk shows.

Many serious commentators are impressed with these developments – and particularly their role in the US presidential election of 1992. They see the 'New News' and 'talk-show democracy' (as the genre has been dubbed) as having at last released talk about civic issues from its constrict-ing straitjacket. Communication for citizenship, then, is being rescued (it is claimed) by the likes of Larry King, Phil Donahue, Oprah Winfrey, Arsenio Hall, and the producers of MTV. As Patterson (1993, p. 170) has enthused:

> Arguably, the new media, in combination with the debates and the return of Ross Perot to the race, 'saved' the 1992 campaign .... The new media helped to energize the campaign, give the public a sense of greater participation, and improve people's opinion .... When turn-out rose in 1992 ... there were clear indications that alternative media such as debates and talk shows were a contributing factor. Those forms were all that the news was not – upbeat, earnest, and packed with issues presented in the context of values.

Graber (1994, p. 344) also considers that:

> The role played by talk and interview shows in the 1992 campaign in restoring a more audience-centered dialog between voters and candi-dates points the way to a future when campaigns will be more genu-

inely informative, more user friendly and attractive, and more apt to generate voter involvement.

These developments have systemic implications in two respects. First, they undoubtedly spring from systemic roots. The expansion of cable- and satellite-based television afforded a technological platform for their emergence. In the more competitive conditions of multi-channel television, many talk shows have achieved strong ratings. They are also relatively inexpensive ways of filling available air time, relying on high-profile hosts and often sensational subject matter to attract viewers. Another source was politicians' need for the more open doors – both to the public and to the news media (via follow-up reporting of their appearances) – that these shows afford, as well as their ability to reach electoral segments not often available in other outlets (e.g. young people and women at home). For the shows themselves, there was the extra bonus of visibility and status associated with the appearance of a top politician. Audience receptivity to a more refreshing and accessible way of hearing politicians' views on problems of the moment than can be found elsewhere may also have been a factor. However we rate them – whether as enablers of democracy or as sideshows – they stand on real foundations and are probably on the political communication scene to stay.

Second, this alternative process does appear like a new political communication system in the making, since it diverges on so many dimensions from the older, more established one:

> More (and less confining) scope for the political advocate to have his or her say.
> The different role of 'media personalities', casting them more like moderators or even bystanders than inquisitors.[9]
> The altered role of the audience member, from that of a mere receiver to an engaged contributor, actually or by proxy.
> A different agenda focus, with more emphasis on topics of presumed personal concern to audience members.
> Different linguistic features, with more recourse to the vernacular.
> A distinctive rhetorical structure, involving a looser, more fluid and less sequential flow of discourse.
> Fuller dialogue, with time for more extended statements.
> And finally, an intermingling of formal political messages with seemingly non-political ones – such that Bill Clinton's saxophone playing on Arsenio Hall becomes a political message.

But how should the civic contribution of 'talk-show democracy' be assessed? While recognizing many of the virtues claimed for it, we should not exaggerate its redemptive potential. From the standpoint of demo-

cratic values, these new forms of political communication are something
of a mixed bag.

Two key features, however, can be welcomed. One is restoration of the
ordinary citizen as a significant point of reference for political communicators and as properly an active participant in public discussion. This
redresses one of the most striking failings of conventional arrangements
as they have evolved under the influence of systemic pressures. As Jamieson (1992) succinctly puts it, the new-style format 'franchises'. In terms
of the criteria spelled out in our 1990 essay on 'Political Communication
Systems and Democratic Values' (Chapter 8), it offers 'Incentives for
citizens to learn, choose and become involved' and implies 'A sense of
respect for the audience member, as potentially concerned and able to
make sense of his or her political environment'.

Another boon is the restoration of substance as a centrepiece of political communication. In contrast to the obsessive preoccupation of professional journalists with political horse races and power games, research
shows that callers in talk shows do ask questions that are 'overwhelmingly
issue oriented', obliging politicians to offer more information about their
proposals (Ridout, 1993). There is also evidence that a sense of civic
involvement – a concern about where their society is heading and not
just how their pockets are faring – animates many of the women- and
men-in-the-street who contribute to these exchanges (Verba, 1993).

There are nevertheless three reasons to temper enthusiasm for this
genre. First, much of it purveys politics as popular culture. Of course
this helps to draw more people into the political process and can serve
as a coin of exchange for lively debate throughout society (Gurevitch and
Kavoori, 1992). But it tends to stage politics as spectacle and theatre
and to suffer from glitziness and shallowness. Its dissolution of boundaries
between political and non-political realms may encourage people even
more than before to perceive and evaluate their leaders as celebrities
rather than as civic problem-solvers. Its agenda tends to be slanted
towards the more immediately riveting issues with strong socio-personal
elements and away from anything more structurally complex. The up-
grading of populism often entails a corresponding downgrading of expertise (Livingstone and Lunt, 1994), and the circle of participants is
rarely structured to offer a considered range of diverse viewpoints and
perspectives.

Second, the genre is not a *dependable* source of civic communication.
It cannot be counted on for a regular and rounded coverage of politics.
When the political situation (say, an election race) or a political personality (say, a Ross Perot) is hot, its vehicles will readily move into the
civic arena. But they will just as speedily depart the scene, as soon as
some more sensational focus beckons (an O. J. Simpson, say, or a Michael
Jackson).

Third, it should be kept in mind that, even at their best, these populist forms of discourse have not *supplanted* the established system of political communication. Much of the latter and its numerous shortcomings – abbreviated soundbites, negative campaigning, 'disdaining' coverage, insider perspectives and, in the US, rampant political advertising – remain in place.[10]

It is also vital to appreciate that one central feature of the old political communication system has not changed and will not disappear. That is the professionalization of political advocacy, including the regular and deep involvement of specialist consultants in politicians' decisions to engage in communication exercises and what to get across when they do. Consequently, the 'new' political communication arrangements are likely to pivot in the future on two related tensions:

1 Between authenticity and manipulation;
2 Between calculation and spontaneity.

There is a real risk, then, of the new system being sucked into the old system's penumbra of cynicism – though a possible safeguard against this could be the greater involvement of ordinary people in the process, whose participation cannot be totally predicted and orchestrated.

RECONSTRUCTING THE PUBLIC SPHERE

Although prescription is always problematic in matters of media and politics, where no Platonic vision of an ideal system could possibly be imposed, one is nevertheless bound to consider how, in these transitional conditions, communication for citizenship might be most suitably advanced. We limit ourselves here to indicating briefly a few directions and priorities for emphasis.

One concerns the aforementioned danger of a capture of the new forms of popular involvement by the old sources of disillusionment. This suggests that those who monitor the further progress of this process should press one demand above all others: any manipulative recruitment and organization of the audience component should be beyond the pale. The audience element should be kept beyond the reach of the professionals' control, and any possibility of deception in its exchanges with politicians should be quashed.[11]

Another concerns the divide that obtains at present between the older and newer forms of political journalism and discussion. Some breakdown of this would be welcome. Now that 'talk-show democracy' has demonstrated the vigour and appeal of political discussion that prominently includes a popular voice, some of the more conventional journalistic outlets should aim to incorporate it into their own coverage. This might release such an approach from its association with the sensationalist excesses of tabloid programming and expose it to more disciplined forms of debate. Communication-for-citizenship requires 'deliberative' not 'simplistic' populism.

In addition, the initiatives of the public journalism movement should be extended and deepened. Faced by so many challenges and fissures in the established patterns, it is surely an opportune moment for professional journalists to transcend stale and sterile notions of their civic role. Any consideration of the inescapably central position of the media in present-day democracy must lead to the conclusion that the time has come for political journalism to accept and embrace its civic responsibilities. In Chapter 8 we recommended exploration of 'the role of "democratic midwife" '. Following a similar line of thought, Hallin (1992) has proposed a move from 'mediating between political authority and the mass public to thinking of it also as a task of opening up political discussion in civil society'. This has many possible implications: no longer covering events and statements that hardly deserve consideration; enlarging the span of voices treated as having something to say worth heeding; exposing advocates both to more informed/expert perspectives and more popular preoccupations; and arranging a multiplicity of forums in which cross-interest dialogue can flourish. And since politicians themselves are powerfully influenced by their perceptions of media requirements when crafting their utterances, the systemic payoff of such journalistic initiatives could be profound. As we point out in Chapter 11: 'how journalists strive to project an election campaign is not just a matter for internal debate. Their choices and decisions have important consequences for all who depend on their coverage of major political events.'

In conclusion, we see grounds for both pessimism and hope at this time. If the grounds for pessimism appear stronger than for optimism, it is because the crisis of communication for citizenship, with which we have wrestled throughout this essay, has deeper structural roots than some of its transitory manifestations. Ultimately it inheres in the massification of Western societies. It is as if, more than a century after the lamentations of the prophets and theoreticians of 'mass society', some of the ills of that oppressive social structure are visited upon us again. Today they are reflected especially in the professionalization of politics and associated attempts to manage and control public communication for manipulative purposes, with the resulting alienation of many citizens. A real basis for hope arises, however, because that very process appears to have incited a several-sided disgust and spurred new forms of communication, admittedly often imperfect and raucous, but pointing tentatively in the direction of democratic values. Mass democracy may be a contradiction in terms – but *both* parts of that equation persist, albeit in contention, in the political communication system of the mid-1990s.

Notes

1 INTRODUCTION: THE CRISIS OF CIVIC COMMUNICATION

1 We use the term 'civic communication' to refer to all forms of public communication that are supposed to serve people in their roles as citizens of a democratic society.

2 LINKAGES BETWEEN THE MASS MEDIA AND POLITICS

1 First published in Curran, J., Gurevitch, M. and Woollacott, J. (eds), *Mass Communication and Society*, London: Edward Arnold, 1977, pp. 270–90.
2 Boundary problems arise in defining what counts as the 'communication aspects' of the activity of political institutions and as the 'political aspects' of mass media performance. For one thing, it is possible to argue that all actions of political institutions have some communication relevance, that is that all the relationships central to political organization – power, authority, obedience, interest aggregation, etc. – imply the existence of a communication function. Similarly, political aspects are so intricately interwoven with all other aspects of the performance of media institutions as to preclude the possibility either of isolating them empirically or even of analytically denoting some part of media content as entirely 'non-political'. Clearly, our definition should not be taken to imply that the communication aspects of the actions of political institutions are separable from other aspects of their behaviour or that the political aspects of mass communication are limited solely to the processes involved in the production of manifestly political content. It depends, rather, on 'the consequences, actual and potential, that communicatory activity has for the functioning of the political system' (Fagen, 1966). Thus, all aspects of the performance of political institutions and of media institutions that are seen or perceived to have such consequences are included in our definition.

3 POLITICIANS AND THE PRESS

1 First published in Nimmo, D. D. and Sanders, K. R. (eds), *Handbook of Political Communication*, Beverly Hills: Sage, 1981, pp. 467–93.

4 JOURNALISTS' ORIENTATIONS TO POLITICAL INSTITUTIONS

1 First published in Golding, P., Murdock, G. and Schlesinger, P. (eds), *Communicating Politics: Mass Communications and the Political Process*, Leicester: Leicester University Press, 1986, pp. 67–92.

5 TOWARDS A COMPARATIVE FRAMEWORK FOR POLITICAL COMMUNICATION

1 First published in Chaffee, S. H. (ed.), *Political Communication: Issues and Strategies for Research*, Beverly Hills: Sage, 1975, pp. 165–93.
2 These may include, for example, breaches of the peace, defamation, slander, libel, invasions of privacy, reporting prejudicial to a fair trial or in contempt of court, publication of obscene material, revealing official secrets and security-sensitive information, and, in the case of many broadcasting systems, fairness and impartiality in presenting opposing views on controversial issues and bans on editorializing.

6 COMPARATIVE RESEARCH: THE EXTENDING FRONTIER

1 First published in Swanson, David L. and Nimmo, Dan (eds), *New Directions in Political Communication: A Resource Book*, Newbury Park, London and New Delhi: Sage, 1990, pp. 305–25.

7 THE FORMATION OF CAMPAIGN AGENDAS IN THE UNITED STATES AND BRITAIN

1 Published in 1991 by Erlbaum Associates (Hillsdale, N.J.), the authors were Holli A. Semetko, Jay G. Blumler, Michael Gurevitch and David H. Weaver, with significant contributions by Steve Barkin and G. Cleveland Wilhoit.

8 POLITICAL COMMUNICATION SYSTEMS AND DEMOCRATIC VALUES

1 First published in Lichtenberg, J. (ed.), *Democracy and the Mass Media*, Cambridge: Cambridge University Press, 1990.

9 PRODUCERS' ATTITUDES TOWARDS TELEVISION COVERAGE OF AN ELECTION CAMPAIGN (UK ELECTION 1966)

1 Written by J. G. Blumler and first published in Halmos, P. (ed.), *The Sociology of Mass Media Communicators*, *The Sociological Review Monograph* no. 13, 1969, Keele: University of Keele.
2 The Independent Television Authority, the body with regulatory powers over Britain's then only advertising-financed channel – Independent Television.
3 Then the Minister responsible for broadcasting.
4 Then the BBC's weekly flagship current affairs programme.

5 Then Leader of the Conservative Party.
6 In Britain, coverage of campaign speeches in television news has always been proportionate to the parties' allocation of party election broadcasts – five each to the Labour and Conservative Parties in 1966 and three to the Liberals.
7 *Gallery* was a specialist late-night programme of serious political analysis and comment; *Tonight* was an early evening magazine programme that occasionally incorporated political items into a more wide-ranging and sometimes entertaining brief.

10 THE CONSTRUCTION OF ELECTION NEWS AT THE BBC (1979)

1 First published, under the authorship of M. Gurevitch and J. G. Blumler, in Ettema, J. S. and Whitney, D. C. (eds), *Individuals in Mass Media Organizations: Creativity and Constraint*, Beverly Hills, London and New Delhi: Sage, 1981.

11 SETTING THE TELEVISION NEWS AGENDA (1983)

1 First published, under the authorship of J. G. Blumler, M. Gurevitch and T. J. Nossiter, in Crewe, I. and Harrop, M. (eds), *Political Communications: The General Election Campaign of 1987*, Cambridge: Cambridge University Press, 1986.

12 THE EARNEST VERSUS THE DETERMINED: ELECTION NEWS-MAKING AT THE BBC, 1987

1 First published, under the authorship of J. G. Blumler, M. Gurevitch and T. J. Nossiter, in Crewe, I. and Harrop, M., *Political Communications: The General Election Campaign of 1987*, Cambridge: Cambridge University Press, 1989.
2 The data presented here appear in a BBC Broadcasting Research Department paper, 'The General Election, June 11th 1987', September 1987.

13 STRUGGLES FOR MEANINGFUL ELECTION COMMUNICATION, 1992

1 First published, under the authorship of J. G. Blumler, M. Gurevitch and T. J. Nossiter, in Crewe, I. and Gosschalk, B., *Political Communications: The General Election Campaign of 1992*, Cambridge: Cambridge University Press.
2 *Newsnight*, however, was allowed to take voting intention readings in connection with polls commissioned to track the electorate's responses to campaign issues.

14 LONGITUDINAL ANALYSIS OF AN ELECTION COMMUNICATION SYSTEM: NEWSROOM OBSERVATION AT THE BBC, 1966–92

1 First published, under the authorship of M. Gurevitch and J. G. Blumler, in *Österreichische Zeitschrift für Politikwissenschaft* (special issue on Political Communication), 1993, 22, 4: 427–44.

15 THE CRISIS OF COMMUNICATION FOR CITIZENSHIP: IN AND OUT OF THE ASHES?

1 We are reminded of the writer-hero of Allan Judd's (1991) novel, *The Devil's Own Work*, who, having first dabbled in and then recoiled from 'something called "fictive realism" according to which reality and fantasy had the same status', declared that:

> You may think that I was opposed to this movement, but far from it. It was only later that I came to see it as a betrayal and to believe that truth in art matters, that part of the role of art is to help us to hear what cannot usually be heard amidst all the noisy nonsense in which we live. I know I am old-fashioned – I who was so keen to be contemporary – but I have been made so by experience. It was the new truths that failed me, not the old ones, and I do now believe that anything that confuses reality and unreality, or that attempts to equate the two, is the devil's own work.

2 One such episode dominated British media coverage of the 1992 election for three days. This centred on a controversial Labour Party broadcast about delays in health service treatment of a child's painful ear complaint, uncovering faulty research and dubious assertions by both Labour and Conservative leaders. This overwhelmed the message of the broadcast but left many bemused voters wondering what all the fuss was about.

3 To be fair, this position is often legitimized by the argument that everything about politicians, including their private lives, is potentially of public significance, as it reflects on the politicians' character, possible influences on their decision-making abilities, their honesty and integrity.

4 As implied in a UK *Guardian* columnist's statement that, 'It is difficult to read a daily newspaper without coming across some scandalous tale of political sleaze, misuse of public powers, or misdemeanour in public office' (Lester, 1994).

5 As in an *Observer* columnist's declaration:

> Public discourse is now disfigured by unrealities that feed on their own mad logic. Nothing is what it pretends to be. Cynicism is the prevailing mood as people accustom themselves to decoding public pronouncements, struggling to make sense of a culture based on lies and ritual games.
>
> (Phillips, 1994)

6 Empirical support for this proposition is presented in Patterson (1980).

7 Consider, for example, the profundity of a phrase such as 'cogito, ergo sum'.

8 As both President Clinton and Prime Minister Major would probably agree at the time of writing.

9 According to Larry King, 'I'm not the star. I'm the conduit. If you turn on the television and I'm talking, something's wrong' (*Washington Post*, 8 November 1993).

10 Perhaps this explains why few commentators seem to be claiming that the rejuvenating role of the talk shows in the US election of 1992 was repeated in 1994!

11 The danger is not fanciful, as Richard Nixon's attempts at such manipulation in the 1968 presidential campaign show (McGinniss, 1969).

References

Alexander, J. C. (1981) 'The Mass Media in Systemic, Historical and Comparative Perspective', in Katz, E. and Szecsko, T. (eds), *Mass Media and Social Change*, Beverly Hills: Sage.

Altheide, D. L. and Snow, R. P. (1979) *Media Logic*, Beverly Hills: Sage.

Arterton, C. (1985) *Media Politics: The News Strategies of Presidential Campaigns*, Lexington: D. C. Heath.

Bagdikian, B. (1987) *The Media Monopoly*, Boston: Beacon Press.

Becker, L. B., McCombs, M. E. and McLeod, J. M. (1975) 'The Development of Political Cognitions', in Chaffee, S. H. (ed.), *Political Communication: Issues and Strategies for Research*, Beverly Hills: Sage.

Bennett, T. (1982) 'Media, Signification, "Reality" ', in Gurevitch, M., Bennett, T., Curran, J. and Woollacott, J. (eds), *Culture, Society and the Media*, London and New York: Methuen.

Bennett, W. L. (1980) 'Myth, Ritual and Political Control', *Journal of Communication*, 30, 1: 166–79.

—— (1992) *The Governing Crisis: Media, Money and Marketing in American Elections*, New York: St. Martin's Press.

—— (1993) 'A Policy Research Paradigm for the News Media and Democracy', *Journal of Communication*, 43, 3: 180–9.

—— (1995) *News: The Politics of Illusion*, 3rd edn, New York: Longman.

Blumler, J. G. (1973) 'Audience Roles in Political Communication: Their Antecedents, Structure and Consequences', paper presented to Congress of the International Political Science Association, Montreal.

—— (1975) 'Mass Media Roles and Reactions to the February Election', in Penniman, H. R. (ed.), *Britain at the Polls: The Parliamentary Elections of 1974*, Washington, D.C.: American Enterprise Institute.

—— (1977) 'The Election Audience: An Unknown Quantity?' in RAI/Prix Italia, *TV and Elections*, Torino: Edizioni Rai Radiotelevisione Italiana.

—— (ed.) (1983) *Communicating to Voters: Television in the First European Parliamentary Elections*, London, Beverly Hills and New Delhi: Sage.

—— (1990) 'Elections, the Media and the Modern Publicity Process', in Ferguson, M. (ed.), *Public Communication: The New Imperatives*, London, Newbury Park and New Delhi: Sage.

Blumler, J. G. and Gurevitch, M. (1991) 'The Election Agenda-Setting Roles of Television Journalists: Comparative Observation at the BBC and NBC', in Semetko, H. A., Blumler, J. G., Gurevitch, M. and Weaver, D. H. (eds), *The*

Formation of Campaign Agendas: A Comparative Analysis of Party and Media Roles in Recent American and British Elections, Hillsdale, N.J.: Erlbaum.

Blumler, J. G. and McQuail, D. (1968) *Television in Politics: Its Uses and Influence*, London: Faber & Faber.

Blumler, J. G. and Semetko, H. A. (1987) 'Mass Media and Legislative Campaigns in a Unitary Parliamentary Democracy: The Case of Britain', *Legislative Studies Quarterly*, 12, 3: 415–44.

Blumler, J. G., Gurevitch, M. and Ives, J. (1978) *The Challenge of Election Broadcasting*, Leeds: Leeds University Press.

Blumler, J. G., Kavanagh, D. and Nossiter, T. J. (1995) 'Modern Communications vs. Traditional Politics in Britain: Unstable Marriage of Convenience', in Swanson, D. L. and Mancini, P. (eds), *Politics, Media and Modern Democracy*, New York: Praeger.

Blumler, J. G., McLeod, J. M. and Rosengren, K. E. (1992) 'An Introduction to Comparative Communication Research', in Blumler, J. G., McLeod, J. M. and Rosengren, K. E. (eds), *Comparatively Speaking: Communication and Culture across Space and Time*, Newbury Park, London and New Delhi: Sage.

Buchanan, B. (1991) *Electing a President: The Markle Commission Research on Campaign '88*, Austin: University of Texas Press.

Butler, D. and Ranney, A. (1992) 'Introduction', in Butler, D. and Ranney, A. (eds), *Electioneering: A Comparative Study of Continuity and Change*, Oxford: Clarendon Press.

Campbell, A., Converse, P. E., Miller, W. E. and Stokes, D. E. (1960) *The American Voter*, New York: John Wiley & Sons.

Chibnall, S. (1977), *Law-and-Order News: An Analysis of Crime Reporting in the British Press*, London: Tavistock.

Chittick, W. O. (1970), *State Department, Press and Pressure Groups: A Role Analysis*, New York: John Wiley.

Clarke, P. and Evans, S. H. (1980) ' "All in a Day's Work": Reporters Covering Congressional Campaigns', *Journal of Communication*, 30, 1: 112–21.

Cohen, S. and Young, J. (eds) (1973) *The Manufacture of News: Deviance, Social Problems and the Mass Media*, London: Constable.

Commission on Freedom of the Press (1947) *A Free and Responsible Press*, Chicago: University of Chicago Press.

Crossman, R. (1968) 'The Politics of Viewing', *New Statesman* 76: 525–30.

Dearlove, J. (1974) 'The BBC and the Politicians', *Index* 3, 1: 23–33.

Dunn, J. (ed.) (1992) *Democracy: The Unfinished Journey*, Oxford and New York: Oxford University Press.

Elliott, P. (1972) *The Making of a Television Series*, London: Constable.

—— (1977) 'Media Organizations and Occupations: An Overview', in Curran, J., Gurevitch, M. and Woollacott, J. (eds), *Mass Communication and Society*, London: Edward Arnold.

Entman, R. M. (1989) *Democracy without Citizens: The Decay of American Politics*, New York and Oxford: Oxford University Press.

Entman, R. M. and Paletz, D. L. (1980) 'Media and the Conservative Myth', *Journal of Communication*, 30, 1: 154–65.

Ettema, J. S. and Glasser, T. L. (1994) 'The Irony in – and of – Journalism: A Case Study in the Moral Language of Liberal Democracy', *Journal of Communication*, 44, 2: 5–28.

Even, M. (1986) 'Television Broadcasting of Post-war Elections and the Case of 1983', in Crewe, I. and Harrop, M. (eds), *Political Communications: The General Election Campaign of 1983*, Cambridge: Cambridge University Press.

Fagen, R. (1966) *Politics and Communication*, Boston: Little Brown.
Fishman, M. (1980) *Manufacturing the News*, Austin: University of Texas Press.
Freedom Forum Media Studies Center (1992) *Covering the Presidential Primaries*, New York: Columbia University.
Frey, F. (1970) 'Cross-Cultural Survey Research in Political Science', in Holt, R. and Turner, J. (eds), *The Methodology of Comparative Research*, New York: Free Press.
Fritz, S. and Morris, D. (1991) *Handbook of Campaign Spending: Money in the 1990 Congressional Races*, Washington, D.C.: Congressional Quarterly Press.

Gandy, O. H. (1982) *Beyond Agenda Setting: Information Subsidies and Public Policy*, Norwood, N.J.: Ablex.
Gans, H. J. (1957) 'The Creator–Audience Relationship in the Mass Media: An Analysis of Movie Making', in Rosenberg, B. and White, D. M. (eds), *Mass Culture: The Popular Arts in America*, Glencoe: Free Press.
Garnham, N. (1973) *Structures of Television*, London: British Film Institute.
Gitlin, T. (1980) *The Whole World Is Watching: Mass Media in the Making and Unmaking of the New Left*, Berkeley: University of California Press.
Glasgow University Media Group (1976) *Bad News*, London: Routledge & Kegan Paul.
Glencross, D. (1983) 'The General Election of 1983: Could We Have Used More Freedom?', *Independent Broadcasting*, 37: 6–8.
Goldenberg, E. N. (1975) *Making the Papers: The Access of Resource-Poor Groups to the Metropolitan Press*, Lexington: D. C. Heath.
Goldie, G. W. (1977) *Facing the Nation: Television and Politics, 1936–76*, London: Bodley Head.
Golding, P. (1977) 'Media Professionalism in the Third World: The Transfer of an Ideology', in Curran, J., Gurevitch, M. and Woollacott, J. (eds), *Mass Communication and Society*, London: Edward Arnold.
Golding, P. and Middleton, S. (1982) *Images of Welfare: Press and Public Attitudes to Poverty*, Oxford: Martin Robertson.
Graber, D. A. (1992) *News and Democracy: Are Their Paths Diverging?*, Bloomington, Ind.: School of Journalism, Indiana University.
—— (1994) 'Why Voters Fail Information Tests: Can the Hurdles be Overcome?', *Political Communication*, 11, 4: 331–46.
Greenberg, D. W. (1975) 'Staging Media Events to Achieve Legitimacy: A Case Study of Britain's Friends of the Earth', *Political Communication and Persuasion*, 2, 4.
Grossman, M. B. and Rourke, F. E. (1976) 'The Media and the Presidency: An Exchange Analysis', *Political Science Quarterly*, 91, 3: 455–70.
Gurevitch, M. and Kavoori, A. P. (1992) 'Television Spectacles as Politics', *Communication Monographs*, 59, 4: 415–20.

Hackett, R. A. (1984) 'Decline of a Paradigm? Bias and Objectivity in News Media Studies', *Critical Studies in Mass Communications*, 1, 3.
Hagstrom, J. (1992) *Political Consulting: A Guide for Reporters and Citizens*, New York: Freedom Forum Media Studies Center.

Hall, S. (1974) 'Media Power: The Double Bind', *Journal of Communication*, 25, 4: 19–26.

—— (1982) 'The Rediscovery of "Ideology": Return of the Repressed in Media Studies', in Gurevitch, M., Bennett, T., Curran, J. and Woollacott, J. (eds), *Culture, Society and the Media*, London: Methuen.

Hall, S., Critcher, C., Jefferson, T., Clarke, J. and Roberts, B. (1978) *Policing the Crisis: Mugging, the State, and Law and Order*, London: Macmillan.

Hallin, D. C. (1992) 'The Passing of the "High Modernism" of American Journalism', *Journal of Communication*, 42, 3: 14–25.

Hallin, D. C. and Mancini, P. (1984) 'Speaking of the President: Political Structure and Representational Form in US and Italian Television News', *Theory and Society*, 13, 4: 829–59.

Hardiman-Scott, P. (1977) 'Some Problems Identified', in RAI/Prix Italia, *TV and Elections*, Torino: Edizioni Rai Radiotelevisione Italiana.

Harrison, M. (1975) 'On the Air', in Butler, D. and Kavanagh, D. (eds), *The British General Election of October 1974*, London: Macmillan.

Harwood, R. (1994) 'Reporting On, By and For an Elite', *Washington Post*, 28 May 1994.

Hertzgaard, M. (1988) *On Bended Knee: The Press and the Reagan Presidency*, New York: Farrar, Strauss & Giroux.

Hirsch, F. and Gordon, D. (1975) *Newspaper Money*, London: Hutchinson.

Hoyer, S., Hadenius, S. and Weibull, L. (1975) *The Politics and Economics of the Press*, London: Sage.

Jakubowicz, K. (1989) 'Mass Communication Research East of the Elbe', *European Journal of Communication*, 4, 3.

Jamieson, K. H. (1992) *Dirty Politics: Deception, Distraction and Democracy*, New York and Oxford: Oxford University Press.

Janowitz, M. (1975) 'Professional Roles in Journalism: The Gatekeeper and Advocate', *Journalism Quarterly*, 52, 4.

Jones, B. (1993) 'The Pitiless Probing Eye: Politicians and the Broadcast Political Interview', *Parliamentary Affairs*, 46, 1: 66–90.

Judd, A. (1991) *The Devil's Own Work*, London: HarperCollins.

Kalb, M. (1992) 'Press-Politics and Improving the Public Dialogue', *Political Communication Report*, 3, 2.

Katz, E. (1974) 'Platforms and Windows: Reflections on the Role of Broadcasting in Election Campaigns', *Journalism Quarterly*, 48, 2: 304–14.

Kavanagh, D. (1995) *Professional Campaigning: Polls, Advertising and the Media*, Oxford: Blackwell's.

Kelly, M. (1993) 'The Game', *New York Times*, 31 October 1993.

Köcher, R. (1986) 'Missionaries and Bloodhounds: Role Definitions of British and German Journalists', *European Journal of Communication*, 1, 1: 43–64.

Kraft, J. (1983) 'Reagan Beats the Press', *Washington Post*, 2 August 1983.

Kumar, K. (1977) 'Holding the Middle Ground: The BBC, the Public and the Professional Broadcaster', in Curran, J., Gurevitch, M. and Woollacott, J. (eds), *Mass Communication and Society*, London: Edward Arnold.

Lasswell, H. D. (1948) 'The Structure and Function of Communication in Society', in Bryson, L. (ed.), *The Communication of Ideas*, New York: Harper & Bros.

Lattimore, D. L. and Nayman, O. B. (1974) 'Professionalism of Colorado's Daily Newsmen: A Communicator Analysis', *Gazette*, 20, 1: 1–10.

Lazarsfeld, P. F. and Merton, R. K. (1957) 'Mass Communication, Popular Taste and Organized Social Action', in Rosenberg, B. and White, D. M. (eds), *Mass Culture: The Popular Arts in America*, Glencoe: Free Press.

Lester, A. (1994) 'A Route Through the Moral Malaise of Public Life', *Guardian*, 11 October 1994.

Levin, M. B. (1962) *The Alienated Voter*, New York: Holt, Rinehart & Winston.

Levine, P. (1994) 'Consultants and American Political Culture', *Report from the Institute for Philosophy and Public Policy*, 14, 3/4: 1–6.

Levy, M. R. (1981) 'Disdaining the News', *Journal of Communication*, 31, 3: 24–31.

Lippman, W. (1922) *Public Opinion*, London: Macmillan.

Livingstone, S. and Lunt, P. (1994) *Talk on Television: Audience Participation and Public Debate*, London and New York: Routledge.

Luhmann, N. (1975) *Macht*, Stuttgart: Enke Verlag.

McCombs, M. E. (1981) 'The Agenda-Setting Approach', in Nimmo, D. and Sanders, K. R. (eds), *Handbook of Political Communication*, Beverly Hills and London: Sage.

McCombs, M. E. and Shaw, D. L. (1972) 'The Agenda-Setting Function of the Mass Media', *Public Opinion Quarterly*, 36, 1: 176–87.

McGinniss, J. (1969) *The Selling of the President, 1968*, New York: Trident Press.

McLeod, J. M. and Becker, L. B. (1981) 'The Uses and Gratifications Approach', in Nimmo, D. and Sanders, K. R. (eds), *Handbook of Political Communication*, Beverly Hills and London: Sage.

McLeod, J. M. and Blumler, J. G. (1987) 'The Macrosocial Level of Communication Science', in Berger, C. R. and Chaffee, S. H. (eds), *Handbook of Communication Science*, Newbury Park, London and New Delhi: Sage.

McLeod, J. M., Kosicki, G. M. and McLeod, D. M. (1994) 'The Expanding Boundaries of Political Communication Effects', in Bryant, J. and Zillmann, D. (eds), *Perspectives on Media Effects*, 2nd edn, Hillsdale, N.J.: Erlbaum.

McQuail, D. (1983) *Mass Communication Theory: An Introduction*, Beverly Hills and London: Sage.

Mandelson, P. (1994) 'Clinton's Lessons for Labour', *Guardian*, 15 November 1994.

Mazzoleni, G. (1987) 'Media Logic and Party Logic in Campaign Coverage: The Italian General Election of 1983', *European Journal of Communication*, 2, 1: 81–103.

Miliband, R. (1969) *The State of Capitalist Society*, London: Weidenfeld & Nicholson.

Morrison, D. E. (1992) *Conversations with Voters: The 1992 General Election*, Leeds: Institute of Communications Studies.

Murdock, G. (1982) 'Large Corporations and the Control of Communication Industries', in Gurevitch, M. *et al.* (eds), *Culture, Society and the Media*, London and New York: Methuen.

Murdock, G. and Golding, P. (1977) 'Capitalism, Communication and Class Relations', in Curran, J., Gurevitch, M. and Woollacott, J. (eds), *Mass Communication and Society*, London: Edward Arnold.

Mutz, D. C. (1992) 'Impersonal Influence: Effects of Representations of Public Opinion on Political Attitudes', *Political Behavior*, 14, 2: 89–122.

Nayman, O. B. (1973) 'Professional Orientations of Journalists: An Introduction to Communicator Analysis Studies', *Gazette*, 19, 4: 195–212.

Nimmo, D. D. (1978) *Political Communication and Public Opinion in America*, Santa Monica: Goodyear.

Noelle-Neumann, E. (1980) *The Spiral of Silence: Public Opinion – Our Social Skin*, Munich: R. Piper.

Nowak, K. (1977) 'From Information Gaps to Communication Potential', in Berg, M. *et al.* (eds), *Current Theories in Scandinavian Mass Communication*, Grenaa, Denmark: GMT.

Ostroff, D. H. (1980) 'A Participant–Observer Study of TV Campaign Coverage', *Journalism Quarterly*, 57, 2: 415–19.

Parsons, T. and Shils, E. (eds) (1951) *Toward a General Theory of Action*, Cambridge, Mass.: Harvard University Press.

Pateman, T. (1974) *Television and the February 1974 General Election*, Television Monograph no. 3, London: British Film Institute.

Patterson, T. E. (1980) *The Mass Media Election: How Americans Choose Their President*, New York: Praeger.

—— (1993) *Out of Order*, New York: Alfred Knopf.

Phillips, M. (1994) 'Shocking Truth of Our Rulers' Cynicism', *The Observer*, 10 May 1994.

Polsby, N. W. (1980) 'The News Media as an Alternative to Party in the Presidential Selection Process', in Goodwin, R. A. (ed.), *Political Parties in the Eighties*, Washington, D.C.: American Enterprise Institute.

Pool, I. de Sola (1973) 'Newsmen and Statesmen: Adversaries or Cronies?', in Rivers, W. and Nyham, M. J. (eds), *Aspen Notebook of Government and the Media*, New York: Praeger.

Ranney, A. (1983) *Channels of Power: The Impact of Television on American Politics*, New York: Basic Books.

Rasmussen, J. S. (1983) 'How Remarkable Was 1983? An American Perspective on the British General Election', *Parliamentary Affairs*, 36, 3: 371–88.

Ridout, C. F. (1993) 'News Coverage and Talk Shows in the 1992 Presidential Campaign', *PS: Political Science and Politics*, 26, 4: 712–16.

Rivers, W. (1970) *The Adversaries: Politics and the Press*, Boston: Beacon.

Rivers, W. L. and Schramm, W. (1969) *Responsibility in Mass Communication*, New York: Harper & Row.

Robinson, J. and Levy, M. R. (1986) *The Main Source*, Beverly Hills, London and New Delhi: Sage.

Robinson, M. J. and Sheehan, M. S. (1983) *Over the Wire and on TV: CBS and UPI in Campaign '80*, New York: Russell Sage.

Rock, P. (1973) 'News as Eternal Recurrence', in Cohen, S. and Young, J. (eds), *The Manufacture of News: Social Problems, Deviance and the Mass Media*, London: Constable.

Rosen, J. (1992) 'Politics, Vision and the Press: Toward a Public Agenda for Journalism', in Rosen, J. and Taylor, P. (eds), *The New News v. the Old News: The Press and Politics in the 1990s*, New York: Twentieth Century Fund.

Roshco, B. (1975) *Newsmaking*, Chicago: University of Chicago Press.

Sabato, L. J. (1991) *Feeding Frenzy: How Attack Journalism Has Transformed American Politics*, New York: Free Press.

Schulz, W. (1983) 'One Campaign or Nine?', in Blumler, J. G. (ed.), *Communicating to Voters: The Role of Television in the First European Parliamentary Elections*, London, Newbury Park and New Delhi: Sage.

Semetko, H. A., Blumler, J. G., Gurevitch, M. and Weaver, D. H. (1991) *The Formation of Campaign Agendas*, Hillsdale, N.J.: Erlbaum.

Semetko, H. A., Scammell, M. and Nossiter, T. J. (1994) 'The Media's Coverage of the Campaign', in Heath, A., Jowell, R. and Curtice, J. (eds), *Labour's Last Chance? The 1992 Election and Beyond*, Aldershot: Dartmouth Publishing.

Seymour-Ure, C. (1974) *The Political Impact of Mass Media*, London: Constable.

—— (1987) 'Leaders', in Seaton, J. and Pimlott, B. (eds), *The Media in British Politics*, Aldershot: Avebury.

Shepard, A. C. (1994) 'The Gospel of Public Journalism', *American Journalism Review*, September 1994: 28–35.

Siebert, F., Peterson, T. and Schramm, W. (1956) *Four Theories of the Press*, Urbana: University of Illinois Press.

Swanson, D. L. (1992a) 'Managing Theoretical Diversity in Cross-National Studies of Political Communication', in Blumler, J. G., McLeod, J. M. and Rosengren, K. R. (eds), *Comparatively Speaking: Communication and Culture across Space and Time*, Newbury Park, London and New Delhi: Sage.

—— (1992b) 'The Political–Media Complex', *Communication Monographs*, 59, 4: 397–400.

Swanson, D. L. and Mancini, P. (eds) (1995) *Politics, Media and Modern Democracy*, New York: Praeger.

Swanson, D. L. and Nimmo, D. (1990) *New Directions in Political Communication: A Resource Book*, Newbury Park, London and New Delhi: Sage.

Tan, A. (1973) 'A Role Theory: A Dissonance Analysis of Message Content Preferences', *Journalism Quarterly*, 50, 2: 278–84.

Tichenor, P. J. (1982) 'Agenda Setting: Media as Political Kingmakers?', *Journalism Quarterly*, 59, 3: 488–90.

Tuchman, G. (1972) 'Objectivity as Strategic Ritual: An Examination of Newsmen's Notions of Objectivity', *American Journal of Sociology*, 77, 4: 660–79.

—— (1978) *Making News: A Study in the Construction of Reality*, New York: Free Press.

Tuchman, G., Kaplan, D. A. and Benet, J. (eds) (1978) *Hearth and Home: Images of Women in the Mass Media*, New York: Oxford University Press.

Tunstall, Jeremy (1971) *Journalists at Work*, London: Constable.

Verba, S. (1993) 'The Voice of the People', *PS: Political Science and Politics*, 26, 4: 677–86.

Verba, S., Nie, N. and Kim, J. (1971) *The Modes of Democratic Participation: A Cross-National Comparison*, Beverly Hills: Sage.

Wakeman, F. E., Jr (1988) 'Transnational and Comparative Research', *Items*, 42, 4: 85–91.

Waltzer, H. (1966) 'In the Magic Lantern: Television Coverage of the 1964 National Conventions', *Public Opinion Quarterly*, 30, 1: 33–53.

Weaver, D. (1994) 'Media Agenda Setting and Elections: Voter Involvement or Alienation?', *Political Communication*, 11, 4: 347–56.

Weaver, D. H. and Wilhoit, G. C. (1980), *News Media Coverage of US Senators in Four Congresses, 1953–1974* (*Journalism Monographs* no. 67), Minnesota: Association for Education in Journalism.

Weaver, D. H., Graber, D. A., McCombs, M. E. and Eyal, C. H. (1981) *Agenda-Setting in a Presidential Election: Issues, Images and Interest*, New York: Praeger.

Weaver, P. (1973) 'Is Television News Biased?', *The Public Interest*, 26: 45–74.

Weber, M. (1925) *Wirtschaft und Gesellschaft*, Tübingen: J. C. B. Mohr.

Index